The
Ancient World

natia

ntus Euxinus

Cappadocia Armenia

Cilicia

Palestina Assyria Media

Babylonia

Mare Caspium

Cyrus

Jaxartes

Oxus

A R I A N A

Indus

ARABIA

INDIA

Arno

The History of the World

IN THREE HUNDRED PAGES

René Sédillot

THE HISTORY
OF THE WORLD

IN THREE HUNDRED PAGES

Translated from the French
by Gerard Hopkins

HARCOURT, BRACE AND COMPANY · NEW YORK

Contents

Preface

To WRITE a history of the world is a vast and ambitious project. It amounts to no less than telling the life-story of men, of peoples, and of states over a period of some five or six thousand years. How can it be reasonably supposed that a writer can, in the space of three hundred pages, compress the achievements of a hundred and fifty generations, make vivid the thoughts of so many persons and periods, speak of wars and describe revolutions, compare empires and republics, set forth the characters of mob-leaders and great generals, show how human beings have lived, set on the page in their true stature and perspective the men who discovered new truths, the men who studied old, the men who transmuted their experience into art, the creators, the discoverers, those who by their daring and their genius have changed and modified the condition of man's life on earth? Is it likely that one will succeed in stirring to life the embers of dead civilizations, in showing with convincing truth the features of old barbarisms rising from their centuries-old graves?

At first sight it may seem a hopeless task. Yet to the geologist or the astronomer, accustomed to measuring all things with a rod which is marked in thousands, in millions, of light-years, its difficulties would seem negligible.

Such a man sees the history of mankind as no more than
an incident of the Quaternary epoch, or our poor planet
as only a speck of dust in a universe of stars. Thus regarded, the history of the world is reduced to the dimensions of a monograph.

This would be the point of view of a watcher on Sirius,
and it is precisely upon Sirius, remote from all human
emotions, that the historian who would record the Passion
of Mankind must take his stand. Only by dominating
space and time can he successfully thread his way through
the tangle of prejudice and legend, of hatreds and imper-
fect knowledge, which besets his path.

But it is hard to wipe the slate clean. We are born, each
one of us, with a native country and natural affections.
We grow up in the company of books. Most of our ideas
are ready-made. Those of us who are writers or scholars
concentrate our attention on special subjects and limited
fields, because the sum of human knowledge is now so
great that a single brain cannot contain the whole of it.
But special study means a narrowed vision. There is danger that when we think we are revealing all truth, we have,
in fact, made known only one aspect of it.

One reef, in particular, we voyaging historians must at
all costs avoid. We must not set out to *prove* anything.
It is attractive, as well as easy, to develop a theory. A
theory gives unity to a book and a sense of continuity.
The theorist can make a cheap reputation for originality
and brilliance. A novel constructed on classical lines is
concerned to develop a single plot. It has unity. Bossuet
once wrote a magnificent *Discourse* which attempted to
show that universal history was the story of providence
in action. It is possible, following his example, to derive
all history from one single principle, one exclusive philosophy: to see it as wholly dependent on the laboring
masses or, alternatively, on the activities of exceptional
individuals; to base it entirely on the achievements of
peace or the conduct of wars; to find it governed by im-

ponderable elements or by chance (Cleopatra's nose or Cromwell's stone), or by the inevitable dictates of Fate. The whole weight of the historian's argument may be laid on military skill or naval supremacy, or the dominant part played by religion. It is open to the historian to concentrate all his efforts on demonstrating the superiority of one particular type of political system, on defending a particular attitude, on praising democracy, lauding aristocracy, glorifying one nation or one race at the expense of others. . . . Such methods are very tempting; nor are they necessarily false. There may be only one truth, but it has a thousand facets.

It is not merely for convenience of demonstration that I have built each chapter of this book round a "people." The facts speak for themselves. Almost every century carries on its front one obvious sign; nor is it merely as the result of chance that in each it is one nation, and one alone, that has shown itself to be preponderant in politics, in economics, and in the things of the mind. The spot of earth which sees the emergence of great statesmen sees, too, that of scholars and artists. Military power goes hand in hand with commercial power.

This small volume was first conceived—why not be frank about it?—as an economic history. Historians who have been trained to regard politics as all-important may be led to conclude that it is the economic structure that alone controls the destiny of mankind. But those bred up to the study of economics have only to study the interrelation of cause and effect to realize very soon that politics remains the determining factor. They may set themselves, for instance, to examine the economic consequences of the discovery of the New World, only to find that this discovery was stimulated by events that were purely political —the cutting of the route to the Indies by the Turkish invasions.

Consequently I have found myself compelled to modify the emphasis of economic developments on the gen-

eral plan of my book; to make room in my scheme for
kings and conquerors, since it was the kings and the conquerors who produced the inventors and the poets.

All those who have figured in the human story deserve
consideration, whether they be called Pericles, Caesar, Li
Shi-min, or Louis XIV; whether they conceived the idea
of baking bread or invented the wheel, the alphabet,
money, or the harnessing of horses; whether they built
the Parthenon, painted the Holy Family, or wrote *Don
Quixote*. Each one of them helped to determine the shape
of the world. This history is their history.

But the man who would write history must learn to
select. The facts are too numerous to be considered all
alike. The historian concentrates on one because it seems
to him to be essential. It may, in fact, be far less so than
another which he has neglected. Possibly the importance
of that other fact may not become apparent for many years
or for many centuries. The contemporaries of Jesus ig-
nored him. Christopher Columbus failed to realize that
what he had found was a new world. It may be that at this
very moment a child has been born who, when he reaches
man's estate, will overturn the world.

This "History of the World" is, therefore, a work of selection. Since it cannot tell the whole story, it aims at con-
centrating attention on its principal features, or on what
to the author have appeared to be its principal features.
It may be found that I have taken the wrong road. I can
say no more than this—that what I have done I have done
in good faith.

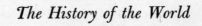

The History of the World

CHAPTER ONE

Prehistoric Man

MYTHS AND SCIENCES

WHEN man first made his appearance on this planet all that he knew was that he knew nothing. But he believed very readily in the myths which he himself concocted. They threw light upon his past; they taught him the nature of his destiny.

"For over seven thousand years," wrote La Bruyère, "there have been men upon the earth." The author of the *Characters* was not hazarding a guess when he thus laid down the chronology of mankind. His authority was the official calendar of his day, the calendar according to the era of Constantinople, which claimed to reckon from the date of the Creation. Everyone, of course, knew that the first man (*homo, humus*) had been made from a handful of clay on the sixth day of Creation.

Within the framework of Christianity there were variants on this system of reckoning. The accepted interpretation of Holy Writ put the birth of Adam at 4004 B.C., and gave 2348 B.C. as the date of the Great Flood, and 1571 as that of the birth of Moses. Every event in world history was carefully ticketed. The historian need not concern himself about such things, nor men's minds be troubled.

It is impossible not to admire these reckless fables.

Their strange beauty, even more than their wealth of detail, seems to have been designed to stick in men's memories. All the legends of the early world, no matter what the religion that produced them, were the work of poets: not only Eve eating the apple in the Earthly Paradise or the dove bringing back the olive-branch to Noah, but Manu, the father of the human race, as he appears in the Vedic tales, dictating the first laws, Prometheus stealing fire from heaven, Deucalion scattering behind him the stones which turned into men, or Pandora opening the chest in which were imprisoned all the miseries of the world. These ancient myths are a confusion of gods and mortals. They raise men to heaven or bring down gods to earth. They attribute a divine origin to such things as the invention of fire and iron, the making of the plow, the finding of the vine, the revelation of language, the founding of races and of cities. They explain the marvelous in terms of the supernatural. They give to man a reason for his pride, and console him for the mediocrity of his condition.

Compared with these grandiose imaginings, science is poor. It has neither gods nor epic deeds to offer. It cannot even propose new certainties in place of those that have died. Timidly it ventures the suggestion that man may have appeared upon the earth a hundred thousand years ago, though even while it commits itself to this computation it knows it to be false. Science asks more questions than it answers. Was man first found in one locality or in several? Was there, at the dawn of history, any such thing as individual property, or did human beings know only some form of the collectivist system? Historians may assert; very rarely can they prove. Their answers to the questions we put to them are contradictory—more contradictory even than the legends.

The hypotheses of science are as insipid as they are deceptive. The sociologists set themselves to explain the earliest men on evidence derived from an examination of

savage races. It is in New Zealand, in Guiana or in Polynesia, they say, that we must seek our ancestors. The Al-
gonquins, the Eskimos, or the natives of Madagascar are,
they maintain, to be regarded as the real brothers of primitive man. They go into raptures at the thought of the natives of Central Australia, and of the pygmies, who are
the most backward of all the human species. In them they
would have us see our forbears summoned from the limbo
of time.

The geologists examine the soil and pore over fossils.
They find no difficulty in distinguishing the age of the
hewn flint from that of the polished, to establish their
culture as earlier than that of the Bronze Age or the Iron.
The terminology which they have invented is a little *too*
expressive, a little *too* close to the language of the legends.
The epoch of the hewn flint becomes the Palaeolithic,
neatly subdivided into the Chellean, the Acheulian, the
Mousterian, the Aurignacian, the Solutrean, and the Magdalenian. As dig follows dig, and discovery follows discovery, a few more stages ending in *ean* or *ian* are light-
heartedly introduced into this stratification of the ages.
The epoch of the polished flints has become the Neolithic,
only in turn to be subdivided. Similarly, the Iron Age has
been learnedly fragmented. It would be too much to say
that these efforts at classification have *no* value. But it
can be only provisional. Man seeks endlessly for his parentage, but it seems doubtful whether he will ever find it.

Archaeologists and natural historians pry at skeletons
which, they will have it, are those of our earliest ancestors,
only to find that the most they can say is that they are
those of our cousins the Australopithecus, the Plesian-
thropus, and the Paranthropus of the Transvaal; the Pithe-
canthropus of Java and the Sinanthropus, which may, perhaps, have stood upright on its hind legs. They examine
the Heidelberg jaw-bones, which are Chellean, the Nean-
derthal skull, and the bones of La Chapelle-aux-Saints,
which go back to the Mousterian, Cro-Magnon man and

Grimaldi's man, and belong to the Aurignacian. Many other poor sketches of *Homo sapiens* do they explore, all of which, no doubt, give evidence of the first uncertain steps taken by the species in its infancy. Man—a vertebrate and mammalian animal belonging to the order of primates of the monkey family . . .

LET US IMAGINE . . .

We should not mock at these patient labors. Let us rather, setting aside the fragile systems of the pedants, try to imagine for ourselves that long unrolling of the aeons which *seem* to have had man as their goal. Let us watch in imagination the vast succession of natural miracles— the formation of the earth, some three thousand million years ago; the first appearance of organic life, maybe two thousand million, in the form of microscopic bacteria living in the ocean depths; the coming of the first vertebrates, five hundred million years ago, of the first mammals, a hundred million, then of the earliest anthropoids, only a few tens of millions of years ago; and, finally, the progressive evolution of the anthropoid into man in the damp heat of the tropical forests.

The ancestors of man lived in the trees. The quadruped became a biped. Two of his paws developed into hands, which enabled him to swing from branch to branch. His head became upright; his body tended to the vertical; his brain grew in volume.

But a further miracle was needed before this primate became a human being. It is to be found, no doubt, in the coming of the Ice Age, which uprooted the forests and left a few droves of anthropoids isolated at the foot of the mountains, deprived of their home (the trees), forced to seek a new life in the security of caves, threatened in their retreats by bears and lions. The choice before them was either to fight or to disappear utterly. They had neither claws nor tusks. But the instinct of self-preservation (unless it were a spark of the divine fire) endowed them with a weapon above all price—intelligence.

In that moment man was born. He was naked in a world of enemies. But the means of assuring his future triumph was within his grasp. Like the child in the cradle, he had at his disposal that potential of intelligence which was to make it possible for him to establish his reign in a world which had greeted him so ill. He was well on the way to assert his supremacy over all those beasts of prey from whom he had escaped. How, but for the gift of thought, could he have resisted them? That gift was his sole weapon, a weapon without compare, but, let us note, beyond his power to perfect. After all the thousands of years that had gone to its making this magnificent characteristic of intelligence was bogged down. We see it today much in the same state as it was at the time of the cave-dwellers.

What *has* progressed is knowledge. Man started from scratch. He had to invent everything, discover everything, beginning with his own body and the planet which he called his home. But all that he had so far learned was far less than what remained for him to learn in the thousands of years ahead. Even today he does not know whence he came nor whither he is bound.

Of one thing, however, we can be certain. The hoarded treasure of his knowledge and his technical skill have increased from generation to generation, in spite of occasional periods of retrogression. This he has been able to pass on, and it is this that we honor with the name of civilization. No other species of the animal world seems capable of enlarging its store of acquired knowledge. Man alone, from the very dawn of his history, has applied his indestructible gift of intelligence to the task of endlessly enriching his cultural heritage.

THE FIRST SUCCESSES

Man's first conquests in the dark night of his past were those which, more than anything else, distinguish him from the beasts. So great was their importance that no subsequent invention has had comparable results, results so enduring that they still control the destinies of nations. There were three of them: language—fire—religion.

There can be very little doubt that humanity in its earliest periods was ignorant of words, of the provision of artificial warmth, of the existence of the gods. But awareness in all three fields seems to have come quickly. No prehistoric culture has been discovered that does not give evidence of the possession by its members of these three things.

Man is a talkative animal. He has vocal cords, and is alone among the beasts in being able to articulate. Nor could any but he practice the art of abstraction. He stammered onomatopoeic sounds and learned to give them a meaning. Language was born, the offspring of instinct and convention, the vehicle of thought, the marvelous instrument of communication. From that moment life in society bore fruit. The first jabbering of the first man must have been rudimentary, but the art of gathering together sounds and syllables soon progressed. Appetites were born, and with them the means of finding their satisfaction—the earliest declaration of love; the earliest quarrels. Human life properly speaking, had begun.

Fire, men had known of old, but as something distant and beneficent in the sun, menacing in lightning and volcanoes, sudden in the spontaneous conflagrations which laid the forest and the underbrush in ruins. At first, by carefully nursing this gift of Nature, they made of it a domestic tool. Then, as knowledge developed, they discovered means of provoking flame. Chance, maybe, revealed to them the truth that from the shock of two flints in

sharp contact a spark would spring. The slow process of
learning from experience taught them how to make fire
by twisting a stick of hard wood in rotting bark. When
that happened they acquired, for the first time, the sense
of power. They never ceased to worship fire, because its
manifestations sowed terror in their hearts. But they
tamed their conquest. Till then they had subsisted on raw
acorns, weeds, roots, and berries. Now they acquired the
art of cooking their food. They were to learn later how to
apply fire to the baking of clay and the smelting of metals.
Later still, after many thousand years of civilization, their
metallurgical science would enable them to build railways
and tanks. But even when that happened they still would
use candles on their altars, and honor with a naked flame
the tomb of an unknown soldier.

Religion early seized upon men's hearts, and never since
has it relaxed its hold. Religion? To apply that word to
practices which had more in them of magic than of organized worship may seem presumptuous. But where does
magic end and religion begin? All peoples take refuge in
one or the other. The first men could not free themselves
from the panic inspired by the forces of Nature and the
threat of wild animals—by the sound of thunder or the
sight of bears approaching their caves. Terror very easily
turns to adoration. The tribes erected totems and established taboos. Religious rites were born in the worship of
animals, of growing things, of the incomprehensible. They
came, too, from the fear of death. What could such utter
immobility at life's end mean? Could the dead help or
torment the living? In their doubt they buried their dead
with pious precautions, adorning them and giving them
funeral furniture and food, binding their limbs to prevent
them from doing harm. After a while they took to invok-
ing their dead ancestors, calling on them for aid against
their enemies. They performed sacrifices, pronounced in-
cantations, invented myths, all in honor of the homeless
spirits and the threatening gods. One man in each tribe

made a special study of the art, became the intermediary between the living and the mysterious forces that lay beyond life. He was the "medicine-man," and, eventually, the priest. In the course of centuries fetishism engendered polytheism, and this, again, gave place to monotheism, until, finally, monotheism yielded to irreligion. But man, conscious of his powerlessness in face of the unknown, has never wholly renounced his superstitions.

With the coming of these three great experiences men were well on the way to triumph over their purely animal beginnings. With their stature increased by the gifts of fire and language, by a consciousness of divinities who gave them arms against their foes and afforded them protection, they were now ready to stand embattled against the world.

THE CIVILIZATION OF THE HUNTERS

The civilization of the chase first gave to men a calling. Their earliest concern had been to ensure security for themselves. They had had to fight with wild animals for the possession of caves in which they might live. They had had to defend themselves against beasts of prey who could crush their heads and their bones in the hug of their shaggy paws. They may, perhaps, have believed that by eating the hearts of that carnivorous foe they could acquire warlike virtues, that by devouring the flesh of the reindeer they might gain his speed, that by drinking the blood of the lion they could make his strength their own. From being vegetarians they became eaters of meat, and grew to like their new food. Thanks to the gift of fire, they learned how first to dry, then grill it; how to roast the carcasses of slain beasts. Hunting, and fishing too, took rank as the main objective of men's lives.

Like elephants and monkeys, men lived in herds. Union was strength. But already they had learned how to counterbalance their natural weakness by fashioning arms.

Fire gave them burning brands with which to set the underbrush ablaze. Wood and stone provided them with clubs and javelins, with lances, knives, and axes. They made handles for their stone blades by wedging them into wooden hafts, and later, with bows and slings, contrived to throw missiles. They could now attack animals at a distance. They could track and deceive, crawl and lie in wait. They made traps and dug pits. In this way did they become cunning and cruel and proud in the thought that, feeble though they were by comparison, they could make themselves stronger than the strongest beast. The spirit of evil possessed them.

Out of hunting grew war. Men had invented weapons, and now they began to turn them against one another. The rivalries of individuals, of families, of clans, could not be allowed to continue unchecked. So men learned to fight, and the conqueror soon claimed the right to kill his vanquished adversary. But he found an alternative, and, instead of killing, enslaved him. Out of war grew slavery. But then, having once learned how to deceive the wild beasts, men took to deceiving their neighbors. They took to parleying with their enemies. They promised eternal peace, and if, so be, they took up arms again they would solemnly announce that they were embarking on the war to end all wars.

In periods of tranquillity men began to organize their lives. They learned games and the dance. They improved their dwellings and their clothes. In order to sew the skins of beasts with which (after the Mousterian Age) they had covered their nakedness they made needles of flint, and the needles had eyes. In order to light their caves they made themselves lamps (after the Magdalenian). For purposes of adornment, and perhaps in the hope of attracting the spirits of good, and averting the spirits of evil, fortune, they devised necklaces and rings and armlets out of shells, amber, coral, and, not infrequently, out of the teeth of wolves, dogs, and chamois. They developed a feel-

ing for the beautiful. Was it solely in order to assure themselves success in hunting that they scratched upon the
walls of their caves the figures of animals pierced by arrows? Art may have begun as an arrangement of magical
symbols, but eventually it acquired a value of its own.
The incised and painted images, of which so many examples have come down to us, are living proof that the
prehistoric hunters were great artists.

THE CIVILIZATION OF THE HERDSMEN

If the civilization of the hunters dates back to at least
a hundred thousand years before our era, that of the
herdsmen, which followed it, can be set at a mere ten thousand—at what seems like yesterday.

The ice-caps, after a period of freakish and dangerous
activity, finally receded. The climate became milder. Men
could emerge from the caves where they had sought refuge
and prance over the young grass. It was as though they
had found the spring. Human life changed. From being
hunters men became shepherds. First they had killed the
wild animals of their world, in self-defense and in the
search for food. Now they tamed them, and watched over
their breeding. They tried their prentice hands upon the
ox, that most peaceable of all the quadrupeds, then turned
their new-found skill to grapple with the donkey and the
camel. They reigned as kings over vast herds of hinds
and stags, of reindeer and of sheep. They trained to their
service the dog, the pig, the buffalo, the llama, the horse,
and the mule. They raised poultry and mastered the ele-
phant. No animal capable of domestication escaped them.

Are we to believe those who maintain that the breeding of cattle was originally undertaken to serve religious
ends, that men were concerned to provide themselves with
victims for the sacrifice, or with winged creatures for purposes of divination? Some such motive may, at times, have
been powerful, but there is reason to suppose that men

were fully aware of the economic significance of this their newest conquest.

From then on animals ceased to be for men merely an immediate source of food and fur, of milk and eggs. A vast world of industry lay open now, awaiting exploitation—a world containing leather and wool, butter and cheese. These capital goods of civilization date from the centuries that saw the rise of the herdsmen.

But when men became shepherds they soon learned that they had assumed constricting duties. They left their caves to live in light tents pitched near the grazing-grounds. They led their herds in search of the grass that was needed for food. They became nomads.

At once a change came over civilization. Art seems to have deteriorated in quality, and such examples of it as we have lack the easy mastery of the Magdalenian legacy. The herding of beasts is not intellectually stimulating, nor does it train the hand as did the acquisition of the hunter's skill. Men now had other and more practical cares. They learned the use of grindstones for the polishing of flints. They acquired the craft of molding clay and turning pots upon a wheel. The Neolithic revolution coincided with the change of life which brought the shepherd.

THE CIVILIZATION OF THE FARMERS

A new stage of development followed hard upon the heels of that inaugurated by the herding and breeding of animals. Here and there it accompanied or preceded it. Men became farmers. No sooner had they triumphed over the wild beasts who were their most immediate threat than they achieved a further conquest, this time over the world of growing things. These encroached upon their homes and were most stubborn. At first men had fought the animals; now they set to fighting the trees and the dense forest creepers. They cleared the ground. They sowed the seed. They harvested the crops.

Again we are faced with a question. Was it from a ritual act that farming was born? Was it in order to bury the dead that men first dug the earth? Was it to provide food for the departed that they first scattered seed upon the ground? Or was it a mixture of chance and observation that revealed to them the miracle of germination? Whatever the reason, men came at last to the knowledge of their mastery over growing things. They calculated the seasons, discovered the virtue of sun and rain, were able to distinguish good soil from bad. They bent themselves in labor above the nourishing earth.

At first they used only the dibble and the hoe, knowing nothing of the plow, nothing of manures. As soon as one patch of earth became exhausted the community moved on to virgin fields. The world was wide, and its inhabitants, so far, numbered only a few thousands.

But soon they realized that by breaking up the surface of the ground they could increase its yield. Then, one fine day, the plow was invented. The name of the man who was responsible for that beneficent discovery is given in the Bible as Tubal-cain, and he is said to have lived some three thousand years before the beginning of our era. The Greeks called him Triptolemus, and made Ceres his nurse. Egypt chose to attribute the invention directly to Osiris. Men were chary of claiming for one of themselves so wonderful a novelty. For once they erred by excess of modesty.

Yet another marvel gave rise to lovely myths. Farmers sowed wheat, milled flour, and baked bread. It was unleavened bread, and was something like a biscuit. But bread of a sort it was, and humanity has never ceased to use it as a symbol of all food. But wheat was not the only crop of the early world. The prehistoric farmer was familiar with barley, millet, and flax. He tended the trees that bore the pear, the apple, and the nut. He pruned the grape and made wine. Saturn, Bacchus, Noah, and many others were honored as the father of this latest wonder.

Once again the nomads had become fixed and sedentary. They settled wherever they could find a well or a water-hole. They made their homes in huts constructed of stone or tree-trunks, or of branches raised on piles at the edges of lakes. These "stilt-dwellings" of the lakeside villages put those who lived in them beyond the reach of marauding animals. Water too, by this time, had become the friend of men. It was crossed by bridges, dammed by dikes, and navigated by canoes.

Industries were born. There was weaving of wool and flax. There was dyeing of stuffs. Clay was baked in the form of pots and vessels. Furniture made its appearance. The craftsmen had at their command tools of flint and wood, or bone and horn, and, before very long, of metal. The invention of the bellows was humanity's first step in metallurgy. First came copper, then, with the admixture of tin, bronze, and finally iron. Thus it was that the world became familiar with knives and hammers and saws.

Here and there great stones were set upright in the earth like giant landmarks, or laid lengthwise on its surface, like immense tables. They are still to be seen in China and in Brittany, in Abyssinia and in Britain, in Java, in the Balearic Isles, and in India. Had these megaliths a religious significance? Were they commemorative of some event or person? What precisely was their symbolism? To these questions we have no sure answer. All we know for certain is that the movement, and sometimes the alignment, of these massive objects give evidence of collective labor and of some kind of social discipline.

THE CIVILIZATION
OF THE TOWN-DWELLERS

No sooner were social groupings organized than they began to tear one another to pieces. Men were objects of fear to one another. Quarrels started. At periodic intervals migrations on an enormous scale brought chaos to our planet. The sedentary dwellers sought a refuge against the nomads or against their neighbors. They crowded together behind defensive walls. Towns grew up, each founded in accordance with exact, accepted rites.

Primarily the town was a stronghold. It was also a public meeting-place and market. Priests and craftsmen elected to live in towns because they provided a sure asylum. Merchants were frequent visitors.

For now it was the turn of trade to make its appearance. What is known as "urban" civilization is always essentially commercial. Previous to its appearance all interchange of goods had been of the crudest description. It had been born in violence, and had known as its media only rape and spoliation. Was not Hermes at one and the same time the patron divinity of brigandage and trade? Did not the same Greek verb mean "to trade" and "to corrupt"? Did not the German tongue tend to confuse *tauschen* ("to deceive") with *tauschen* ("to exchange"); *Handel* ("trade") with *Händel* ("dispute")? To piracy pure and simple succeeded robbery by consent and subsequent compensation. In some consecrated spot, preferably a temple, one clan would leave its offering. When night had fallen a neighboring clan would take possession of the goods thus deposited, leaving in their stead some object adjudged to be of equal value. Later the exchange of goods became direct—in short, a matter of barter.

With what *type* of goods was early commerce concerned? With blades of flint or obsidian useful for the making of tools or weapons; with yellow amber, much sought after for the adornment of women; with salt, with slaves, and, at a later stage, with various metals—tin, copper, zinc, and iron.

Where once barely perceptible paths had threaded the forests, where tracks through the undergrowth had been trodden by men and beasts, the first caravan routes came into being. At long last the towns were joined by regularly marked highways.

Towns, by their very nature, were the crossing-points of roads, and it was as such that they were symbolized in the earliest Egyptian picture writings, which show a town as a cross within a circle, a junction of roads within a defensive wall.

At this point man becomes the subject of history.

CHAPTER TWO

The Ancient World

THE DAWN OF HISTORIC CIVILIZATIONS

AT THE dawn of historic civilizations man, despite his achieved conquests, was still strangely naked. He was ignorant, for example, of writing, of the One God, of money, of the wheel. He did not know how to ride the horse, and if he counted at all it was by saying, "One, two, many." Man was like a puling child in a cradle.

Not all the agglomerations of peoples had reached the same level of civilization. Some men were still nomads in a world where others tilled the fields. There were those who had knowledge of iron without having first passed through the stage of bronze. In parts of the world men were still raising megaliths when Athens was carving marbles. In our own twentieth century there are still tribes at the level of the prehistoric hunters.

But two or three millenniums before the birth of Christ certain centers of high civilization had already arisen. While the rest of the world was content to live on in the conditions of prehistory, these favored spots were embarked upon the sea of history proper. Issuing from the anonymous mass, *some* peoples were growing to maturity, *some* capital cities were already built, *some* empires were in course of construction. This flowering was concentrated in a number of definite localities. All were in the old hemisphere, and in its northern part, between the twentieth and fortieth degrees north latitude, and between the twentieth and the hundredth degrees east longitude. The area thus delimited was a comparatively small part of our globe stretching from the Eastern Mediterranean to the China Sea. Here lay the countries of the sun.

Within these narrow boundaries the zones of advanced civilization were confined to the muddy deltas of certain large rivers—the Nile, the Euphrates, the Tigris, the Indus, and the Yellow, because their valleys, periodically enriched by flooding, gave to man the means of prosperity.

These civilizations, though by no means shut off from one another, had each its own character and its own excellencies. Each was inventive in a different manner. They introduced political systems all different in kind, ranging from absolute monarchy to anarchy of the feudal type. Their economic systems were opposed, appearing here under the guise of liberalism, there of State socialism. This very variety added much to the general load of human experience.

But our knowledge of these civilizations is very incomplete. At some we can only guess, basing our conclusions on such ruins and legends as have come down to us. Because the traces that we find have often to do with religion, because temples and tombs which were built to last have survived the institutions of the living, we are left with the impression that religion played in them a capital rôle. However that may be, then, as always, human beings must have lived, loved, and laughed. These cultures had, no doubt, their free-thinkers, their daring theorists. But all that our archaeologists can find are their fables and their gods.

But if the fables and the gods differ the fortunes of these societies were much alike. Beyond the limits of the fertile valleys in which they came to birth the nomad shepherds muttered and snarled. From their deserts and their up-

land plateaus they wondered at, and envied, the easy lives
led by the peoples of the plain. A day came when they
swept down to attack the centers of civilization. They
left the sandy wastes of Africa and Arabia, the steppes
of Tibet or of Mongolia, and hurled themselves on the
defenseless prey. A day came when they made themselves
their masters. Then one of two things happened. Either
the attackers became assimilated with the peoples they
had conquered and helped to raise them to new heights
of achievement, or they stifled them beneath a weight of
barbarism.

THE CIVILIZATION OF THE NILE

* 5000 B.C.   Some five thousand years B.C. nomads, coming, perhaps, from Abyssinia, explored and traveled down the
Nile, where there had already been a flourishing Neolithic
culture. So greatly were they struck by its fertility that
they settled down, became farmers, and intermarried with
the original inhabitants.

From their past of shepherding they retained a Pantheon of animal divinities. They worshiped Sekhmet, the
lioness, Ta-urt, the hippopotamus, Anubis, the jackal,
Khnemu, the ram, Hathor, the cow, and in addition, the
ibis, the cat, the hawk, the falcon, and the crocodile, all
of which were represented in human form with animal
heads. A special cult was devoted to Apis, the bull, to
whom they dedicated a curious tomb not far from Sak-
kara. It may, too, be from some totem that the Sphinx
was derived, that crouching lion with a woman's face
whose impressive presence is one of Egypt's legacies to us.

When they became farmers in the rich valley lands the
Egyptians completed their collection of gods. They extended their worship to include every influence that might
assure good crops—the sun (who is Ra), the Nile (which

---

* Hereafter, all B.C. date references will be preceded by a minus
sign: e.g., −5000.

is Osiris, the god of vegetation), fecundity (which is Isis, the daughter of the earth).

But the Nile, which brought down each year its rich alluvial deposits, is no tranquil stream. Its flow had to be controlled. Had this not been done Egypt would have alternated between periods of flood and drought. Great works, therefore, had to be constructed to mitigate the capricious moods of the waters and the heavens.

This task imposed a discipline and a special form of social organization. Egypt chose the formula best suited to her condition—that of a socialist monarchy.

Her kingship was based on divine right. The Pharaohs were the children of the sun. They were absolute sovereigns and monopolist landowners. All the territory of their realm belonged to them of right. Though it might be willing to let the district governors transmit their office from father to son, and play at being feudal lords, the New Monarchy kept them well in hand. The Pharaoh, master of men and things, never ceased to be the living God, "the giver of water to the earth."

The socialism that prevailed in Egypt was State socialism. To find its like we have to go to the empire of the Incas or to the U.S.S.R. of our own day. Private property was unknown. Every Egyptian was a civil servant incorporated into an immense hierarchy of bureaucratic administration. District governors and village headmen were responsible for finding the labor needed to maintain the canals, the dams, the cisterns, in a state of repair. They kept a watchful eye upon the farmers, and to these officers a return at harvest-time had to be rendered. Technicians were in charge of the hydraulic installations. Official storekeepers collected the various fruits of the earth, which by law or custom had to be delivered up to them.

This system of collectivism could not but be costly. One-quarter of each harvest was shared among the inhabitants of the district which produced it; the other three-quarters were absorbed by the "expenses of administration"—in other words, in paying the salaries of the officials and in maintaining such of the citizens as were not farmers, the priests and the Pharaoh himself. A proportion of the annual yield was laid aside as a reserve with which to meet the eventuality of a lean year. Of all this, it is true, only a fifth part went to the person of the monarch in whose hands lay the sole power to appoint both priests and civil officers.

With the building of ships, the exploitations of mines and quarries, the weaving of textiles, the sending out of expeditions to seek incense and spices, and as closer contact became established with the Eastern Mediterranean, a commercial chapter opened in the history of Egypt. And all these various activities were controlled by the socialist machine. Industry and trade were State monopolies.

In a system which made no distinction between free men and slaves the provision of man-power was regarded as being a tax on the community. Labor could be enlisted at will. It was thus possible to carry through enormously ambitious programs of public works—such, for instance, as the construction of a canal equipped with locks, to link the Nile with Lake Moeris, and the conversion of the latter into a huge reservoir by the aid of which the river-flow could be controlled.

—2600   To this mobilization of the population, too, we owe the building of the pyramids, those grandiose tombs within whose walls the Pharaohs believed they could brave the menace of eternity. Nothing in the ages to come ever surpassed the funerary architecture of Gizeh and Memphis and the Valley of the Kings. In the old age of the world, cities like Rome and Paris could find no more impressive adornment than that supplied by the obelisks of Egypt.

But it was not only in the production of tombs and bas-reliefs, of fables and poems, that the Nile civilization showed its creative genius. It flowed over into more practical fields. The art of writing was invented, first in the form of marks incised in stone, and then in the setting down on papyrus rolls of signs corresponding to objects, and later to ideas, to sounds, to syllables. The Egyptians came very early by the knowledge of counting and computing. In their regular periodic measurements of the rise and fall of the Nile they produced the first known instance of economic statistics. They could reckon the quantity of land lying under flood-water, and were the first to apply to daily affairs the principles of geometry and surveying. They could calculate the extent of surfaces, and handle volumes and weights. They knew how to employ common fractions, and established a relation of equality between π and $\sqrt{10}$, that is 3.1623—no mean approximation. They observed eclipses, discovered the movements of the planets, and fixed the solar year, which they divided into twelve months of thirty days each, with five additional days. Some investigators, carried away by enthusiasm, have even claimed that the dimensions of the Pyramid of Cheops provide the answer to mathematical and astronomical problems far beyond the power of the elementary science of those days to solve.

The horse and the wheel reached Egypt from Asia, but —1680 even in her earliest recorded period her people had known how to make glass. They had weighing-scales and windmills, which they used for grinding corn and for raising the water used in irrigation. In Egypt too began the arts of medicine and surgery—a medicine still constructed on a basis of exorcism, but rich in empirical cures. Egyptian belief in human survival resulted in a very high degree of skill in the craft of embalming, thanks to which the "double" of every dead person might hope to find his own body again. Chariot-races and running were popular, and from these activities came other sports. The use of sheets and stuffed pillows for beds was common, as was that of gloves and chessmen—early items in the development of comfort and recreation.

These innovations were scattered over a long and variegated history which filled the glorious annals of thirty-

one dynasties. This method of computing periods in terms of dynasties was arbitrary and traditional, but it has, for us, the advantage of convenience. The first sovereign to
—3200 reign over a united Egypt was Menes. Those of his successors who left the most durable monuments to future
—2800 ages were Zeser, the builder of the stepped pyramid, and
—2600 Mycerinus, to whom archaeologists are inclined to credit the three great pyramids. In this competition for sepulchral glory Tutankhamen played his part by immortalizing his
—1350 pride in a golden sarcophagus weighing more than six hundredweight. The most famous of all the Pharaohs to be commemorated in Western text-books was for a long
—1300 time Rameses II, to whom, under the name of Sesostris, were attributed a number of legendary campaigns in the course of which he was supposed to have reached points beyond the Ganges. In fact, his military exploits amounted to no more than the defeat of certain Hittite bands from Syria, and even this was accomplished only with considerable difficulty.

—1680   Security was more important for Egypt than conquest. At an early date the Hyksos, or Shepherds, a nomad tribe from Asia, invaded the Lower Nile Valley, and held it in fee for more than two centuries. Though freed from these conquerors by the Kings of Thebes, the Egyptians always went in fear of greedy neighbors, whether they were wandering desert folk or the great empires which had come into existence beyond their frontiers. Ultimately
—730 they succumbed, first to the Ethiopians, then, in succession, to Assyria, Persia, Hellas, and Rome. They learned at the last that neither pyramids nor embalming can make a civilization immortal.

THE TIGRIS AND EUPHRATES CULTURES

The banks of the Nile had seen the rise to greatness of a single people. Those of the Tigris and Euphrates served as the cradle and the tomb of numerous civilizations. Different races and various systems of government prospered, sometimes simultaneously, sometimes in succession, in those twin and parallel valleys. The Tigris and the Euphrates have a unity neither of history nor of culture. Mesopotamia, which means, etymologically, "Between-two-rivers," seems to have been one of the main crossroads of the ancient world. Tribe followed tribe, as in some temporary resting-place, some stage upon a journey. No sooner had one settled than it was chased out by a newcomer. None of them ever managed to achieve that thousand-year permanence which made the greatness of Egypt.

The Mesopotamian basin, even more than the Nile Valley, needs the work of men's hands. Without it nothing grows there: all is sand and desert—or else flood. The story of the Deluge is a lasting monument to one of these —3600 recurrent catastrophes. But with man's help Mesopotamia can become a flourishing area of the world's surface. It demands constant irrigation. The health-giving waters need to be forever led through the soil in a close network of canals and trenches.

The first farmers who settled in Lower Mesopotamia early came by that knowledge. Their civilization was highly developed. They invented the wheel, and they were —4000 familiar with copper, which, no doubt, reached them from the Caucasus, that home of all metals. In the necropolis of Susa shards have been found bearing stylized designs, mirrors which seem to have been mounted on bone or wood, and painted pottery—all going to show the existence of an industrial output which, though primitive, was of high quality.

A thousand years later, almost in the same spot, the founders of the Sumerian culture were quick to realize —3000 the debt they owed to the rivers. In the land of Sumer, lying in the delta, there was a multiplicity of those hydraulic works which brought moisture to the soil and filled the barns with garnered crops. The Sumerians worshiped the god of inundation, the god of growing things, the goddess of seed. They sowed barley and cultivated the date. They

—2900 mastered the secret of manuring the earth and of the use of the plow. Very soon they learned how to weigh out silver, the white metal which must have come to them from the mountains where the rivers rose. They used it in ingots for making payments. It was money in an embryonic form.

These Sumerians were an amazing people. They invented a cuneiform script, and employed light carts drawn by oxen or by donkeys. They left behind them, in the royal tombs of Ur, delicately wrought jewelers' work, in which precious stones were combined with rare metals.

Is it safe to assume that the Sumerian civilization was destined to be prematurely overrun by the tide of encroaching barbarism? It is true that for nearly four cen-

—2875 turies the land fell into the clutches of Semites from Akkad—that is to say, from the north—and that at intervals during the same period savage hordes of mountain folk descended upon the plain, pillaging everything they found.

—2622 But Sumer freed itself and rose again. Its institutions became a model of administrative organization. State func-

—2500 tionaries received the animals handed over in payment of taxes, herded them into a great park, and used them either for purposes of sacrifice or in ways that served the national economy. They loaned oxen for plowing and donkeys for draught work. Scribes kept the public accounts in terms of barley, dates, or oil. The king's couriers sped along the roads. Barges loaded with fruit and grain moved along the canals. Sumer was a rich land.

—2358 It was, indeed, too rich. The Semites infiltrated into the kingdom, and finally submerged it. But even under foreign masters, the Sumerian civilization continued. It showed its mark in the works of irrigation, in the methodical upkeep of the canals, in poems, and in the sculptures which first made Babylon famous. Especially was its influence

visible in the legal institutions which were the glory of
King Hammurabi.

The Code of Hammurabi was at once a civil code, a   —2120
code of procedure, a penal code, and a commercial code.
The civil code recognized three classes of citizen—freemen, semi-freemen, and slaves. It established a monog-
amy; it controlled the power of fathers over their children;
it made every landed proprietor responsible for the upkeep
of the canals on his estate. The code of procedure set up
courts, laid down rules for the appointment of judges,
both civil and religious, and compiled rules of evidence.
The penal code apportioned penalties to the various types
of crime and misdemeanor—death by drowning, death by
burning, death by crucifixion, the bastinado, and the fine.
The commercial code fixed prices and wages, organized
the caravans into transport companies, regularized loans,
whether in money or in kind, and laid down the interest
to be charged at 20 per cent for money transactions and at
33 per cent for transactions in barley.

In contrast to socialist Egypt, Babylon dealt with its
economic problem in the spirit of liberalism. Private property was formally recognized; individual enterprise was encouraged. All the machinery of capitalist trading was set
up—contracts, promissory notes, and letters of credit.
The State was no more than the referee and regulator.
More than two thousand years before the Christian era the
Code of Hammurabi contained much from which we
might profit today.

But a day came when the last traces of Sumerian civilization were swept away. Once again the nomads descended from the mountains. The Hittites settled on the   —1925
site of Babylon, and later still the Kassites established
themselves there for six centuries. Beyond the frontiers of
Mesopotamia there was a flurry of newcomers. Hourrites,   —1760
Phrygians, Aramaeans founded kingdoms or dreamed
of founding empires. It was a time when whole nations   —1200
were on the march over all the Middle East, men, women,

and children, with their carts, their herds, and their treasures, seeking cities to pillage or to occupy.

In the end it was a people from the valleys who succeeded in establishing a hegemony over all this motley rabble. The Assyrians, in whose veins ran some tincture of Semitic blood, became the heirs of Sumer. They settled at Assur, in the Tigris plain. War was the dominant passion of their lives. They thrust their neighbors from their path, held whole tribes to ransom, enslaved the conquered. Assyrian imperialism aimed at world conquest.

—1100

The Assyrians realized that it was not enough to irrigate the plain. They must defend it, too, and in their eyes offense was the best form of defense. To reduce the unruly nomads of the highlands and the mountains, to make themselves the masters of their wealth, which was all in timber, metals, and precious stones, they set light-heartedly about becoming soldiers and conquerors.

—731

In turn they subdued Babylon, Damascus, and Samaria. Their empire extended from the Mediterranean to the Persian Gulf. Megalomania led them at last to the possession of Egypt.

—663

Their war-chariots, their cavalry, and their archers spread terror wherever they appeared. They burned villages. They decapitated, impaled, flayed, or walled up alive their prisoners. They disemboweled the women, and systematically enslaved and deported the inhabitants of whole tracts of country.

Their civilization was too bloodthirsty to be creative. Their legal system was far cruder than its predecessor in the century of Hammurabi. Their religion was largely a matter of warrior gods. Though their astronomers could group stars in constellations and distinguish the planets, their science was closely akin to astrology. Their medicine, it is true, made use of diet, of poultices and dressings, but it also had recourse to amulets and was not far removed from magic. Barley and silver, as a medium of exchange, had given place to stamped ingots, but these were of lead.

The royal palaces were luxurious, but built of brick. Their sculptures were of gigantic size, but treated only of battle and the hunt. They were more successful in their rendering of animals than of men.

Assyria was a brutal master. It diffused and transmitted more than it created. The library of Nineveh—the first-known library in history—contained a wealth of Sumerian material. But the warriors of Sennacherib and Sargon did little to enrich it. They were content to live on the past, and to devote the present to massacre and pillage, rather than to literature and philosophic speculation. By what —810 process of fantastic transmogrification did Queen Sammuramat, the obscure wife of Samsirammon, become the beautiful Semiramis, who, by unveiling her loveliness, quelled a revolt? As the result of what confusion did the —668 King Assur-barni-pal, that hardened warrior, find himself changed into the effeminate Sardanapalus, who burned himself in his palace with his wives and his eunuchs? The Greek imagination remade history in its own image.

But the Assyrian monarchy collapsed. Its fighting-men were exhausted; its subject peoples were ground beneath its heel. Hordes of barbarians—Medes, Scythians, and Cimmerians—stormed Nineveh and liberated Babylon. —612 A wave of new peoples spread over the valleys of the Tigris and Euphrates.

THE CIVILIZATION OF THE INDUS

Like the Nile, the Tigris and the Euphrates, the Indus saw a civilization come to birth upon its banks. It too suffered from annual floods. They brought natural wealth to a valley which was more extensive than that of Egypt, more temperate than the plain of Mesopotamia. But though there was water under its soil, and though its irrigation was, to some extent, unaided, man's handiwork was still necessary. There, as elsewhere, the inhabitants had to work hard for a living.

What we know of the civilizations of the Nile, the Tigris, and the Euphrates is little enough, but of the mysterious life of the Indus Valley we are almost entirely ignorant. The most the archaeologists have achieved is to bring to light the ruins of two big cities which constitute the oldest known urban communities—Mohenjo-Daro, —2800   on the Indus, and Harappa, on the Ravi, a tributary of the larger stream, some 450 miles to the northeast. They appear to date from about 3000 years before Christ. The houses are equipped with running water and modern sanitation. Shops too have been unearthed which prove that this city civilization was familiar with trade.

But that is about all we know. Excavation has revealed no palace, temple, or monumental tomb, nor has it provided any evidence of the political or economic organization of the dwellers in the Indus Valley. Of what their religion was we have no idea. Seals, it is true, have been found, adorned with pictographs and representations of animals, which are reminiscent of Sumerian art. It is possible that some sort of relation existed between the valley —1300   of the Indus and Mesopotamia. But at least we know how and when this civilization perished. It too was a victim of the great migrations. At a given moment nomad Aryans, coming from Iran, descended upon the Indus plain. They are still there.

THE CIVILIZATION
OF THE YELLOW RIVER

At the eastern end of the Asiatic continent China was born of the Yellow River. Flowing down from the clay uplands, which are the source of its distinctive coloring, the river has made of the Great Plain, from the dawn of time, a land of corn and millet and soya. Alluvial deposits have raised the natural level of its bed, to the danger of the

low-lying country along its course. But men have always
preferred soil that is rich and dangerous to soil that is poor
and safe. It has never been their habit to flee from the
slopes of volcanoes or the flood-areas of rivers. According to the Taoist legends, the Yellow River emerged from
one of the arteries of P'an Ku, the first man, whose head
became a mountain, and whose eyes are the sun and moon.
The symbolism, even at this early stage, is that of a race
of poets.

The Chinese have never been agreed about the period
at which their ancestor P'an Ku lived. Some said 276,479
years before Christ, others 96,962,219, and various inter-
mediate dates have been named. Whatever the truth of
the matter, it is clear that they had a far greater sense of
man's antiquity than had the Jews of the Bible.

The Westerners, who think of themselves as the true
reference-point of all chronology, long refused to admit
that the Chinese were the first and original inhabitants of
China. Heroditus traced their descent from the Egyptians; the Hebrews thought of them as the grandchildren
of Shem; and Gobineau believed they came originally
from India. Voltaire, showing more sense, said, "The
Chinese are no more likely to have derived from Egypt
than from Lower Brittany." Actually there is no trace in
ancient China of any immigration. From its earliest period
the "Middle Empire" has existed in solitude, cut off from
the rest of the world by the immense distances of the
steppes. It would be foolish to maintain that it had no contacts whatever with foreign peoples, but one can at least
say that such contacts were few.

In the basin of the Yellow River the Chinese cleared
and drained the land, provided a system of irrigation, and
sowed their crops. On the microscopic scale of gardeners
they turned the Great Plain into a garden. They had
knowledge of the orange, the lemon, and the mulberry.
From Southern China they brought rice, eight centuries
before the beginning of the Christian era. They bred silk-

worms, and wove the wonderful textiles for which those creatures provided the raw material. It was more than fifteen hundred years before the silk industry reached Europe by way of Constantinople and Sicily.

The Chinese led a settled, agricultural life, living in houses of mud and wattle. They knew nothing of building in stone or brick. But on military expeditions, two thousand years before Christ, they were making use of horses, having learned the art from the Mongols. About the same time they showed themselves to be past-masters in the manufacture of ceramics. Later they made the acquaintance of bronze, which reached them by way of Siberia, and quickly learned to handle it with the skill of artists. The pots, cups, and tripods dating from this period are genuine masterpieces.

—2000

—1500
—1200
—1000

At a somewhat more advanced date they passed from bronze to iron and became metal-workers. It may have been about this time that it occurred to them to do what no one had ever done before—exploit their natural deposits of coal.

Nor were they less advanced in intellectual activities. They claim, with pride, to have invented five thousand years ago, the art of music—"an expression of the union of heaven and earth." At a very early period they used writing, at first in the form of knotted cords; later by scratching arrangements of lines on bones and scraps of tortoiseshell; finally by inventing ideographic symbols.

—3300

—2500

Thanks to this medium of expression, the Chinese were able to embark on scientific and literary work. They developed the earliest theories of astronomy, and they were passionate students of history—in so far, that is, as it concerned themselves. They collected the records of their own past in a work consisting of four thousand volumes, beginning with Fu Hi and the five emperors who ruled in the name of the elements of earth, wood, metal, fire, and water—symbols which probably go back to prehistoric times.

—2953

Their history is a tedious chronology of dynasties and sovereigns, of slaughter and of palace intrigues. It is hard to remember all the names consisting of singing monosyllables, many of which belong to legend more than to history. All we need to know is that the king, the Son of Heaven, was the great pontiff who presided over the festivals of the seasons and uttered the invocations for rain, and, at the same time, was the political head of a State organized on feudal principles. The great lords lived in their walled castles, and the mass of the people was divided into five classes, determined by profession. The function of the State was to organize enterprises of hydraulic engineering, to encourage or impede the sowing of certain crops, to share and assign the available land.

All would have been for the best in this fruitful land of China had it not been for the watchful nomads on her borders. There seems to be little doubt that it was the Chinese who took the initiative of spreading outward from the Great Plain and of breaking up the wilderness that lay to the northwest and to the south, as far as the Blue River. The barbarians were forced back, and waited   —771
patiently for their revenge. They invaded the northwest marches, looted what they could find, and compelled the reigning dynasty to withdraw into the Great Plain the capital which it had imprudently pushed forward. But the true miracle of China always has been, and always will be, in her power to assimilate the invader and conquer the conqueror.

THE CIVILIZATION OF THE SEA

It was not only the rivers that attracted men. The sea too, once it had lost its power to terrify, was a strong seducer. Just as on the plains men became farmers, so on the coasts they turned themselves into sailors.

The first maritime civilization came into being on an island—Crete, the natural stepping-stone between Europe, Asia, and Africa. Her prosperity was built on sea-borne trade.

—5000   A number of Mediterranean tribes settled on the island and established their suzerainty over the Aegean archipelago at a very early period. They exploited the obsidian deposits of Melos, and trafficked in it among the islands. Their genius for trading seems to have been due in part —3400 to the new blood brought by invaders of unknown origin from the north. The Cretans knew how to work gold, silver, and copper. They established relations with Egypt, and learned the art of writing.

With the coming of the Bronze Age the Cretan economy entered on a new phase. The new alloy became their monopoly in the whole of the Mediterranean area. To develop their growing skill in metallurgy the Aegeans made expeditions to the harbors of Greece and Spain in search of the tin which reached those places from countries situated in the far north. They obtained it, as well as ivory and copper, by trading agricultural products—their oil and their wine. In Egypt they sold perfumes and wood in exchange for gold and pearls. Their sea-power grew. The civilization of Crete, at first confined to the east coast, spread to the center of the island. It was there that the Palace of Knossos was built, and linked to the southern coast by a royal highway dotted with villas.

—1700   A single family of Knossos ultimately established its authority over all the princes of Crete, who in consequence became a feudal aristocracy. It gave to the island a chief who combined in his sole person the functions of ruler, commander-in-chief, and priest. It may be that, as the Greek legend tells, he was called Minos, and that he imposed on Attica a yearly tribute of seven youths and seven maidens. This fiction probably symbolized long memories of Cretan oppression, and served to recall the toll levied by sea-rovers on the peoples of the mainland. Not everything perpetuated by legends is untrue, and

there is almost certainly a substratum of fact in the story
of Minos. The existence of a Cretan despot, the magnificence of his palace labyrinth (marked with the sign of
the double ax—*labrys*), and the extent of the Minoan
Empire—these things are beyond doubt.

The Aegean civilization was highly sophisticated. What
distinguished it was not so much a system of centralized
monarchy as a way of life. Woman was enthroned. There
was gallantry of manners, and the Court was the arbiter of fashion. This Cretan world of the eighteenth century B.C. may be, in some sort, compared with that of
the sister-century of our own era. Knossos was a forerunner of Versailles, with its elegancies, its marquises in
their low-cut dresses, and its noblemen. The Cretan
courtiers, too, had a taste for pastoral artificiality. They
played chess, they organized fêtes, they danced. There
were, in the kingdom, workers in gold and silver; there
was even a royal factory devoted to the production of
ceramics. The walls of the Cretan houses were decorated
with painted plaster and brightly colored frescoes. The
whole island lived in a whirl of pleasure and luxury.

But the Achaean barbarians, who had long been set- —1450
tled on the Greek mainland, cast envious eyes upon it,
and a process of infiltration began. Whether the burning
of so many palaces was due to them we do not know, but
they were certainly responsible for the looting and de- —1400
struction of Knossos. The age of Minos was no more.
The Aegean Empire vanished from the stage of history.

Their heirs were the Phoenicians, who rebuilt for their —1100
own profit a seaborne civilization. The coastal lands from
which they came were arid and constricted. They left
them to seek their fortunes elsewhere.

They were of Semite race, and transferred to the open
seas the nomad habits of their people. They used their
native country as no more than a base of operations. The
world was their oyster. They first appeared in it as humble fishers of the murex (from which they extracted the

purple used in the dyeing of wool). But after a while these fishers became mariners and merchants sailing the seas at will.

Tyre and Sidon, situated on two small islands off the coast, were their main supply-depots. The two cities were rivals, often at odds, but united in a common determination to retain the monopoly of the Mediterranean trade. They were linked by a number of economic agreements, and both worshiped the same marine deities—Astarte, goddess of the moon and Lady of the Sea, and Melkarth, the wandering hero. In co-operation they built heavy vessels for ocean sailing and light galleys with which to frequent the new coastal trade-routes. The cedars of Lebanon furnished the keels, the ribs, and the masts; oaks of —1000 Bassou the oars. The sails were woven of Egyptian cotton. Over the deep green billows went the Phoenicians, buying slaves everywhere, as well as pottery in Rhodes and Crete, oil, figs, and wine in Greece, mother-of-pearl, coral, and sulphur in Sicily, silver in Spain—the root of the name is Semitic, and is connected with its silver-mines —tin from Andalusia, or from the islands of the Cassiterides, lying not far from Britain. For they passed the gates of the Atlantic and ventured into the wide ocean. They —500 are said to have made the circuit of Africa (taking forty-eight months for the journey) two thousand years before Vasco da Gama doubled the Cape of Good Hope.

They were not wholly innocent of piracy, but, whatever they did, they brought to bear on it a practical good sense. They made no attempt to colonize the hinterland of the harbors in which they traded. It was enough for them if they could set up their trading-stations, get a concession from the inhabitants, and avoid competition. There were not enough of them to provide the troops necessary for territorial conquest. They preferred to increase the number of their "factories" from the Black Sea to the Atlantic coast. Beyond the Strait of Gibraltar they founded Gades —814 (the later Cadiz), and Carthage on the littoral of Africa.

It was this latter city which became the heir of their enterprise and their policy.

Where trade was concerned they showed themselves to
be inventive. They developed a system of numerals which   —1300
lacked only a conventional sign for zero, and from the
clumsy Egyptian script evolved an alphabet of twenty-   —1300
two letters. This was the father of the Greek alphabet and
of all the alphabets that followed it.

In the long run the power of Phoenicia was weakened
by the armed might of Assyria, whose armies took Sidon
and razed it to the ground. Their final destruction came   —677
at the hands of Macedonians. But the legacy of Phoeni-
cian teaching remained.

THE NOMAD INVASIONS

Sooner or later the civilizations of the river-valleys and
coastal strips died out. Either they devoured one another
or were overwhelmed by the nomads. The struggle was
long, but the nomads finally prevailed. They made their
homes in the plains, became settled and sedentary, and
gave birth to fresh empires.

It is by no means sure whence came these wandering
peoples who forced the ancient cultures into the melting-
pot, absorbing some of them, and bringing with them
the gift of new blood. They were destroyers, but they
gave birth to new communities; they were barbarians, but
they fathered a new world. By definition they were ubiquitous. They came from everywhere. The ethnologists have
done their best to identify the localities of their earliest
migrations. They were of many races, and they numbered
many tribes. There were some from Abyssinia, some from
Mongolia. But two groups in particular were marked out
by destiny for great events, and these were to be known
to history as the Semites and the Indo-Europeans.

The Semites came from Arabia, or, more precisely, it   —3000
seems, from the remoter parts of Palestine. In successive

waves, and more often as a result of infiltration than of
conquest, they penetrated into the whole of the Middle
East, settling in Upper Syria and drifting down into
Mesopotamia. It was they who made their home among
the Sumerians, and inherited the rich legacy of their cul-
—2800 ture. It was they who, under the leadership of Abraham
and driven forward by the spur of famine, moved from
—2100 Chaldaea into Egypt. It was they, perhaps, who, hand
—1680 in hand with the Hyksos, conquered the land of the Pharaohs. Both the Assyrians and the Phoenicians were, to some
extent, impregnated with Semitic elements. Semitic were
—1500 the Aramaeans, who swarmed over vast tracts of country
from the Mediterranean to the Euphrates, continuing on
land the mercantile activities of the Phoenicians. Semitic,
too, were the Hebrews.

The Bible contains the long story of their unhappy wan-
derings. About the "chosen people" one thing is certain:
they were nomads, moving from water-hole to water-hole
with their herds, their tents, and their women. The gods
they worshiped were the gods of shepherd-folk. The calf,
whether golden or not, was to be numbered among their
totems. They sacrificed lambs, and regarded certain kinds
of food as impure.

One of Abraham's descendants, Jacob, surnamed Israel,
shook from his feet the inhospitable dust of Canaan, and
migrated to the alluvial Nile Valley. But his people did
not long prosper there. Oppressed, and forced to work
as slaves, they preferred to flee once more. Moses led
them. For a long time they wandered in the desert, but
finally returned to Canaan. There they fought against the
Moabites, the Philistines, and ultimately settled.

From the days of Moses, who, on the mountain of Sinai,
had heard the Divine Voice, the Israelites worshiped but
one God. It was their destiny to teach the truths of monotheism to the world. Their gift to mankind was a universal
God, a just God, but a God Who had chosen His people.

But this chosen race was dogged by misfortune. It was

split by a schism which set Israel against Judah, Sichem against Jerusalem. They bred murders and palace revo- —935 lutions. Finally the Assyrians intervened, deported the in- —731 habitants of Samaria, and replaced them with their own colonists. The Babylonians made themselves masters of —587 Jerusalem and led the Judaeans into captivity. At a later date the Jews returned to Palestine, only to come under the domination of foreign conquerors—Macedonians, Syrians, and Romans. They revolted in vain. The Temple was destroyed, the people of Israel dispersed. In country after country the individual Jew resumed the old nomadic life which once had been the destiny of the whole tribe.

The Indo-Europeans were more successful than the Semites in finding a permanent home. Where they first came from is uncertain. It was long held that they had originated in the highlands of Pamir. Later theories placed them in Turkestan or Siberia. Some have supposed that they came from the Baltic coast, from the German-Polish —3000 plain, or from the Danube Valley. The most probable supposition is that they had lived for a long time as no- mads in Southern Russia, between the Dnieper and the Volga, and, perhaps, between the Danube and the Ural.

Tamers of horses, breeders of sheep and oxen, they looked on livestock as the only wealth, confusing *cheptel* with *capital*, *pecus* with *pecunia*. Their industries were those of herdsmen—milk, wool, and honey. They were not ignorant of agriculture, and could use the plow and till the fields. They settled in villages, building rec- tangular houses with fixed hearths. They were grouped in families and tribes. Unlike the Jews, they had a stronger sense of hierarchy than of equality. They did not know how to write.

They were ignorant of gold and silver even after they had made the acquaintance of copper. From this latter metal they made murderous axes which served them well —2500 in the conquest of a continent. Their other weapon was the horse, which gave them enormous superiority over all their adversaries.

Whether they used wagons for longer journeys is by no means certain, but with or without them they moved freely and loosely. Most of them left the lands of cold and fog for the countries of the sun.

Their advance-guards reached the Balkans and Asia Minor on their way to the Mediterranean and the Indian

—2100 Ocean. Almost certainly the route they took was the one that led them through Turkestan, the Caucasus, and across the Bosporus. In the course of their migration they overwhelmed a city on the site of which the later Troy was built.

When their tribal unity was broken the various sections adopted a variety of manners and tongues. The

—2000 Achaeans settled in Greece, whence they set out on the
—1450 conquest of Crete and the Aegean. The Cimmerians and,
—1200 later, the Scythians made their homes on the Russian
—1925 steppe. Other groups penetrated into the Middle East—
—1300 the Hittites, who took Babylon, the Aryans, who made
—1200 their way to the Indus; the Thracians and the Phrygians, who occupied Asia Minor and Syria, the Medes and the
—612 Persians, who invaded Mesopotamia and completed the ruin of the Assyrian Empire. Of similar origin were the
—500 Slavs, the Germans, and the Celts, who, strong in the possession of iron weapons, spread over the European plain. Five hundred years before the beginning of our era the Indo-Europeans were masters of the whole of the West from the Atlantic to the Ganges.

From these scattered groups of an identical parentage almost all the great peoples of the world were born. Sprung from that root, the Greek and Latin branches prospered, and the later barbarian shoots grew ever stronger, until at length they overshadowed the whole earth.

Such was the sequence through the ages of those great invasions which merged the races, and ground the nations beneath their feet.

CHAPTER THREE

The Age of Greece

THE STRENGTH OF GREECE

THE NOBLEST lesson in civilized living ever given to the world came from a tiny province, at one and the same time insular and peninsular, lying at the point upon the map where the Balkan ranges fall to the Mediterranean. Greece was a mountainous country, sunbaked, poor, unprovided with rich farming lands, and devoid of most of the raw materials of industry. But the sea made up for what the earth lacked. Many and various peoples had already prospered in the coastal areas of the Mediterranean, and that long stretch of water was to make the fortune of the Greeks. They entered on the stage of history as traders, pirates, and mariners.

The enlarged promontory which we know as Greece, where the invading Achaeans had mingled their blood with that of the hypothetical Pelasgi, became a melting-pot of races. The Cretans had sailed as merchants to Argos, and Mycenae—pale reflection of Aegean greatness —had watched the growth, within its high walls, of the first civilization to take root upon the mainland of Europe. The Aeolians and Ionians, both of them sprung from wandering Indo-European bands, made there renewed contact with the Achaeans. The Dorians, in their turn, another branch of the same Nordic tree, thrust aside

—2000

—1300

—1200

the peoples who, before their coming, had been settled in Greece. They arrived as marauders, and they stayed as masters, subjugating, as in Sparta, the original inhabitants. Elsewhere these latter were compelled to face the perils of emigration. But there were few places to which they could go. The only road open to the displaced Achaeans was the sea, and they set out to colonize the coasts of the Mediterranean and of Asia Minor.

In the course of their exodus they came up against the peoples who were already living in the territories where they proposed to settle. It seems almost certain that the —1180 legendary Trojan War is nothing but a poetic expression of the clash which occurred when the peoples of Asia met these Achaean emigrants led by Agamemnon of Mycenae. We cannot be even certain of the actual site —800 of Priam's city, or know whether Homer who sang of the famous siege three or four centuries later was a poet of genius or the name given to a group of rhapsodists. It is at least probable that the name Achilles is an evocation, or an abridgment, of that of the Achaeans. It is possible that the episode of the Trojan Horse symbolizes the triumphant appearance of the first mounted warriors at a time when war was normally waged by infantry and chariots. All that we can regard as certain is that the Hellenes, reacting to Dorian pressure, or struggling to get away from the poor land of an overpeopled continent, spread over the length and breadth of the Aegean.

Cities were born of this migration. Phocaea, Ephesus, Miletus, Smyrna, Samos, and many others were centers of Hellenism, and became commercial capitals. The real Greece was not, at that time, to be found upon the mainland. The Greeks had learned the way of the sea, and it was upon the sea that henceforward they were to seek their fortunes. Younger sons and political refugees carried to distant lands their country and their native tongue. Very soon the Greek sailors made themselves masters of the declining empire of the Phoenicians. All the way along

the tin-route they colonized the Mediterranean littoral. —700
Eastward they founded Byzantium, passed the Bosporus,
and established settlements up and down the Black Sea. —658
To the south they set up trading-stations in Egypt, and
founded Libyan Cyrene. In the west they swarmed over
Sicily, where later Syracuse was to grow great, and Italy,
the future home of Greater Greece. They built Parthenope, —600
to be known in after-years as Naples, and Massilia, or
Marseilles, which owed its existence to the Phocaeans. It
was from there that Pytheas set out on a voyage of adventure which took him as far as mysterious Thule, hidden in its northern mists. Seeking trade, the Greeks —400
reached Spain. They bought, sold, peddled, and bartered,
realizing enormous profits. But the foreigners with whom
they did business were the principal gainers from this
interchange, for they learned the lessons of civilization.

In Greece what had been humble villages became opulent cities. Corinth had all the characteristics of a capital.
Aegina was a clearing-house for big business; Chios, a
slave market. The Piraeus, according to Isocrates, was a
"storehouse where merchandise abounded." All this
wealth came from the sea, or from countries to which the
sea gave access.

For the mainland of Greece remained inexorably sterile. Athens, in her heyday, could produce only one-third
of the wheat that she consumed. The secret of her expansion and her power lay elsewhere than in her figs and
olives and her bees. Greek industry was still in a primitive stage. Craftsmen did their work by hand with simple
tools of iron, a few wooden levers, a few sets of leather
bellows. The roads were no better than rough tracks.
Goods were carried on mules or donkeys, but, because
the knowledge of harnessing four-footed beasts was still
in its infancy, men were more often than not used for
drawing carts.

It is true that the difficulties presented by sea-travel
were no less formidable. In the Homeric epic navigation

ceases in winter and during the hours of darkness. Ships, when possible, never moved out of sight of land; the swift currents of narrow straits were usually avoided, and sailors were at the mercy of the winds. In those days there was no such thing as a fixed rudder, and consequently tonnage had to be kept light. But the Aegean and the Mediterranean are well suited to coasting. When need arose the three banks of oars of the Hellenic triremes could supplement capricious breezes. The Greeks were natural sailors, and carried Greece with them beyond the seas.

THE WEAKNESS OF THE GREEKS

These same Greeks, on whom heaven had showered her rarest gifts, had also very serious defects. Not only were they thieves but liars as well, braggarts and babblers. They were born politicians. In workshops, villages, and trading-stations fierce jealousies were rife. Competition was the law of their being, and indiscipline their method. Mutual slaughter was commoner than mutual understanding. Even when peril threatened from outside they were incapable of calling a truce to their ruling passions or of uniting in self-defense. With them private interest was always of more importance than the general good. Greece perished because her cities could not federate.

Greece is merely a geographical term. The history of the ancient world was familiar only with Greek factions, divisions, and rivalries. Rome gave birth to the State. Hellas could produce only warring cities, and even within each one of them individualism was rampant. To the credit side of the Greek character can be put inventiveness and daring. But there was a debit side as well which showed in endless internecine struggles which led to ultimate collapse under weight of party politics.

It seems almost certain that every Greek city was, in its earliest phase, monarchic. They passed, like families,

through a patriarchal stage. In historical Greece all that
remained of this period of absolute kingship were certain figures of popular myth: Theseus, King of Athens,
Bellerophon, King of Corinth, Danaus, King of Argos,
Perseus, King of Mycenae, Menelaus, King of Sparta,
Oedipus, King of Thebes—all of them more demi-gods
than men. These city monarchies collapsed after the coming of the Dorians. The Greeks regarded this early form
of government as something primitive, whereas, in fact,
it was the arrival of the barbarians that had brought it
to ruin.

What really happened after the Dorian invasions was
that the heads of clans seized on the sovereign power and
turned it to their advantage. The Greek cities made the
transition from monarchy to aristocracy. Political power
and the possession of land became an appanage of the
nobility. But with the rise of trade a new phase started.
The business middle class evicted the feudal lords. The
privilege of wealth was substituted for that of birth. This
new system was based on property. The rich man's word
was law.

But the people were restless and unsatisfied. Social strife
became common. In such uncertain conditions the need
was felt for someone to arbitrate. Sometimes a single individual succeeded in imposing his authority, and, whether
he came from the nobility, the merchant class, or the
proletariat, provided only that he could solve the prevailing problems and rule, he was welcomed. He was
called "tyrant"—which means no more than "master."
There were plenty of benevolent tyrannies, that of Poly-
crates in Samos, of Pisistratus and Pericles at Athens, of
Gelon and Dionysius at Syracuse . . . but there were
many instances, too, of the plotter and the incompetent
seizing power. Tyranny, which had been born of the
people, became unpopular when the violence of its methods was turned not against the nobles but against the

plebs. Besides, indiscipline, which was endemic to the Hellenes, could not long endure dictatorship. The mob overturned the tyrants.

It was the turn of democracy to triumph. It was hailed as the ultimate goal, as the crowning mercy, of a long process of political evolutions. Demos was king, and Demos was proud of his kingship. The people forgot the precept enunciated in ancient days by Odysseus that "the government of the many is never good." They grew drunk on freedom, on argument and talk. This was the great age of Greek particularism, which produced masterpieces and paved the way for disaster.

—450   Greek democracy, however, remained curiously oligarchic. At a time when the total population of Athens numbered 450,000 it included about 250,000 slaves, more than 80,000 aliens, resident or otherwise, and only 120,-000 citizens proper. That means, if one deducts the women and the children, that only thirty to forty thousand persons were eligible to take part in public affairs. Democracy was confined to the privileged, and only one man in fifteen could exercise political rights. Athenian democracy was rigorously exclusive of all who were not citizens by right of birth, and, because it needed manpower for carrying loads, drawing vehicles, and working at the oar, it did not even so much as discuss the rights and wrongs of slavery.

It carried the seeds of destruction in itself. Greek democracy yielded to the temptations of mediocrity, self-satisfaction, and wastefulness. It turned to demagogy, and condemned its best men because it had a horror of leadership. It annihilated its élite, and by so doing weakened the power of the city to resist aggression. The result was that Athens had to bow to Sparta, and Greece as a whole to surrender to the barbarian.

SPARTA; OR,
LIFE ON THE BARRACK SQUARE

Sparta was an exception among the cities of Greece. The normal processes of their evolution passed it by. Having moved from monarchy to aristocracy after the Dorian invasions, it remained obstinately fixated at that point, and knew neither tyranny nor democracy. Its political immobility was but one aspect of a failure to evolve. Another was the nature of its economy. Sparta would have no more to do with trade or colonization than with the vainglories of art and literature. It lived with its eyes turned inward, self-sufficient and protectionist, knowing no other business than that of war.

The whole of life in Sparta was subordinated to military needs. The young were the property of the State; the old lived and died under arms. The normal condition of the city was one of perpetual mobilization. The army, which meant all citizens who were physically fit, had to be ready to take the field at any moment.

Nothing must be allowed to distract the Spartans from their warrior mission. They needed neither poets nor temples. They held philosophy in contempt, except in so far as it exalted the doctrine of force. They despised architects save as builders of fortifications. They turned from gold and silver, and used only iron bars as internal currency.

Family ties counted for little in the Lacedaemonian barracks, where life in common was the rule. A husband was a soldier. A mother was nothing but a mother of soldiers. A child was a potential soldier.

Society was organized in a strict hierarchy of four classes. The nobles, who descended in direct line from the Dorians, enjoyed full political rights. They numbered no more than a few thousands, and between them all available land was divided in equal and inalienable lots. Territorial property passed at death to the eldest son. These full citizens were strictly forbidden to possess any of the precious metals. They must beware of the temptations of luxury! They must be warriors, and nothing more.

The perioeci were free men, but without property rights. They might be artisans or traders, and could own land outside the boundaries of the city. On the other hand, they paid permanent and regular taxes, and were eligible for military service.

The helots were State serfs, attached to the land on which they worked. They could be killed with impunity. The young Spartiates would often make concerted attacks on them at night. But, though the law did not protect them, it made use of them in the army. They served as light infantry, and were the anonymous "cannon-fodder."

Below them came the slaves, who were private property serving their masters in peace and war.

In this way was the whole city dragooned. Those who governed, those who paid, those who worked, must all, in their condition, fight and die, if necessary, for the greatness of Sparta.

—750　　It is doubtful whether Lycurgus, to whom this system was attributed, ever existed. Nor is it certain whether this mythical figure was responsible for the strange political constitution of Sparta, which provided for two hereditary kings, who performed the functions of priests, judges, and generals under the eyes of watchful and suspicious magistrates. There were, in addition, a senate of elders, and a legislative assembly of which all full citizens were members. Oligarchy in Sparta served as a mask to what, in fact, was a gerontocracy and a double monarchy.

Despite all precautions which she took to maintain her strength, Sparta was not invulnerable. She carried the seed of destruction within herself. Though she might forbid the possession of gold or silver, her citizens evaded the law by depositing their capital abroad. She might legislate against the alienation of State lands, but she could not prevent her nobles from running into debt, from mort-

gaging and ultimately transferring their property, and so
helping to create an opulent minority. She might limit the
rights of the perioeci, but she could not forever dam their
growing power. Her constant terror was lest a day might
come when the helots would rise against their oppressors.

ATHENS; OR,
SHOPKEEPERS OF GENIUS

Sparta—Athens; the antithesis is just a shade too facile,
but it expresses admirably the particularism which was
the outstanding characteristic of classical Greece. The
two cities were less than 100 miles apart, yet they dif-
fered utterly from one another—in politics, in manners,
in ideals. Sparta lived for war, Athens for trade. Sparta
has been the delight of German historians, Athens the
pride of English.

To regard Athens as merely a liberal democracy rich in
ennobling and perilous lessons for humanity is to shut our
eyes to other aspects of the city. It had experienced, in
succession, kingship, aristocracy, and tyranny before blos-
soming at last into democracy. It came into existence at
the foot of the Acropolis, under the protection of its
tutelary divinity, the virgin goddess Athena. It grew as
the result of hard work on the part of craftsmen, potters,
smiths, and fishermen—to say nothing of the farmers of
Attica. The first kings were expelled by the nobles, whose   —682
assembly, sitting on the hill of Ares, formed the Areopagus. But already the tide of democracy was setting, and
it proved to be irresistible. The penal code drawn up by   —621
Draco is remarkable less for its harshness than for its
equity. Justice was to be pitiless, but it was to be the
same for all. Some years later the reforms of Solon did
away once and for all with the privileges of birth. The   —594
insolvent were relieved (by the abrogation of mortgages,
the abolition of arrest for debt, and the devaluation of
the drachma). The whole body of the citizens was divided

into four classes, based not on birth but on property. Solon was the father of the plutocratic revolution.

He had intervened as the benevolent arbiter of civil strife. All that now remained was for him to see that he was obeyed. Pisistratus, who carried on his work, had at his disposal means of which Solon had known nothing. —561 He seized power, and he laid down the law. As popular dictator he forcibly divided up the lands which had been confiscated from the nobles, and silenced the factions. As a patron of the arts he built on the Acropolis a temple of one hundred feet, the Hekatompedon. Athens became one of the metropolitan centers of Greece.

A century later another tyrant set the coping-stone upon the city's glory. Though his reign lasted for only —446 fifteen years, he gave his name to a period. Though he was a master whose hand never weakened, his name finds a place in the scroll of Athenian democracy. Pericles was the champion of democratic imperialism.

It was under him that the word "democracy" was born, and under him that the democratic system reached its apogee. The Areopagus was now no more than a tribunal with strictly limited powers. Other assemblies, of more popular origin, drafted and voted the laws. The magistrates who administered them were elected or appointed by lot, which was a way of associating the gods in the government of the city.

Athens has remained an inspiration for mankind: first, as an example of the genius that shone resplendent on the Acropolis, and radiated an influence upon the civiliza- —438 tions of more than a thousand years. It built the Parthenon, that poem in marble with the Propylaea as its epigraph. Never, in future ages, was the human spirit to rise to greater heights.

But she is an example, too, of liberty—of the liberty of free association on which has been built the prosperity of commerce, companies, and banks; of the liberty to say, to write, and to think all that man's mind can conceive,

which has created the climate in which masterpieces can
grow; of liberty in religion, to believe or to abstain from
belief, with its legacy to mankind of dreams built round
the lovely legends of the pagan mythology, and of delight
in the feasts and mysteries which expressed and perpetuated them.

She would have liked, too, to be for the world an example of human equality. She made, it is true, no distinction between noble and commoner. But equality is not
of this world. Even she made a point of distinguishing
those of her citizens who were born of Athenian parents
from foreigners, and it was not in her power to suppress
slavery, which, though a social scourge, was for her an
economic necessity. Nor was it possible even for her to
prevent the antagonism that rises between classes—the
great landowners of the plain, the ship-masters and traders of the coast, the peasants and shepherds of the mountains. Strife multiplied and grew big in a city where the
word was all-powerful.

Finally, she would have liked to remain an example of   —484
prosperity. The silver of the Laurium mines, extracted by
slaves, did, it is true, assure for her the hegemony of
Greece. Her fleet was mistress of the seas. The Piraeus,
main center of big business, admitted free of duty grain
and all raw materials, and other imports were subjected
to a duty of only 2 per cent, which was tantamount to
free trade. The islands of the Aegean sought her out as   —478
a protector and became her satellites, paying her a tribute, adopting her coinage, her weights and measures, and
her institutions. She became an empire. But the prosperity of the few is not the prosperity of all. There were rich
and poor. Poverty was rife in the home of democracy. In
vain were the indigent invited to emigrate and found colonies; in vain was an attempt made to develop the system
of pensions, allowances, and public assistance. The only
effect of these increased charges was to cripple the treasury. Liabilities exceeded assets. The taxes weighed heav-

ily on a minority which grew smaller year by year. Athens had recourse to desperate expedients—to confiscations and voluntary contributions. But, in the long run, her

—494   wars brought ruin. When her mines were exhausted, even though her empire was enfranchised, what remained to her? Nothing but the memory of dead greatness.

For Athens did die. Her death-agony was slow, but it was sure. It worked itself out in an atmosphere of indiscipline and corruption, of excesses and bribery. She persecuted the best of her children. Miltiades died in prison; Themistocles saved his life by fleeing abroad; Aristides was subjected to the rigors of ostracism; Socrates was made to drink the hemlock; and once even Pericles was condemned to death. The legislature sought to assume the powers of government. The executive found it impossible to fulfill its functions. While orators orated the birthrate fell and civic sense grew weak. When, spurred on by

—338   Demosthenes, Athens tried to rouse herself to one last effort, it was already too late. The barbarians were at the gates.

CIVIL STRIFE
AND WATCHFUL BARBARIANS

The history of Greece is, in large part, the history of cities devoured by envy of one another, and endlessly fighting to acquire a supremacy that was never more than temporary. In this continuing warfare Sparta, thanks to her army, held all the trumps on land; Athens, because of her fleet, at sea. But other partners took a hand and queered the pitch.

No good purpose would be served by our following in detail these recurrent wars, in which a few thousand men met in a clash of arms with the object of defending interests that were of purely local significance. Sparta managed very early to establish her suzerainty over the Pelo-

—459   ponnese, and Athens hers in the Aegean. Coalitions were

formed. Successes alternated with failures. There was a
patched-up peace which recognized spheres of influence.   —446
It was agreed that both sides should have recourse to arbitration in the event of disagreement. But the two adversaries kept watchful eyes on each other, taking advantage
of the cessation of hostilities to get their second wind.

It had been solemnly laid down that the peace should
be for thirty years. Needless to say, it was broken before
that period had elapsed. There was a new war, from which   —421
only the army contractors emerged with profit. It was
followed by a new peace and new promises of arbitration, which were soon forgotten. Because Athens wanted
to extend her power in Sicily, Sparta went to the help of
Syracuse on the plea that she was concerned to liberate
the Greek cities from Athenian imperialism. Brute force
always has the better of eloquence, no matter how cou-
rageous. Athens collapsed and surrendered. By the terms   —404
of the treaty she had to demolish the "long walls" which
linked the city to the Piraeus, evacuate all her foreign
territories, and accept the humiliation of a Spartan alliance.

But Greece had done no more than change masters.
Sparta pounced like a beast of prey on Hellas. Athens
waited for an opportunity to take her revenge, and found
it in co-operating with Thebes, whose turn it now was to
enter the lists. The Theban Epaminondas defeated the   —371
Spartan armies. And so the interminable hurly-burly went
on between cities which could never be reconciled, but
exhausted themselves in base intrigues and vain hero-
isms, until the day came when a foreign sword quelled
their differences.

There was nothing lacking to this tragi-comedy—not
leagues or congresses, not pacts or oaths or treacheries.
Not even foreign intervention which the Greeks sought
in their blindness.

For all this civil strife was taking place under the eyes
of the barbarians, and often with their complicity and

support. They were close at hand, waiting for civilization to founder that they might seize its treasures. In the west the Semite Carthaginians were hungry for the rich empire of Syracuse. But they, at least, did not endanger Greece itself, and Dionysius the Elder succeeded in saving his country. It was otherwise in the east and north, for there the enemy was more nearly threatening: in the east the Persians, heirs of Assyrian Asia; in the north the Indo-European bands, the settled Macedonians, the still nomadic Celts. Greece, which for two centuries had held at bay the Persian danger, could stand up to the Macedonian hurricane for no more than twenty years.

PERSIANS VERSUS GREEKS

In the eyes of the men who built the Parthenon the Persians were barbarians. Who, in comparison with themselves, was not? And, indeed, the Persians, like the Medes whom they had evicted, were scarcely more than Indo-European nomads when from Iran they thundered to attack the old Assyrian Empire which later they were to rebuild. Cyrus took Babylon and rich Lydia. Cambyses conquered Egypt and Ethiopia. It was left for Darius merely to organize this universe which stretched over all the Middle East and included a large bite of the African continent.

—545

—500

Though these conquering Persians might be barbarians to Greek eyes, they were no longer savages. They knew how to build palaces, though these great edifices were marked more by luxury than elegance. They had acquired a taste for wealth. Their religion, at first confined to the worship of the sun, the moon, fire, and the winds, underwent reform as the result of the astonishing preaching of Zoroaster. This curious man held that there was only one God, the Maker of the Universe, the King of Heaven and dispenser of all good things, a God of purity and justice. Six centuries before Christ, thus spake Zarathustra. But the

—550

Persians were not ripe for monotheism. They achieved a compromise between their primitive beliefs and the teaching of Zoroaster. Their wise men retained Mithras, the god of light and protector of kings: they adopted Ormuzd, the almighty deity and the spirit of good. But they set up in opposition to him the spirit of evil and gave him an attendant train of satellite divinities.

The Persians had a gift for administration. Their empire was divided into satrapies. Their fiscal system, of which a tax on land was the foundation, was coherent. Their currency, which comprised a golden daric and a coin of silver, was in use throughout their dominions. In more than one way they were equipped to teach a lesson to kaleidoscopic Greece.

It was but natural that they should take advantage of the double superiority conferred on them by unity and numbers. They had a professional army, while the Greeks, with the single exception of Sparta, could put only a civic militia into the field. The prey was tempting and close at hand. The armies of Darius landed in Attica. The defense of Hellas depended on Athens alone.

In a plain which has remained forever famous the Athenians repulsed the invader. The battle of Marathon saved Greece. It was a triumph of militiamen caparisoned —490 in iron against half-naked barbarians. The Athenian phalanx was armed with lance and sword. The men who composed it wore helmets and breastplates, had shields upon their arms and greaves upon their legs. The Persians were equipped only with bows and wicker targets. The heavy-armed infantry of Miltiades established its superiority over the archers of Darius.

"The victory is ours!" cried the soldier who had run from Marathon to Athens. But victory merely delayed the peril. Xerxes, the son of Darius, returned to the charge. He forced the pass of Thermopylae, where the Spartans had left no more than a rearguard. In spite of —480

Salamis, in spite of Plataea, in spite of Greek historians, the Persian threat continued.

The cities of Greece had proved once again that they were incapable of coming to terms. They had refused to accept unity of command, and some of them had talked of concluding a separate peace. The Persians had been not so much conquered as contained. Even though their reputation had suffered, their power remained intact. They were still masters of those provinces of Asia Minor which formerly Greeks had colonized. They took a hand in the —412   disputes of the Greek cities, allied themselves with Sparta, were prodigal of gold in an attempt to assure the defeat of —404   Athens, then turned against Sparta, intrigued with Thebes, enrolled Greek mercenaries, and acted as arbiters in the local conflicts of the Greeks. These barbarians were clever diplomatists.

Actually they were strong only because Greece was weak. When it came to action it was found that the Persian colossus had feet of clay. They could never carry their warfare to a triumphant conclusion, because they lacked that irresistible drive which took the Macedonians into the heart of Greece and out to the boundaries of the known world.

THE MACEDONIAN SAGA

To the north of Greece, between Epirus and Thrace, stretched the mountains, the grazing grounds, and the forests of Macedonia. Its people lived as horse-breeders in an inhospitable land. It seems doubtful whether they can be called Greeks. Demosthenes included them in the anonymous horde of barbarians, and his countrymen regarded them as being little better than beasts. The Mediterranean civilization had scarcely touched this mongrel Balkan race, a mingled product of Thracians, Illyrians, and Epirotes. The Greeks laughed at the archaic and old-fashioned institutions of a country which, ignorant of democracy, lived still in a system of hereditary monarchy more suited to the Homeric age.

This hereditary monarchy, however, was to make the fortunes of the Macedonians. There came to the throne an ambitious king, a great lover of wine, women, horses, and sports. His name was Philip. Ever since he had started —359 to work the mines of Mount Pangaeus he had never been —356 without resources. He minted money which bore his name, and this made it possible for him to maintain an army and to buy men's consciences and the alliance of powerful neighbors. His troops were well equipped with very long lances, thanks to which several ranks of the phalanx could move simultaneously to the attack. His cavalry was trained not to seek out occasions of single combat, but to operate in unison. It became a tactical body with an ease of movement which enabled it to envelop the enemy's flanks. More important still, the whole Macedonian army was controlled by a General Staff which kept a watchful eye on its communications and saw to it that the men were well provided.

With such means to his hand Philip went from success to success. He took Thessaly, Chalcidice, and Thrace. In vain did Demosthenes sound the call to arms. At Chaero- —354 nea Philip crushed the combined armies of Athens and —338 Thebes. Corinth opened its gates. The Spartan posses- sions were mutilated. Greece became unified, but in the interests of a foreigner.

Philip had a son who continued his work. Alexander set out to unify the East. He was nineteen when he mounted the throne; he died at thirty-three, after a reign —336 of epic achievement. Not only were those fourteen years rich in actions calculated to strike men's minds with won- der, to leave behind them a wealth of legends, and to thrill the poets. They turned the world upside down, and, through the triumphs of this young, half-barbarian con- queror, revealed to it the splendors of Hellenism.

The operative principle of Alexander's career was an

insatiable pride and a thirst for booty that nothing could slake. At heart he was still a nomad, never happy unless he were on the move with his horsemen about him. He was handsome and healthy, a god-made man, Achilles risen from the grave.

Like Achilles, too, he appeared before Troy. He had crossed the Dardanelles and thrust his javelin into the —334 soil of Asia in token of possession. He had assured his rearward communications by completing the submission of Greece, by razing Thebes to the ground after an ineffectual revolt, and by silencing the Illyrians and the Celts of the Adriatic fringe. Asia lay open before him.

Persia was decadent, and crumbled. Its ill-led soldiers could not stand before the advance of this commander of —333 genius. Phrygia fell, Lydia, and the whole of Asia Minor. At Issus the Persian army melted away, and Darius fled, abandoning his family to the conqueror. Within the empire of Persia the satrapies were taken over by Mace- —332 donians. Alexander tirelessly pursued his course. He defeated first Syria, then Egypt. In the course of the campaign he founded Alexandretta and Alexandria, and sent a scientific expedition to explore the Upper Nile. Then —331 he turned back on Mesopotamia, took Babylon and Susa, crossed the Euphrates and the Tigris, pursued Darius into —330 Persia, and found there only his dead body. From Persepolis he moved up to the Caspian, penetrated the country which was later to become Turkestan, occupied the future —329 Samarkand, swept on towards India, and broke through the line of the Indus. He reached the banks of the —326 Hyphasus and dreamed of reaching the not far distant sources of the Ganges, which for the ancients marked the limits of the world.

But the conqueror's army was tired. The distance it had covered was approximately that of the North Pole from the South. After seventy days of rain the summer monsoon proved to be too much for the spirit of his men. They refused to go farther. Alexander gave way to his "old

sweats." The ebb of the tide had set in, and the *Grande
Armée* was now embarked upon its Odyssey. It recrossed   —323
the Indus, returned to Susa and to Babylon. It was in the
latter place that Alexander died, carried off in a brief fort-
night by malaria. The meteoric adventure was over.

To the question, "What was it that Alexander wanted?"
the answer can scarcely be in doubt—universal empire.
It was not enough for him to sit upon the throne of the
King of Kings at Babylon, or in Egypt to be the heir of all
the Pharaohs. He dreamed of reducing Carthage to
slavery. He wanted to be acknowledged as the son of
Zeus.

At heart he was still a barbarian: civilization had been
no more than a veneer. Those of his relations who got in
his way he had murdered. At Persepolis, after a drunken
orgy, he set fire to the Palace of Xerxes. He was shameless
in his bigamy. There was more in him of the Oriental
than the Greek.

But he had been blessed with a high order of intelligence. He could not only conquer, but administer. He did
more than defeat his enemies: he made them his partners
in governing. His despotism was creative. He made a
melting-pot of the nations, and crushed old empires beneath his feet. He carried the Greek genius to the ends
of the earth. He molded a new world.

DEATH IN SPLENDOR

Alexander's empire had been cut to the measure of a
hero. It was too large for his successors. There had been
no time for the conqueror to make known his wishes before he died. Even had he been able to do so his heritage
would almost certainly have been too heavy for human
shoulders to carry. His empire fell to pieces, and the frag-
ments became the booty of his lieutenants. Antigonus laid
claim to Greece, Antiochus to Asia, and Ptolemy to Egypt.

Greece was well on the way to decadence. More than

ever the cities were at one another's throats. The parties
quarreled endlessly. Social revolutions alternated with
political. The rich dreaded reforms on communist lines.
The barbarians were threatening as never before, and
—279   this time they were savages indeed—Illyrians, Thracians,
Celts—who advanced as far as Delphi, and then flowed
back again towards the north, finally settling in the tract
of country lying between the Danube and Byzantium.
But even now the flame of Hellenism was not quite ex-
tinguished. Its dying sparks could still dazzle the world.

The Middle East fell to the lot of the Seleucidae, who
established a dynasty in which the incapable and the
drunken outnumbered the able. Its sole distinction lay in
having inspired the Ptolemies in the matter of political
economy.

For it was Egypt that truly carried on the Greek tradition, though in a version peculiarly its own. The intellectual climate was Greek, at least so far as the rulers were
concerned. The people might remain Egyptian and opposed to all forms of Hellenism, but the Ptolemies themselves were Greek, as were their civil servants and their
troops. Greek was the official language. It was the ambition of Alexandria to become a new Athens, and this in
some sort it was. Commerce flowed into its harbor, at the
entrance to which, on the island of Pharos, stood a light-
house three hundred and sixty feet high, and learning
filled its great library—nearly 500,000 scrolls stored close
to a former temple of the Muses. The city was laid out in
rectilinear blocks, and the buildings were on an enormous
scale. Each of its five districts was designated by a letter
of the alphabet. If, to some extent, it evoked memories of
Athens it also vaguely prefigured New York.

But in spite of everything Egypt was Egypt still—the
old Egypt of the Pharaohs, at once monarchical and so-
cialistic. The Ptolemies carried on the tradition of absolute monarchy wedded to State socialism. All land belonged to them; every form of produce was theirs by right.

Public functionaries were in charge of agriculture, industry, and trade. They organized reserves of foodstuffs. The production of oil and salt, the tanning of leather, the making of papyrus, spinning and weaving, were all State monopolies, as, too, were the mines and the working of metals. The State was the chief industrialist and the chief trader. It held a monopoly in the export of oil, wine, and cereals. It alone could import and sell incense and perfumes, spices and precious stones. On all other imports a customs duty of 25 per cent was levied. Individualist Greece would scarcely have recognized herself in this all-absorbing State economy.

Big business had come into its own all over the Eastern Mediterranean. Navigation had progressed since the days of the Argonauts. Ships were better designed, more adequately decked, and swifter. Rigging, it is true, was still somewhat rough-and-ready, and an oar, hand-controlled at the stern, remained the only means of steering. Nevertheless a regular service linked the Mediterranean ports, at least during the fine season. To Hippalus, a pilot of Alexandria, belongs, it is said, the credit of having discovered the periodic rhythm of the monsoons, and he is believed to have had the idea of using his knowledge for the purpose of trading with India. Delos was a great slave-market; Rhodes, with its harbor straddled by a gigantic statue, a vast clearing-house for grain. It was a citizen of Rhodes who thought out the first known system of insurance. Everywhere banking and credit were at their zenith. Foreign exchange, deposit accounts, loans at interest, ledger transfers, were now normal. Bank checks were in common use.

But the opulence of the rich was a standing insult to the destitution of the urban and rural proletariat. Alexander's foreign wars, by revealing the existence of unsuspected mines and hidden treasure, had at first given an impetus to depreciation and rising prices. But very soon the over-production of food reversed the tendency. Wages fell, because it was necessary to compete with slave-labor, and life for the poor became hard.

There was a gradual break-up of the family. Women no longer stayed at home, but went out into the world of men, where they practiced law, took up architecture, and even engaged in chariot-racing. With the coming of Cleopatra a woman was actually to rule as queen. But children were now more and more scarce, and the threat of depopulation lay over Greece and the whole of the Aegean. A falling birth rate is a logical consequence of the simultaneous existence of great wealth and extreme poverty. When life tends to be concentrated in a few great cities, the countryside is left to run to seed.

Hellenism in its decadence sinned by an excess of civilization. Everything was turning soft—courage, faith, virtue, and even language. Greece had finished her course. It was for a more virile nation to carry on the torch.

THE CULTURAL CONTRIBUTION
OF GREECE

From the time of Mycenae to that of Alexander, from prehistory to the centuries of the Alexandrine inheritance, Greece had been enormously prolific. She had taught many lessons to mankind which future ages have not let die.

First, and above all, in the realm of the spirit Greece was the teacher—nay, the high-priest—of beauty. The Hellenes were not content merely to carve marble and make poetry. They had the passion and the pride of the beautiful.

Egyptian temples are larger than Greek temples. In the centuries to come the Gothic cathedrals struck more deeply into men's emotions; but no human architecture has ever been more flawlessly lovely than the Greek in its heyday. A beauty of line was achieved which has never been surpassed.

Temples on the summit of the Acropolis or on the slopes of Attic hills, theaters open to the light of heaven, stadia, market-places, cities, all bear witness to the master-touch of Hellas. Nor was Athens alone in achieving such perfection. Delphi, Epidaurus, Aegina, Corinth—these places had the same message to give: the Doric order is the purest, the Ionic the lightest, the Corinthian the most elegant, known to man. In them we can trace the evolution of Greek art—almost, one might say, of human thought.

There were Phidias and Apelles, Homer and Aesop, Herodotus and Thucydides. There was Socrates, who wrote nothing but said a great deal. At the Academy was Plato; at the Lyceum, Aristotle. There were also Aeschylus, Sophocles, and Euripides, who, followers of the car of Thespis and the rites of Dionysus, invented the drama; Aristophanes, devoted to comedy; and Pericles, the statesman. The primitive age could give us the Heraion of Olympia, the age of decadence the *Victory of Samothrace.* Athens was a capital, Tanagra no more than a village, but beauty was everywhere. It dwelt in the hearts of the Greek people, and they made of it the first of all the virtues. Aphrodite, goddess of beauty, lorded it on Mount Ida over the wife of Zeus and over the goddess of Reason. Helen, queen of beauty, expressed in her one person all of Hellas. Phryne, the courtesan, won with her beauty the pardon of her judges. What other country in the world has ever given so high a place to beauty and intellect?

With the cult of beauty went respect for strength and dexterity. Zeus with his thunderbolt crushed the Titans. Apollo with his arrows slew the Cyclops. Herakles with his club accomplished many more than twelve labors. Milon of Croton carried a bull upon his back and felled it with a blow of his fist. The Greek athletes measured their strength with one another at those Olympic Games, which, in their recurrent four-year rhythm, served the Greeks as a measurement of time.

The Greeks had the cult neither of the good nor of the true. They made their gods in their own image—liars, thieves, adulterers, murders. Of morality and justice they were ignorant. Life at Olympus was made up of scandals, small and great. The world of the gods was a world imagined on the human scale, accessible, familiar. The gods were no more than men endowed with immortality, subject to weakness and to passions. In them the Greeks saw themselves reflected.

They took them where they found them, and adopted them into the life of Greece. Rhea was Cretan, Zeus Indo-European, Apollo was a Dorian importation. Poseidon was from Aeolis, Dionysus a Thracian, Aphrodite from Cyprus. At a later period the Greeks borrowed Mithras from the Persians, Isis from Egypt. They came in time to think that divinities were universal, but in assimilating them they had a feeling that they had made them peculiarly their own. Anyhow, what did it matter, provided the legends were sufficiently beautiful to inspire sculptors and poets, orators and dramatists?

Truth counted for little with the Greeks. Their philosophers constructed systems that were not, all of them, rational. The lessons which they proffered or sold in the streets were more often sophistical than wise. Diogenes might mock at human folly, but Epicurus lauded human instinct. Plato believed that the heavenly bodies were gifted with intelligence, that the compass was a divine instrument. The progress of arithmetic was hindered by prejudice. The Greeks were barely beyond the stage of counting with pebbles: etymologically the word "calculation" means no more than that. For figures they used the letters of the alphabet, and gave to numbers a mystic significance. Both Aristotle and Plato were in this respect much to blame.

Mediocre arithmeticians though they were, the Greeks had a natural gift for geometry. To the lovers of lines and planes geometry had in it something of architecture. It is by no means certain that Thales and Pythagoras ever existed, but there is nothing legendary about their theorems. Euclid gathered together into a bundle the first triumphs of geometry. Hipparchus was the creator of trigonometry. Apollonius made a shrewd guess at analytic geometry. Archimedes of Syracuse, one of the greatest geniuses of all time, succeeded, without any knowledge of the decimal system, in establishing the truth that π exceeds 3 by a fraction lying somewhere between $1\%_0$ and $1\%_8$ (roughly 3.141). This same Archimedes conceived the infinitesimal calculus, and opened vast horizons to physics and mechanics—specific weights, floating bodies, centers of gravity. . . .

—285

In the realm of biology Hippocrates, by establishing a method, became the father of medical science—though that did not stop men from saying that he could cure the incurable malady of love! The dissection of the bodies of animals advanced the science of anatomy, though it was not until the time of the Ptolemies that the dissection of human corpses was permitted.

Knowledge of the earth and sky progressed. The Greeks knew that yellow amber—which they called electron—when rubbed acquired the property of attracting light bodies. They knew that the earth is spherical, and tried to calculate its circumference. They discovered that our planet turns on its own axis, and Aristarchus of Samos even advanced the theory that it revolves about the sun, and that the sun is the center of a system of which the earth forms part. Seventeen centuries were to elapse before mankind rediscovered this explanation of the world. But the Greeks rejected the hypothesis, and accused Aristarchus of impiety. They preferred the sublime myth of Apollo's chariot—another example of the triumph of the beautiful over the true.

—250

THE MATERIAL CONTRIBUTION
OF GREECE

As the centuries pass, so do technical achievements in many different fields grow nearer to perfection. The age of Greece gave to the world the endless screw, the cogwheel, the waterwheel, the windmill, the hydraulic clock, and the organ. It introduced into Egypt the camel, which was to conquer Africa. It invented the anchor, and thus facilitated the use of harbor moorings by ships. These material triumphs may seem of secondary importance. But there was one which struck to the very center of human life. By developing a system of currency Greece revolutionized economics. In the *Iliad* the only money was oxen. The single animal was the unit of calculation. A beautiful slave was worth four oxen. Achilles sold the son of Priam for a hundred oxen.

—750 Later tripods of bronze or iron and, at a still more advanced period, ingots of metal served as currency. It was in Lydia, a country of Hellenized Asia, that pieces of stamped gold and silver first made their appearance. They were to remain for thousands of years the media of exchange, the measure of value, the means of accumulating wealth.

The country where money first emerged into the light of human knowledge has something almost legendary about it. It was, to some extent, the Eldorado of the

—700 ancient world. Was it money that made Lydia rich, or was it Lydian riches that produced money? King Gyges possessed a golden ring which made its wearer invisible. Is it not arguable that his ring was a symbol of metal coinage

—550 —that is to say, of transferable wealth, which is both anonymous and ubiquitous? The wealth of King Croesus has remained proverbial. In neighboring Phrygia, King Midas could turn to gold all that he touched—for Phrygia, like Lydia, was watered by the river Pactolus, which swept down grains of gold in its current.

From Lydia money spread over the whole of the East. In Persia men minted the daric. In Aegina coins were is- —670 sued bearing the mark of the tortoise. In Athens the coinage carried the emblem of the owl. Philip of Macedon made the use of golden coinage general. After Alexander, the mines of Colchis and the Urals, of India and Arabia, fed the mints of the world. Very soon the cities learned the art of debasing and devaluing their money. The Greek world grew intoxicated with this pastime.

The minting of coinage brought with it the trade in money. Changers operated at street-corners, and later became bankers. The Greeks, true sons of Hermes and Odysseus, discovered the miracle of credit. On this score alone their material contribution to the history of mankind amounted to a revolution.

But Greece's contributions occurred in every field, and their value has stood the test of time. Many centuries after the Age of Greece civilized man continued to talk and to think Greek. Two thousand years after the fall of Athens the scientists of every country are still using Greek words for the tools and instruments of their own new world.

IN THE LAND OF BUDDHA

Alexander, in the course of his journey to the rising sun, halted, after crossing the Indus, at the approaches of the Ganges. In his person Greece made contact with the civilization of India.

The Aryans had for a considerable while imposed their rule upon the original inhabitants of that country. Like them, they worshiped the divinities of nature—the sky and the fire. Their Sacred Books, the Vedas, written in Sanskrit, ascribed great importance to rites and sacrifices. Their priests, or Brahmins, had early remodeled the Vedic

religion in their own interest, making of Brahminism a
system of castes in which Aryan priests, warriors, and
peasants were set apart from the great mass of non-
Aryans. Hierarchy is an Aryan conception.

—560   But somewhere to the north of Benares, in the noble
family of the Sakyas, a prince was born who, at the age
of nineteen, renounced the pleasures of the aristocratic
life, and became a monk. One night, as he sat meditating
under a fig-tree, he had a revelation. He became the Il-
luminated, the Buddha. From then on he taught his doctrine which was all compact of charity and compassion. It
denied the value of sacrificial rites, and offered men what
was more a discipline than a religion. After a lifetime of
—483   alms-giving and good works the Buddha died, his head
towards the north, between two trees which burst into
flower, though it was winter, and covered him with their
white petals.

Buddhism, which knows no distinction of castes or
races, and aids the humble, soon became popular. It had
—326   already spread through India at the time of Alexander's
—260   expedition. After the Macedonian epic had run its course
the king Asoka himself accepted this new religion which
knew no gods. His conversion, so legend says, was due to
the remorse into which he had been plunged by the murder
of his ninety-nine brothers, or, in another version, by the
burning of his five hundred wives. In strict truth, Asoka
seems to have been a monarch who was more concerned
with the digging of wells and the planting of trees along
the roads of his kingdom than with cutting his neighbor's
throat. However that may be, his conversion marked a
turning-point. Thereafter, Buddhism swept India, took
root in Ceylon, moved into China, and, by way of Kash-
mir, came face to face with Greek culture.

Greece, which had failed to reach the Ganges, was still
in evidence west of the Indus. Greek was actually spoken
on the banks of that river. Money bearing the heads of
Olympian deities was in circulation there. An art devel-

oped as a result of this contact, filled India with statues draped in the Greek manner, and produced a version of the Buddha himself with the features of Apollo. This conjunction gave birth to a Graeco-Buddhist civilization which, moving along the silk-routes, ended by inspiring the artists of China.

CHINA CONTINUES

While in Europe so many countries were still wrapped in the slumbers of prehistory, China had been pursuing its destiny. The Age of Greece was also the Age of China.

The differences between the Hellenic civilization and the contemporary civilization of the Yellow River are profound. The significance of the Greek Parthenon is far from being the same as that of the Chinese bronzes, and the influence of Greece upon the world has been far more direct than the influence of China.

Nevertheless the destinies of Greece and of China were almost parallel. The cities of Greece, heirs of a common culture, were continually engaged in fratricidal warfare. Similarly, China was fragmented, and emerged from feudal chaos only to be split up into hostile kingdoms.

The feudal period of China is reminiscent of the *Iliad* —quarrels of great lords, chivalrous encounters of handsome knights. But it is reminiscent, too, of philosophizing Athens. Wise men in China were rated higher than priests. Lao-tse taught that men should identify themselves with —600 the Tao, who is the harmony of the world. K'ung Fu-tse, whom the West was to know by the charming name of Confucius, exalted the authority of tradition, and long —500 before Socrates told men that they must know themselves before they could hope to grow better. By a singular coincidence, in the very same century that heard the voice of Confucius, the Jewish prophets were disseminating the idea of the One God, and Solon, Zoroaster, and Buddha were speaking to mankind. It was the era of sages.

But Chinese wisdom remained, at bottom, an affair of magical formulae and hieratic movements. Built on a system of rites and rhythms, it was the appropriate instrument of a civilization of scribes and musicians.

But the China of the "Warring Kingdoms" presents a different and an uglier face. Gone from battle was all its former chivalry. Even the technique of war had changed. The two-wheeled chariots had given place to hordes of mounted archers on the Mongol model. The conduct of the victors was atrocious. They boiled children alive in caldrons; they dismembered and devoured the women; they cut off sometimes 80,000, sometimes 240,000, sometimes 400,000 heads—trophies calculated to turn the Assyrians pale with envy.

The Chinese Alexander was called Che-Huang-ti. He eliminated in succession all his rivals. The kingdoms fell into his hands, and he succeeded in building a Chinese Empire which he exploited for his own profit. He imposed upon it by force a centralized administration, and broke the back of regional liberties by carrying through transfers of population on the largest possible scale. He unified the laws, standardized weights, measures, and money—which was of bronze—the width of the roads, the wheel-base of vehicles, and writing. The philosophers he despised. The China of Che-Huang-ti extended from the Yellow River to the Blue, and even farther. Canton was occupied by an army, and convicts were forcibly removed from prison and sent as colonists into the southern districts. The Great Wall was built to protect the Empire against the Huns—those Turko-Mongolian nomads who galloped across the steppes.

The Empire of Alexander failed to outlive its maker. Similarly, when Che-Huang-ti died there were no successors capable of carrying on his work, and China once again relapsed into anarchy. The barbarians, whom no Great Wall could ever hold in check for long, awaited their moment to strike.

(Margin notes: —335, —307, —230, —214, —215)

CHAPTER FOUR

The Thousand Years of Rome

THE DIM BEGINNINGS

IF THE apogee of Rome came later than that of Hellas, the Roman age encroached upon the Greek. The two civilizations interlocked in time like the links of a chain. The birth-pangs of Rome occurred at the very heart of the Greek centuries.

Not only must we travel back in time. In space we must adjust our eyes to a wider vision, break from the limits of the older civilizations, and move westward. The leadership of the world was shifting from the Eastern to the Western Mediterranean before moving northward.

Italy saw its first Indo-European invaders several centuries later than Greece, nor was it ever able, subsequently, —1200 to make up for the time-lag. Rome never achieved a refinement of culture comparable to that of the Greeks. Her shepherds might become farmers, her soldiers turn into lawyers, but deep in the heart of every Roman lay a heritage of fierceness and savagery. Marius had the heads of the proscribed brought to him at table; Caesar had his enemies slaughtered in cold blood; Tacitus welcomed a good massacre with cries of delight.

It is true that a little of everything can be found in the

history of Rome. Cruelty did not exclude greatness. If the Greeks taught beauty, the lesson of Rome was wholly one of unity. Rome, from being a village of herdsmen, became a city—the City. Round Rome as its center coalesced an immense empire, but Rome remained Rome, and only Rome: twenty peoples with a single heart; fifty provinces with a single head—*caput,* capital, Capitol—eighty millions of subjects all bearing the same stamp.

Rome, with her feet firmly set upon the highway of glory, sought to construct a past which should be worthy of her ambitions. Like a newly enriched tradesman, she concocted a family tree of gods and princes. She unearthed tales of her beginnings all compact of patriarchal rulers and tutelary beasts, ranging from a nursing wolf to a flock of guardian geese.

Not that her legendary origins need be regarded as wholly false. It is quite possible that after the taking of Troy a number of fugitives *did* make contact with the aboriginals of Italy, and take root at Latium. Farther to the north the Etruscans may also have traced their descent to immigrants from Asia Minor. It is quite certain that in the south the Greeks had carried the treasures of their civilization to Italian soil.

—750   It may be that the fable of the twins expressed the plurality of Rome's origins—Albans, Sabines, Latins, Romans—for all these small ethnic groups, neighbors and enemies alike, did ultimately combine. They mingled their blood; they adopted one another's gods, Saturn was a Sabine deity: Romulus, later deified under the name of Quirinus, and worshiped on the Quirinal, hailed from Alba: Jupiter, god of the day, could claim an Indo-European parentage. The very name of the "Flamens" has a family relationship with that of the Brahmins. Tarquin was Etruscan. Rome was a melting-pot in which myths and men alike were fused.

But for many centuries Rome was no more than a small market town among the villages of the Latin Confederation. She attached great importance to the building of a bridge over the Tiber, to her exploitation of the salt-marshes, to the construction of a harbor at the river's mouth. She placed her destinies in the hands of a king who was at once soldier, judge, and priest, and came not seldom from the ranks of the populace. Suffrage was given by general acclamation (which is the precise meaning of the word *suffragium*). Quite early she showed that hers was a lawyer's vocation. Her earliest code is thick with rites, and might well be part of a magician's textbook.

All about her in that early Italian dawn were other prosperous groups which seemed destined for a greater future. The Etruscans understood land-drainage, and could tear the iron and copper ore from the bowels of the earth. They had the secret of modeling vessels of a strange perfection. The Greeks of Sicily and Campania knew how to build temples and discuss philosophy. But Greek and Etruscan cities alike lacked precisely what was to make Rome great—strength of will.

THE REPUBLIC; OR, THE REIGN OF THE NOBLES

Early royalty at Rome was plebeian. But this popular system of government was not to the taste of the heads of the local clans, who were jealous of their authority. Consequently they imposed upon the State a republic which was patrician in complexion. For an elected king who occupied the throne only for life they substituted a dy- —500 archy of aristocrats. Two consuls, appointed for one year only, directed the affairs of the State—in such a way as not to give offense to the patricians. The real master of Rome was the Senate—the Assembly of Elder Statesmen. It was this body that drafted laws, granted credits, authorized the levying of troops, and controlled foreign

policy. The Senate was Rome—S.P.Q.R. It took precedence of the Roman people.

A time came, it is true, when plebeians were admitted
to its ranks, but this influx of "common" blood merely had
the effect of making it more vigorous. The Senate still remained an assembly of the privileged—whether aristocrats or rich men. The virtuous Cato was nothing but a
capitalist who was in reality defending the interests of the
senatorial aristocracy when he claimed to be defending
Rome. Cicero, the conservative, the champion of republican corruption, was, in fact, a man of the Senate against
the people.

For centuries the plebs were ranged against the entrenched patricians. Only if we realize that can we understand the domestic politics of the Roman Republic. It
becomes important, therefore, to ask what precisely was
this exploited plebeian class which looked back with nostalgic longing to the days of the kings? It may, in early
days, have consisted of Albans and Sabines conquered by
Rome. At a later stage, however, it numbered in its ranks
the whole of the urban and rural proletariat, the members
of which were systematically excluded by the aristocracy
from all administrative posts and all honors.

The plebs had both time and numbers on their side.
With patient obstinacy they advanced their claim to equal
rights. Their earliest success is to be seen in the creation
of certain magistracies the function of which was to defend them against their enemies. They acquired the right
of meeting publicly, and their decisions were known as
"plebiscites." They forced through a measure abolishing
slavery for debt, and compelled the Senate to adopt a law
regularizing marriage between the two orders. Gradually
they managed to gain access to the very offices from which
the nobles had tried to keep them—the military tribunate,
the quaestorship, membership in the College of Pontiffs
and Augurs.

They still, however, remained the disinherited. They

were poor. Whether as artisans or as salaried employees,
they had to reckon with the competition of slaves whose
unpaid labor introduced an artificial element into the price
pattern. As farmers they suffered from another form of
competition—that of the corn supplied by tributary territories. Not seldom they found themselves compelled to
leave their land and swell the ranks of the urban unemployed.

The reforms put through with the object of improving   —134
their condition were precarious. The Gracchi might succeed in getting grants of land for them, but the agrarian
laws soon neutralized any advantage they had gained.
After the Second Punic War the Senate utilized a party
truce to centralize all the powers of the State, and to draw
the teeth of the tribunate. The privileged were giving
nothing away.

Only when the safety of Rome was in jeopardy was the
Senate prepared to take a back place. When a serious
crisis arose full powers passed to a dictator chosen by the
consuls. But, no matter how great the danger might be,
the Senate was careful to hedge the office of dictator with
every possible safeguard. He was appointed for six months
only, and was not allowed to draw on the public funds.
His field of action, therefore, was much reduced.

Not all the dictators were docile; not all of them agreed
to bow to these restrictive ordinances. A time came when
civil strife imposed its own dictatorships. The first of these
was held by Marius, the champion of the plebs. This suc-   —108
cessful soldier built up his popularity on a number of
demagogic measures. By throwing open the army to members of the proletariat he offered them the chance of loot.
He reduced the price of corn, distributed the State lands
among his veterans, and, on occasions, confiscated some
of the large private estates. He bullied the Senate, called
the populace into the streets, and stood aside while patricians were massacred. He was the idol of the people.

After Marius came Sulla; after revolution, reaction.

Sulla was an aristocratic dictator who re-established the Senate in all its privileges, and took from the plebs most of the concessions they had won. His reprisals were ruthless. Then, suddenly, at the height of his powers, he abdicated. That he should do so was not very surprising. It was but natural that he should withdraw as soon as the Senate had recovered its sovereign rights.

—79

But the civil war was far from being over. The plebs were too strong passively to accept defeat. The suburbs and the country districts were seething with discontent. Spartacus called on the slaves to revolt. Capital took fright and fled from Italy. An embargo had to be placed upon the movement of gold. There was a panic on the Stock Exchange.

—73

Faced by the threat of social and financial collapse, the Senate looked about for a strong man. Sulla was dead; so, too, was Crassus, who had brought the slaves to their senses. Pompey was not reliable. Who was to save Rome from anarchy? The man of destiny was not an aristocrat, but the nephew of Marius. His name was Caesar.

—49

GROWING PAINS

Meanwhile Rome had expanded. At moments of crisis, when faced by external threats, she had managed to subdue domestic discord. She had carved out an empire for herself. Her victories were due to her army—an army solidly organized and magnificently disciplined. Failure to obey orders, desertion, and cowardice were all punished with death. If cavalry played but a small part, the heavy infantry could outclass any adversary it was likely to encounter, thanks to the completeness of the soldier's equipment, which consisted of a coat-of-mail, a helmet, a long shield, a throwing-spear, and a sword. Action was opened by a discharge of spears, after which the men went in with the sword.

Elephants were another military innovation. They had

first appeared in the field during the campaigns of Alexander, and had subsequently come to play a great part in
warfare. Rome procured them from the Atlas Mountains
in Africa. Their rôle as a mobile weapon continued until
the end of the Republic.

The art of fortification, too, had made great progress.
When on active service the Roman armies entrenched
themselves in rectangular camps, carefully constructed for
defense. These camps quite often grew into cities. Siege
methods had also been much improved. Rams were used
against standing walls, as well as catapults and ballistas,
which could discharge heavy stones against the enemy.

Thus equipped both for offensive and defensive tactics,
Rome was in a position to attack or to repulse. She had
long since reduced her neighbor cities and the hostile
mountain-folk. She had conquered, or was soon to conquer, Latium, Etruria, and Campania. She had to face,
one after the other, two powerful foes—the Celts, who
swept down from the north, and the Carthaginians, who
were masters of all the Western Mediterranean.

The Celts were Indo-European nomads who had ranged
all over Europe from the mouths of the Danube to the
Atlantic coast. They were as clever in the things of peace
as they were redoubtable in the arts of war. They must
have been great lovers of drinking and eating, for it was
they who invented the barrel and found out a method of
curing hams. But they were ready, too, to die for their independence. They used battle-cries which they called "slo-
gans." The Celts had long been established in Bohemia
and in Gaul, where they had driven back the Ligurians;
in Spain, where they lived side by side with the Iberians; in
the Northern Islands, where they were known as Britons.
By way of Switzerland and the valley of the Ticino they
now descended upon Italy. They reached the Po, marched   —383
on Rome, remained encamped in the Forum for several
months, and then withdrew northward. But they were

more than once to move on Rome, and so serious was their threat that the Republic had to come to terms with them. They sprawled over Central Europe, penetrating into Serbia, Hungary, Thrace, and even into Asia Minor, where they appeared later as Galatians. Had they been able to unite, Rome would have had cause indeed to tremble.

The Carthaginian peril was less intangible. The Celts were everywhere and nowhere. The Carthaginians were at Carthage. It was a question of Rome or Carthage. One of the two cities had to be wiped from the map of the world. There was no room in the Mediterranean for two such ambitious communities.

The Semites of Carthage, heirs of Phoenicia, claimed the right to forbid the coasts of Africa to foreign shipping. Their aim was to establish that maritime empire which for so long they had disputed with Athens. Their colonies swarmed over the coastal areas from Senegal to the Cameroons. The Romans championed the freedom of the seas. It was a case of peasants against traders; of landsmen against sailors.

The first clash came in Sicily. After twenty-three years of exhausting warfare the Romans succeeded in driving —241 the Carthaginians from the island and in making them pay a heavy indemnity.

Next it was Spain that became the prize and the pretext of a new conflict. This time the fighting lasted for —218 eighteen years. Italy was not spared the devastation of —216 war. Hannibal's cavalry crushed the Roman infantry at Cannae. If Rome had not been inspired with a spirit of fanatical determination, if Carthage had not been weakened by the necessity of dealing with insubordinate subjects at home, the Romans would have been permanently eliminated, and the course of history changed. The three Scipios, father, brother, and son, were the instruments of Rome's vengeance. The Carthaginians were driven out of —202 Italy and Spain, were harried even in their native Africa, and finally suffered defeat at Zama. They abandoned Spain for good and all—its silver-mines were to provide the basis of Rome's wealth—surrendered their elephants and their fleet, and were at the mercy of the conqueror.

But Rome was neither generous nor hoodwinked. Fifty years later, jealous of the territorial wealth which Carthage had succeeded in building up afresh, she determined to have done with her rival once and for all. The haughty —149 city was destroyed in accordance with Cato's wishes. Her population was sold into slavery and dispersed. Her lands became a Roman province.   —146

For Rome the struggle for existence was now over. But her people had developed a taste for conquest. It had brought treasure pouring in on them. Slaves and land were theirs for the asking. A dishonest diplomacy served the interests of a new imperialism. The Romans completed the occupation of Italy, absorbed Illyria, Greece, Numidia, Syria, and Asia Minor. They adventured as far as the country of the Parthians, those nomads who, moving from their base in Turkestan, had taken over the legacy of older civilizations in Iran and Mesopotamia. They were within an ace of making contact with the Chinese, who —55 about this time had sent out an expedition in the same general direction. They did not fail to lay hands on Egypt, —50 where the Hellenism of the Ptolemies was in its decline. Rome was now mistress of the whole area of the Mediterranean. Nothing was lacking to her glory.

CAESAR; OR, THE POPULAR DICTATOR

If nothing was lacking to Rome's glory a great deal was lacking to her security. The northern barbarians had not been reduced, and she never forgave the invasion which had brought the Celts to the foot of the Capitol.

But the Celts were not the only danger. They had been concerned only to preserve their freedom. The Germans presented quite a different threat. Nothing could quench

their thirst for loot. They were a nation in arms. The god
they worshiped was a god of battles, whose throne was
set among slaughtered warriors. They streamed down
from the north and menaced the Roman peace. Once already they had crossed the Rhine and devastated Gaul.
—102 Marius had defeated them at Aix, but they renewed their
pressure, and the Celts of Gaul turned to Rome for help.

Julius Caesar answered the call. His armies, guided by
the Gauls, advanced into Belgium and reached the Rhine.
—57 Once in Gaul, a rich country with access to the four seas,
whose rivers brought down gold in their waters, the
Romans would not readily relax their hold. It became
their colony.

In vain did the Celts revolt. They had opened the gate,
and the wolf was in the fold. Caesar succeeded in con-
—54 taining Vercingetorix, the Gaulish leader, at Alesia. He
—52 slaughtered and enslaved. He became proconsul of the
Gauls.

But Gaul, for him, was no more than a springboard.
His eyes were set on Rome. The Senate feared him, and,
at Pompey's suggestion, sent word that he should disband
his army before returning to the capital to give an account
—49 of himself. Caesar crossed the Rubicon and marched on
Rome. Pompey and the senators fled in dismay. Caesar
pursued them, defeated Pompey at Pharsalus, and re-en-
—49 tered Rome. The Republic of the Nobles was at an end.

Caesar was fully aware of the debt he owed to the
plebs, his allies. He made grants of land, and created
colonies for the poor and for the veterans of his armies.
He inaugurated a vast system of public works in the interest of the unemployed. He gave assistance to the fathers of large families, promoted humble men to great positions, and laid a heavy hand on the financial corporations. In order to relieve the wage-earners, who had suffered from slave competition, he issued an edict that at
least one-third of the workers on the great estates should
be freemen. With the object of protecting Italian agri-

culture he forbade the growing of vines and olives in
Spain and Gaul. He reorganized the free issue of corn,
and legislated against luxury. He reduced the Senate to
the position of a mere council, and brought new blood
into it by recruiting members from the ranks of the provincials and the sons of freedmen. Caesarism was a popular dictatorship.

But he aimed at being above all parties. It was his wish
to issue an amnesty, to embark on a policy of pacification.
He did not hesitate to reduce the number of those in receipt of public assistance. As head of the army, and the
man responsible for the laws and finances of his country,
he started on a program of far-reaching and genuine reforms. He undertook to bring the year into harmony with
the movement of the sun by instituting a new calendar of   —45
three hundred and sixty five days, with an additional day
once in every four years. He started a kind of newspaper,
almost certainly the first ever known to history, the *Acta
Urbis.*

Wherever he went he triumphed—in Britain, in Egypt,
in Asia, and in Spain. He came, he saw, he conquered.
He was absolute master. He wore the purple and the
laurel-wreath. He accepted divine honors. He was perpetual dictator. In ages to come his name was to symbolize
unquestioned authority. The heir presumptive of the
Roman Empire was henceforward to be known as Caesar.
The emperors in centuries yet to come were to be known
as Tsars and Kaisers.

But the senators had long memories. They conspired
against the man who had undermined their privileges.
Maybe the financial corporations, regretting the easy op-
portunities of the Republic, joined in the plot. In the
name of liberty oppressed the daggers flashed. Brutus was   —44
the hero whose name gave sanction to the murder. Legend
was to make of him a rigid republican, and legend was
right, if by republican we are to understand aristocrat.

Caesar fell beneath the knives of twenty-three con-
spirators. But Caesarism, backed by plebeian armies, was
to rise again.

AUGUSTUS

The Republic of which the patricians still dreamed had
not been without merit. It had built Rome's greatness.
But because it went in mortal terror of kingship it had de-
generated into anarchy. The régime, in its last years, had
concealed behind a façade of political triumph a deep-
seated moral decadence. The workers lost the love of
work. The middle classes dreamed only of speculation.
Leisure and money were the twin objects of a world
grown oversophisticated and slightly effeminate. Half
asleep, crippled by debt, given over to speculation, Rome
was fast heading for ruin. The public funds were raided,
—42 and it was necessary to institute a form of income-tax.
The Romans had lost their faith, and cared no longer for
religion. They had ceased to take their own gods seriously, and viewed with indifferent tolerance the new divinities who came to them from overseas. At the same
time, perhaps because their blood was beginning to show
a mixture of African and Oriental strains, they were losing their warlike spirit and forgetting the virtues of the
soldier. They preferred the comfort of their homes to the
hurly-burly of the battlefield. Military service was no
longer obligatory, and the army now consisted only of
mercenaries. Furthermore, it tended to become more loyal
to its generals than to its country.

It seemed doubtful whether Caesar's murder could
really save Rome once again from civil strife. The Senate
claimed to have resumed full power. Antony, one of
Caesar's lieutenants, and Octavius, his grand-nephew,
challenged it. Octavius finally won the day. Off Cape
—31 Actium his fleet defeated Antony's. Rome, weary of party

strife, accepted Octavius as its master. The Republic was dead.

Once upon a time the augurs had predicted that Octavius would achieve the empire of the world. Mindful of this prophecy (*augustum augurium*), he assumed the title of Augustus, which set him above all other magistrates. He was at one and the same time princeps, Augustus, tribune, consul, and censor. He became Pontifex Maximus. He was named Father of his Country. He was *imperator*—in other words, commander-in-chief of all the armed forces. *De jure,* he had merely accumulated all the honors of the Republic, holding them for life. *De facto,* he was the one man who could maintain internal order and foreign peace. —27

Like Caesar, he based the Roman system on the plebeian masses, though he was careful never to call them into consultation. He achieved popularity by abolishing all debts to the State, by doubling the pay of his guard, by giving the people "bread and circuses," by taxing capital and legacies. But he drew sharp lines and built a hierarchy of social classes, ranging from the senators, whose ranks he purged, to the slaves, whom he protected.

He restored the traditional cults—those of Apollo, Mars, and Venus—nor did he refuse to let his own name be added to the catalog of gods. Rome, before his day, had been a city of brick; he made of it a city of marble, with a population of some 500,000. The poets sang the praises of Divine Augustus. Rome's great century had dawned.

Augustus lacked Caesar's military genius. Nevertheless he extended Rome's patrimony, and carried the fame of the Eternal City into distant lands. He completed the conquest of Spain, and throughout the Iberian peninsula this event served as a starting-point from which the years of the era just opening were dated. He gave audience to embassies from India, and sent an expedition into Arabia. He organized the conquered territories, giving them roads, —39

—12　bridges, and amphitheaters. The eagles of the legions
　　　crossed the Danube and the Rhine, winging their way as
—7　far as the Elbe. Augustus annexed Germany.

　　　It was there, however, in Germany, that his policy received a setback which was to determine the whole destiny of the West. Where the Gauls had failed the Germans succeeded. They rose against the Roman yoke, and
A.D. 9　their chief, Hermann (called by the Roman chroniclers
Arminius), decimated the legions of Varus. The frontier
of the Empire was withdrawn to the Rhine, on the banks
of which Augustus hurriedly constructed a series of fortifications designed to contain the barbarians.

　　　Hermann, Germany's first national hero, had liberated
his country, but in so doing had deprived her of the benefits of a civilization. While Gaul, the Rhineland, and Hel-
vetia became Romanized, Germany remained savage for
centuries, and so technically ignorant that her people
could not even use stone for building. The Rhine, which
might have been a great highway of communication, was
turned into a sundering moat. As such it remained.

THE EMPIRE

　　　After Augustus came absolutism. Despot succeeded
despot, each rivaling each in cruelty. Claudius had his
wife, Messalina, murdered; Nero, his mother, Agrippina;
Commodus, his sister and his wife; Caracalla, his brother.
Such gentle attentions appear to have been the rule in the
imperial families. To make up for this, out of the fifty
emperors who occupied the throne in the first three centuries of the régime thirty-seven died violent deaths—
were poisoned, beheaded, stabbed, had their throats cut,
or committed suicide. They were the victims of their relations, their wives, their mistresses, their soldiers, or—
themselves. The Roman Principate was to offer an inexhaustible supply of subjects for the tragic writers of future centuries.

But let there be no mistake about it: this Roman Empire in many ways resembled a dictatorship of the proletariat. Nero, acclaimed by the lowest slum-dwellers and 54 the vilest slaves, was essentially a gutter-emperor. Others who were raised to, and retained, the Purple by the will of the people appointed the sons of freedmen, or those whom they had themselves freed, to the greatest offices in the State. Under Heliogabalus there were, among the highest Ministers, a dancer, a coachman, and a barber. Most of the emperors sought to win the franchise of the streets by making free issues of corn and bread, of wine and oil, by distributing great sums of money, and by raising the pay of the army, without worrying about the effect such liberality might have upon the Treasury, or how it would tend to inflate the currency. Alexander Severus extended the scope of public assistance, and multiplied 222 the number of State bursaries for poor children. Caracalla decreed a blanket-amnesty for condemned criminals. The condition of the slaves was improved, as much from reasons of policy as because of economic necessity. For now that foreign conquest had ceased the flow of slaves to Rome had dried up. They had become a rare commodity, and, as such, were worth taking care of.

While the status of the lower classes rose, the ranks of those who had formerly enjoyed privileges were mercilessly thinned. Ever since the days of Tiberius the nobility had been attacked by the emperors with unrelenting hatred. Under Nero the members of the great families were exiled; under Caracalla, killed. The ancient Senate of Rome, still, in theory, the chief legislative body, was persecuted, degraded, and rendered harmless. The property of those who composed it was freshly assessed and made the object of a special tax. Senators were removed from positions of military command. To mark his contempt for the assembled elders, Domitian forced them to debate how turbot should be cooked. Caracalla reduced their function to registering such laws as were laid before them. By the time of Constantine the Senate had sunk to being no more than Rome's municipal council. Nor were the rich treated any more gently than the noble. Crushed under a weight of taxation, they lived in constant dread of seeing what remained of their fortunes confiscated by the socialist State.

The emperors themselves were caught in the process of general leveling down. In the early days they had been drawn from the ranks of the patricians or of the rich middle class, though the nature of their origin did not keep them from playing the demagogue. Often they were soldiers or officials. In the latter years of the Empire they tended to be proletarians. The father of Pertinax had been a freedman; Maximinus and Galerius were the sons of shepherds, Aurelian came of peasant stock, Philip was the son of a robber chief.

What was far more serious, these later emperors were no longer Roman. Even the Flavian family was only Italian. The Antonines were descended from émigrés. Trajan was born in Spain. Both Hadrian and Marcus Aurelius had Spanish blood. Then came the reign of provincials, of foreigners, of barbarians. With Septimus Severus, the African, Carthage took her revenge: it was as though Hannibal had risen from the grave. Heliogabalus was of pure Semitic extraction. Maximinus was born in Thrace. Philip was an Arab. Diocletian came from Dalmatia.

Needless to say, the subjects of Rome were to be found in all the great offices of State, and rose to the highest eminence. Under Claudius, the Senate was made accessible to non-Italians. In the reign of Tiberius, Gauls achieved the consulate; under the Flavians, Spaniards and Africans; under the Antonines, Asiatics. Caracalla granted Roman citizenship to all the peoples of the Empire. Thereafter all distinction between Roman and Roman subjects vanished. Colonies and colonials ceased to exist. The Empire became more Roman as Rome became less so.

The city lost even the name of capital. Diocletian preferred to reign from his palace at Split, in Dalmatia. Constantine transferred the seat of government to Byzantium, 283 to which he gave his name. Julien established his Court at Lutetia, of the Parisii. Valentinian lived at Treves. Honorious made his residence at Ravenna. Rome declined even before the Roman Empire fell.

BUREAUCRACY TRIUMPHANT

The drama of the Roman Empire was that of discontinuity. The régime lacked everything that would have made it hereditary. There were times when it was not even a monarchy at all, and more than once two, three, four, or more emperors divided among them the title of Augustus and of Caesar, sharing the powers and territories of the Empire, and quarreling among themselves, each treating the others as usurpers. In no sense was the Empire hereditary. It knew nothing of laws of succession, and only very rarely did a son follow a father in the Purple. Sometimes an emperor would try to designate his heir by the process of adoption, or by having him recognized as future monarch. But it frequently happened that the praetorians sold the Empire to the highest bidder. In most cases an emperor gained his throne by being acclaimed among the armies, or as the result of a plot hatched by his supporters. The system gave free rein to every sort of intrigue, and set the stage for drama. By encouraging competition for the throne it opened the way to catastrophe.

The only continuing element in all this instability was the bureaucracy. Emperors might come and emperors might go, but the civil service went on forever. Within the framework of its organization Rome strove to remain Rome. Its officials were creatures of routine, the instruments of a centralized government, omnipotent. In their persons the State triumphed.

Because it eliminated private enterprise from every

sphere, because it intervened more and more in the life of the community, the machinery of State became more and more expensive to run. In order to meet the drain on the Treasury taxation was increased to a point at which it became intolerable. The burdens laid on private enterprise ended by killing it. Inevitably bureaucrats gave birth to more bureaucrats, and State action produced more State action.

The imperial administration imposed taxation by decree. In course of time it had become the owner and exploiter of an immense landed property. As a result of nationalizing the mines, of instituting a monopoly in purple dye, in having wool and cloth woven in State factories, it found itself involved in the day-to-day business of trade and industry. Under Alexander Severus it constituted itself a National Bank, and issued loans to the poor to enable them to buy land. It controlled all companies which operated on accumulated capital. It prohibited the exportation of cereals, of wine, of oil, and of military weapons. It built up a controlled economy. Under Domitian, in order to check over-production, it ordered vines to be uprooted. Under Vespasian, in order to help unemployment, it laid a ban on mechanization, and forbade the use of a winch for hoisting columns into position on the Capitol. Under Diocletian, in order to combat a rise in the cost of living, it laid down maximum prices and wages, threatening death to any who should be found guilty of contravening the new ordinances. But the laws of supply and demand rebelled against this pattern of arbitrary administration.

301

The system inevitably produced inflation and devaluation. The denarius had its silver content progressively reduced until it contained more of copper than of white metal. The weight of the gold piece, called at first *aureus*, and, later, *solidus,* was reduced by 50 per cent between the reigns of Caesar and Valentinian. The decline in money values would have been still more severe if Rome

had not had at her disposal the treasures and natural resources of the conquered countries—silver-mines in Spain,
silver-bearing lead-mines in Britain, gold-mines in Gaul
and Dacia.

But Rome's commercial budget showed a hopeless deficit. She had to import and pay for foodstuffs of every
kind, as well as raw materials. The Arab caravans were
her middlemen. Through them she bought from Asia and
the Far East jewels, silk, and perfumes. While her mines
became progressively worked out, her gold and silver reserves melted away—to the profit of the Indies, that
tomb of the precious metals. Rome was impoverished as
a result of her luxury; and not only impoverished, but
weakened.

THE LEGACY OF ROME

The history of Rome, from her foundation to the
break-up of the Empire, covers a thousand years. But the
period of her greatness was very much more limited. In
the realm of culture it was especially short. Latin literature came early to birth, and met an early death. Plautus
and Terence apart, it extended from Cicero to Juvenal—a
period of two centuries at most. Even so, Phaedrus ill
stands comparison with Aesop, and Virgil is not the equal
of Homer. In the sciences her contribution was almost nil.
Similarly, Roman art was neither precocious nor original.
Very soon, under Eastern influence, it became theatrical
and gaudy. Rome did not create—she copied.

But when the model happened to be Greek it was so
beautiful that it has the power to move us to admiration
even in the hands of its plagiarists. It was Rome's great
merit that she acted as a transmitter of Hellenism. Though
the Latins might despise the Greeks as men and politicians, they could recognize the superiority of their culture.
Even before she had conquered Hellas, Rome had shown
honor to Greek gods, and taken pleasure in assimilating

them to her own. No sooner was the conquest an established fact than Rome made herself the mistress of the works of art she found at Corinth. It was in the Greek language that the Emperor Marcus Aurelius composed his *Meditations*. After living for twenty-five years in Rome Plutarch was still ignorant of the Latin tongue. Galen came from Pergamum. Ptolemy wrote his geography in Greek, as did Longus his *Daphnis and Chloe*. Public education in Rome was still being conducted in Greek as late as the seventh century. Thanks to Roman civilization, Hellenism was revealed to the world.

The true legacy of Rome was essentially material. The Romans were practical and hard-working people who did not waste their energies in idle dreaming. Art was never, for them, an end in itself, but the means by which they increased their comfort and satisfied their vanity. For them the art of writing took second place to that of speaking. Cicero asserted that there was nothing more glorious, more admirable, than eloquence—doubtless because the orator is a man of influence and can make a lot of money.

Mediocre as painters and sculptors, the Romans were excellent architects, and even better masons. From the Etruscans they had learned the secret of building arches and constructing vaults. They mastered the intricacies of the dome. They were past-masters in the use of brick. They had a feeling for size, which flattered their self-conceit: the word *Coliseum* conveys the sense of "colossal." The monuments they built were designed for use— drains and aqueducts, baths, circuses, and harbor jetties. Their forums were mass-produced, and they laid out their cities in rectangular blocks. Their *castra* ("camps") left a legacy of *castres*—La Châtre, Chester, Manchester. They covered Europe with an admirable network of roads —and from the word *strata* ("roads") came Estrées, Strasbourg, Stratford. It was an astonishing system of communication by reason of its extent rather than of its technique: Roman paving may give the impression that it has been constructed to last forever, but, in fact, it is over-rigid and is difficult to keep in repair. Their waterways are still the great economic arteries of Europe, but the roads, which drove straight onward, over hills and valleys, were a superb instrument of military penetration and political control.

Rome had the love of order, and a passion for uniformity. That was her real lesson to the future. It found its expression in the systematization of the laws, and in the technique of government, commerce, money, and taxation. Augustus inaugurated a postal service; Marcus Aurelius created civil status. From the Laws of the XII Tables to the Institutes of Justinian, Rome codified her customs with such thoroughness that the jurists of every later age have learned from her.

To all the peoples whom she subjugated, to all the countries which she conquered, Rome taught the lesson of "the State." She gave them the example of an organized—of an over-organized—civilization, and for centuries they have looked nostalgically back to Rome. Her traditions and her language left a mark on them which nothing will ever efface.

PAX ROMANA

Roman orderliness moved hand in hand with Roman peace. But Roman orderliness was self-evident, whereas "Roman peace" was nothing more than a formula. Not only was it an armed peace, but it was a peace made up of innumerable wars—offensive wars waged for expansion, defensive wars waged to retain what had been won; foreign wars which brought booty and slaves, internal wars which repressed the restlessness of conquered peoples.

At first under the Empire the territorial possessions of Rome were multiplied. Britain was subdued (including Scotland); Mauritania, Thrace, Dacia, and Arabia were annexed, and the frontier was pushed beyond the Danube and the Euphrates. Nerva received an ambassador from China; Trajan sent a Roman embassy to India. Egypt provided Rome with one-third of her cereals. Greece was a favorite center for tourists from Italy. Syria wove silk and linen for the Roman market, and dyed them purple. The provinces were becoming latinized. Africa contributed both Apuleius and St. Augustine to Roman letters; Cordova gave her Lucan and Seneca; Bordeaux was the birthplace of the poet Ausonius.

This Roman world had its belt of fortifications, as China had its Wall, and sheltered behind a series of ditches equipped with palisades, watch-towers, and a road for lateral communication. The Peace of Rome was well defended.

But within the Empire all was not peace. At times there was war between the classes. The poor became clamorous. Strikes broke out in Asia. But most of the upheavals were political in character. Under Vitellius the Gauls and Batavians revolted; under Antoninus, the Dacians; under Trajan and Hadrian, the Jews. But already the Jews were scattered through the world. There were millions of them in the Roman Empire—in Egypt alone, one million, and anti-Semitic murmurings begin to be heard in Alexandria. In Africa, among the Berbers (or barbarians), the Numidians (in other words, nomads) were showing signs of restlessness. At one time they provoked a nationalist movement; at another they swept down towards the Sahara, which, now that they were mounted on camels, they were able to penetrate.

On the frontiers of the Empire the greed of the have-nots was on the increase. Why should the barbarians not be tempted by the insolent luxury of a world in its decline? They were waiting for the first sign of weakness to show itself. By and large, Rome kept them out, though she could not always prevent disastrous raids from occurring. The Goths looted first Greece, then Asia Minor. The Parthians, who dreamed of rebuilding the Empire of Darius, advanced as far as Antioch. Rome's thousandth year was marked by a German invasion of Thrace. The Alamanni got a footing in Northern Italy. Rome was not everywhere victorious. There were occasions on which she had to pay tribute to the barbarians, or to accept them as allies—a cure that was worse than the disease. 248 261

In the long run, the Roman world cracked. The lines of fissure followed the two languages of the Empire—Latin and Greek. There came into being a Western Empire and an Eastern. The latter lived for many centuries longer. The former collapsed under the weight of the invading hordes. There was nothing beautiful about Rome's death-agony. Plague and inflation were rife. The bureaucracy struggled on to the end. The last of the Western emperors was called Romulus, as, according to legend, had been the first of the Roman kings. 476

Rome fell because she was no longer Rome. What had once been a warrior nation broke down through lack of soldiers. The Italian youth would no longer serve in the field, not even when they were promised that this time it should be a "war to end wars." Trajan had to take action against those found guilty of procuring self-inflicted wounds. Tibullus, in one of his *Elegies,* played at being a pacifist: "Let us leave fighting to men of barbarian race." There could be no surer way of being forced into surrender. Vespasian followed the poet's advice and released all Italians from military service. The armies of Rome came to consist only of mercenaries, of paid barbarians. But the pay was not always forthcoming. Germans were charged to defend the Empire against their fellow-countrymen. Rome had ceased to care.

True, there was a shortage of soldiers, but there was a shortage of children as well. Rome, once so prolific, had become sterile. The Empire was suffering from depopulation. The countryside was deserted. Laws could avail nothing against this particular scourge. Hand in hand with the

demographic crisis went one of morals. Vice was everywhere in the ascendant. The most "enlightened" of the emperors, Trajan and Hadrian, practiced forms of sexual in-
dulgence which are usually regarded as unmentionable,
though Catullus hymned them in verse. Luxury and irreligion gave strength to debauchery. Rome had ceased to believe in anything, except, perhaps, in quacks and fortune-
tellers.

Once Rome had been rich, but she was rich no longer.
She had fed upon her wealth. She had destroyed her natural leaders and ruined her middle class. She had undermined the spirit of enterprise. She had come to hate hard
work. Incapable of producing, she could only consume.
As a result of her decadence the economic axis of Europe
moved from the Mediterranean to the Rhine-Danube line.
Rome was no longer the center of the world.

PAX SINICA

The peace of Rome was balanced by the peace of
China, just as the Roman world had been balanced by the
Empire of the Hans. Each contained close on eighty million souls. China, like Rome, had built her strength upon a
formalist tradition and a firmly constructed administrative
framework.

The unlettered son of a peasant father turned soldier of
fortune and founded a dynasty which was to last for four
−202 centuries. It was to enjoy such prestige among the inhabitants of China that for a long while they found their
chief glory in being the "sons of Han." Liu Pang achieved
the throne at the very time when Rome, at Zama, was
triumphing over Carthage.

The most famous monarch of this line was Wu-Ti. He
consolidated the imperial authority, brought the feudal
−140 nobles to heel, and expanded the empire as far as Korea in
the north, Tonkin in the south, and the approaches of
−87 what was later to become Russian Turkestan in the west.

His long succession of wars landed Wu-Ti in financial difficulties. To resolve these he determined on heroic measures. He minted and issued coins made of an alloy of tin and silver, the value of which he fixed at the equivalent of 300, 500, and 3000 pieces of bronze. He also invented a new currency of squares of white doeskin, to which he gave an arbitrary value of 40,000 pieces of bronze. This was near the first recorded instance of paper-money, of a fiduciary currency.

The Emperor also devised a tax on capital of 5 per cent, but had to abandon it when capital began to flee the country. He established State monopolies in salt, iron, and alcohol, and entrusted the running of all transport to a central administration. He also attempted to control prices.

The reign of the Han emperors was not untroubled. For three-quarters of a century there was struggle against usurpers. The educated classes, who were hostile to the Hans, triumphed for a while in the person of Wang Mang, who experimented with a species of State socialism more radical than anything enforced by Wu-Ti. Wang Mang established the State as sole proprietor of land and slaves, and made a redistribution of the great estates. At each season of the year he fixed the prices of all commodities, and compelled the banks to lend money at 3 per cent per month, instead of at their former exorbitant rate. He instituted a system by which all those in receipt of salaries had to declare their incomes, and these were made subject to a tax. He increased the number of State monopolies, notably in metals, timber, and fisheries. But this experiment in controlled economy ruined peasants and businessmen alike. China rose against Wang Mang, and, after a period of famine and rebellion, restored the Han dynasty.

A.D. 9

22
27

The new Emperor, Kouang Wu, repaired the injuries done by the civil war, and developed still further the Chinese hegemony in Asia. His most notable success was the conquest of the Tarim oases, on the far side of the Gobi Desert. Thereafter the land route followed by the silk

trade was through these oases, while the sea route led
from Tonkin to the Red Sea. The precious fabric reached
Antioch and Rome, where its iridescent substance gave
rise to enthusiastic admiration. By the oases route, too,
60   Buddhism—that philosophy which had been transformed
into a religion—originating in India, reached China. The
Han Emperor did not persecute the disciples of Buddha,
but the cultivated followers of Confucius watched its progress with jealous eyes. The general mass of little yellow
men was prepared to assimilate all imported novelties,
whether they took the form of religions or invaders.

China grew in splendor and in wealth. The art of the
Han dynasty was marked by a noble purity of line. Its
bronzes, bas-reliefs, and prints turned men's thoughts back
regretfully to the vanished palaces. A definitive text of the
180 Confucian teachings was established and widely distributed through the medium of stamped stones—forerunners
of printing. About the same time paper made its appearance, and was brought to Europe by the Arabs and the
Persians eight centuries later. As a result, perhaps, of their
search for the philosopher's stone, the Chinese discovered
also the secret of gunpowder, which, twelve hundred years
afterwards, the Europeans were to employ in their warlike
operations. They devised, too, a breast harness for horses
at a time when the Western nations were still clinging
obstinately to the strangulating neckband, and it only remained for the Chinese to invent rein and bridle for the
world to get full value from the use of draught animals.

The Hindus of the same period were scarcely less productive. It was a Hindu who thought out the symbol for
"zero," which served to open up vast arithmetical horizons. The same unknown genius, or another of the same
quality, invented the system which later swept the West
in the form of Arabic numerals, and, by supplanting the
sterile conventions of the Greeks and Romans, opened the
way to advances in every field of science. India, which
had recently emerged from feudal chaos, formed with

Iran a compact empire. But the Persians ultimately broke from it, and the Aryan family, then ruling India, lapsed into decadence.

For neither dynasties nor empires are eternal. As in India, as in Rome, the Han rulers fell into decline and collapse. Three pretenders dismembered China into three kingdoms. In spite of foreign threats, the sophisticated ruling class of China preached pacifism and brought the career of arms into disrepute. Like India and like Rome, China was an easy and a tempting prey. From the Roman *Limes* to the Great Wall the barbarians were on the watch. Now, at last, they felt that their hour had struck. **223**

THE BARBARIAN FLOOD

Each chapter of history ends in a flood of barbarians. The first historical civilizations were submerged beneath a tide of Semitic and Indo-European invaders, and now it was from the steppes that a great wave broke on the Chinese and Graeco-Roman cultures, and almost overwhelmed them.

Whence came these conquering nomads? In Eastern Asia, round the periphery of China, was a constant eddy of Turco-Mongol tribes, the main element of which was **300** Hun. The Alans were squeezed down towards the Caspian and the Caucasus. Farther north, spaced out along the Baltic coast, lay the Finns, the Lithuanians, and the Slavs. Scandinavia was the home of Norwegians, Danes, and Swedes. The vast area stretching from the Vistula to the Rhine was peopled by various Germanic groups—the Goths, who had moved down into the Ukraine, the "shining" (or Ostro) Goths to the east, the "wise" (or Visi) Goths to the west. There were Vandals on the Danube, Angles in Schleswig, Lombards on the banks of the Elbe, Saxons on the Weser, Alamanni on the Main, and a spearhead of Burgundians and Franks on the Rhine.

All these peoples were barbarian, though not to the

same degree. By the Romans, as by the Greeks, the word was used to designate foreigners in general, and it carried an implication of inferiority. These nomads, whether of Mongol or Germanic stock, were, as far as civilization was concerned, a good thousand years behind the people of the Mediterranean. They moved from one stretch of grazing-ground to another, taking with them their women and their children. They were ignorant alike of writing and of city life. They wore long trousers, as opposed to the civilized races, Chinese as well as Romans, who dressed in robes. They were herdsmen, hunters, and warriors.

Were they so numerous that they lacked freedom to move in the untamed immensities of Europe and Asia? The answer to that question would seem to be "no." But, since they never cleared encumbered land, they avoided settling in forest areas, and the plains across which they galloped were bound, sooner or later, to bring them to the frontiers of one of the forbidden empires. Its conquest would give them booty beyond reckoning. They might even draw from it a permanent supply of food, and so become converted to the sedentary life.

Already a number of profitable raids had taken them within the fortified lines, and the emperors, unable to evict them, had tolerated their presence, settling them in one or other of the provinces, and treating them as "guests" or allies. The barbarians, once across the frontier, were, quite literally, given "billeting orders," and the local landowners had to share with them their fields and their farming implements. In this way the Huns became established in Northern China. In this way the Goths were authorized to settle in the Balkans. Rome wanted to think that they would supply a source of man-power and soldiers. Formalists to the end, they deluded themselves into believing that the treaties entered into with these strangers would be honored.

But the barbarians still outside the Promised Land grew ever more eager to taste of the forbidden fruit, especially now, when it seemed ripe for plucking. The Huns, whom the rulers of the Han dynasty had driven back or contained, now dashed on their prey and broke through 308 the Great Wall. They were born horsemen. It was, observed a Roman officer, as though they were riveted to their little ponies. On horseback they ate, drank, and slept. They were a race of centaurs. The China into which they advanced had lost all cohesion. The Confucian pacifists preached non-resistance. The newly established Ts'in dynasty was incapable of resisting the invaders, who swept onward, massacring, burning, looting, and enslaving.

The Ts'in emperors and their successors took refuge in Southern China, where Nankin became their capital. The Huns remained masters of Northern China. They broke 318 open the imperial tombs and stole their jewels. One of their chiefs had the loveliest young girls of his harem served up roasted at table, though it is only fair to point out that another sought to have the teaching of Confucius explained to him. The barbarians were making contact with civilization.

Perhaps it was because they were growing soft that the Huns let themselves be caught napping. Other nomad bands, Mongols from the borders of Manchuria, drove them from Northern China and took over their settlements. This incident marked one of the turning-points in the history of the world, for the Huns, pressed back towards the interior, with the Mongols at their heels, swept across the continent. In their turn they drove westward all the nomads whom they encountered, giving an increasing impetus to vast human migrations, forcing the Germans against the frontiers of the Roman Empire, and so making the Great Invasions inevitable.

The Huns crossed Asia, reached and passed the Volga. They left the Slavs undisturbed upon their right, but crushed the Ostrogoths, who, in their turn, streamed to- 374 wards the Danube and broke into North Italy. They prized 375

376   out the Visigoths, who were forced to take refuge, first in
Thrace, then in Illyria, whence they moved on into Italy,
pillaged Rome, entered Gaul, and came to a halt only
when they reached the Atlantic on the coast of Aquitaine.
Another tribe dislodged by the Huns was that of the
406   Alamanni, who, set in movement, pushed the Vandals before them, the latter doing the same by the Burgundians.
The Vandals crossed the Rhine, swept through Gaul,
passed into Spain (where one province was to be known
later as Vandalusia or Andalusia), and subsequently into
Africa, where they stopped their forward movement at
Carthage. The Burgundians went no farther than Savoy.
The Franks too, playing their part in the general surge towards the West, moved gradually into Northern Gaul.
430   The Saxons and the Angles crossed the sea and took possession of Britain, which had been left undefended when
the legions were recalled to Rome. One group of Britons,
after a long resistance, made famous by the legendary exploits of King Arthur and his companions of the Round
Table, took refuge in Armorica. From this great melting-
pot of the peoples came the molten stuff from which the
nations of the future were formed.

    It began to look as though the Huns would never settle
down. Their domain now extended from the Caucasus to
the Elbe, and their king, Attila, a hirsute and many-wived
warrior, who wished to be initiated into the secrets of
Roman luxury, possessed a palace built of timber somewhere in the Danube plain. But the Huns were still in-
447   curable nomads. They roamed on horseback through
Thrace and Macedonia, and the Emperor of the East kept
them at bay only at the cost of heavy ransom-money.
They moved towards the Rhine, entered Lorraine, and
wandered as far as the neighborhood of Orléans. Gallo-
Roman and Visigothic forces made a joint attempt to stem
the advance of the "Scourge of God," who was finally de-
451   feated near Troyes (and not Châlons). But defeat mat-

tered little to the Huns. They threw themselves upon an- 452
other prey, and next it was the soil of Italy which trembled 453
beneath the hooves of the Mongol horses.

Only Attila's sudden death put an end to their adventuring. Bereft of their chief, divided among themselves,
beaten by the Ostrogoths, they withdrew towards the
North Sea. Their empire crumbled. They left an emptiness
behind them into which came the Slavs from the Vistula, 470
who drove forward as far as the Elbe. But the Huns returned in different forms to be the terrors of a later Europe
—as Bulgars, as Turks, as Mongols. The first wave of
barbarian invasions was followed by others.

Already the Roman Empire of the West was little more
than a name. A day came when the Vandals of Africa
landed in Italy, put Rome to the sack, and left again, carry- 455
ing their booty with them. The Ostrogoths made the last 476
of the Western emperors prisoner at Ravenna. It was the
end. Flowing onward in the wake of the Huns, a great tide
of barbarism swept over the civilized world.

CHAPTER FIVE

The Thousand Years
of Christendom

OUGHT not the thousand years of Christendom which followed the thousand years of Rome to be called, rather, the Age of the Barbarians? The nomads descended upon the world in successive waves and dictated their laws. After the Huns, after the Germans, came the Arabs, the Norsemen, the Magyars, the Turks. . . . The barbarians were as the sands of the sea; the Christians were a mere handful. But barbarians destroyed, whereas the Christians built. The barbarians strangled civilization; the Christians preserved it. The Christians started from nothing, but in the end they succeeded in imposing a spiritual domination. They gave to the period which bears their name its true glory.

The Roman world had paid, it is true, little attention to the teaching of Jesus of Nazareth. We cannot even be sure when it was he was born in a stable at Bethlehem. Clement of Alexandria clung to the 25th of May, but the traditional 25th of December has come, finally, to be accepted. As to the year, all chronologists agree that it should be put at least four, some say five or seven, years earlier than the one adopted as the beginning of the Christian era. In this respect our knowledge of these times has been obscured by the lack of contemporary records.

Rome in her decadence was crying out for a new religion. Caesar and Tiberius believed in none of the gods. Marcus Aurelius took counsel of a serpent with a human head. The Romans, too blasé to attach any importance to the gods of their ancestors, adopted foreign divinities, as the Greeks had done before them. Caligula permitted the cult of Isis; Nero, that of Mithras; Aurelian, that of the sun. Rome was seeking a faith.

Virgil had predicted the birth of a divine child who should "put an end to the age of iron and bring back to all mankind the happiness of the Age of Gold," though doubtless the author of the *Bucolics* was thinking only of a "scion of Jupiter." But the Jews were awaiting the coming of a Messiah, the liberator foretold by the Prophets. The times were ripe.

The Four Gospels brought the "good news," the good word. Christianity was born. It combined the monotheism of the Jews with the ethical teaching of Zoroaster. It displayed a Roman gift for organization. It reveled in a Greek love of hair-splitting. It admitted many different interpretations, and from these flowed many heresies. It seemed to teach respect for the established order; at the same time, it announced the coming of a social revolution. Its rich fermentation was to bring a new world to birth.

By stressing the importance of the individual, and in giving release to egalitarian sentiments, primitive Christianity did, in its own way, proclaim the Rights of Man. Among Christians, said St. Paul, "there is neither Greek nor Jew . . . Barbarian, Scythian, bond nor free." Such a statement seems to come little short of a faith in internationalism. Did it mean that all national loyalties were to be abolished? Christianity taught submission to the civil power. Did this mean the suppression of slavery? The Church, though it honored the slaves who had suffered martyrdom, though it permitted marriage with slaves, though it raised a former slave to the Holy See, was careful not to commit itself on this point. Besides, slavery was an unavoidable economic necessity.

Another claim made by Christianity was that it had brought freedom to women. It had made of her man's equal; but it refused to admit her to the priesthood. Was not woman, in the Rome of decadence, already too free? Was she not abusing her emancipation?. The Christian doctrine may not have much improved her material condition, but it certainly ennobled her moral qualities.

Whatever the answer to all these questions, Rome, faced by so subversive a form of teaching, was scornful. Tacitus, in the first lay reference to Christians, condemns their "execrable superstition." Nevertheless he expressed compassion for the martyrs whom Nero had condemned. The emperors, at first, hunted down the "anarchists" who were undermining the cult of the Throne. But by degrees they weakened, and finally surrendered. Alexander Severus tolerated the Christians; Gallienus allowed them freedom of worship. To such an extent did the power of the young Church grow that Diocletian feared it might become a State within the State. Constantine was converted. Theodosius persecuted the country-folk who were still attached to the "old legends"—the peasants (*pagani*), who now began to be known as pagans, and thereby multiplied the number of those adepts of Christianity whom public contempt denominated "cretins." Thus it came about that just as Rome had once been a "carrier" of Greek culture, so now she became a "carrier" of the Christian faith.

The new religion had, to a high degree, the gift of adaptability. It had begun in poverty, at a time when the Apostle Peter lived in a squalid Roman slum, when the faithful had found sanctuary in the catacombs. The martyrs had supplied admirable material for propaganda, and on them it had flourished. It nursed its legend very carefully, surrounding with miraculous circumstances its more spectacular conversions—those, for instance, of Constan-

120

222

310
370

tine and Clovis—and taking to itself the merit for many victories—St. Genevieve driving the Huns from Gaul, St. Leo keeping them from Italy. Very cleverly it drew the teeth of paganism, tracing crosses on the menhirs, transforming the ancient pagan festival of the sun to St. John's fire, turning the cult of Isis into that of Mary, metamorphosing the Roman Pantheon, which had been dedicated to all the gods, into a church of all the martyrs. Of the cross-armed signposts used to mark road-junctions it made calvaries, and because those pagans who came from Germany knew nothing of temples or of statues it quickly charmed them with rites and images. It established itself firmly in success. The Lateran Palace became the seat of the Bishops of Rome. Churches arose on all sides—luxurious organs of publicity. Christianity triumphant was no less at home in opulence than the primitive Church had been in poverty.

WHO SHOULD BE ROME'S HEIR? BYZANTIUM?

Though the Empire of the West was dead, the Empire of the East remained. Constantinople claimed to be Rome still. The empire that fought for survival was even now the "Roman" Empire. But Latin was only the official language; the current tongue was Greek. Court ceremony was Oriental rather than Roman. The Emperor had become a Persian potentate. Constantine had made Byzantium Catholic, but her Christianity carried, more often than not, a taint of heresy in one of its many forms.

At a time when the rest of the world was plunged in barbarian darkness the Eastern Empire was regarded as a refuge of civilization. There were moments when it did attain to a spiritual greatness, as when Justinian built the Church of St. Sophia, with its domes, its marbles, its mosaics, and caused to be drawn up the Digest of those Institutes which were the monuments of Roman Law; a

548

political greatness, as when that same Justinian drove the
Vandals from Africa, beat the Ostrogoths in Italy, the
627 Visigoths in Spain, and, for a brief spell, restored the
unity of the Empire, or when Heraclius triumphed over the
Persian profaners of the Holy Places, and threw them back
to the Tigris; and an economic greatness, too, because
Byzantium remained the last commercial center of a world
which had forgotten trade. Byzantium exported wines,
spices, cottons, and textiles. Her foreign customers had almost nothing to give in return, unless it were slaves, who,
for the most part, were of Slav nationality. As a result of
her trading, built on a firm foundation of customs duties
and State control, the Empire of the East grew progressively richer, and built up a reserve of gold, which was
rapidly disappearing from the West.

But the brilliance was little more than glitter. Even
Byzantine art, which spread from St. Mark's in Venice to
the domes of Kiev, set gorgeous decoration above purity
of line. It was an art of ornamentation rather than of structure. Similarly, the whole imperial edifice was sump-
tuous rather than solid. Byzantium had to struggle against
evils both within and without. At home an urban lower
class, unappeased by the free distribution of bread, oil,
and wine, voiced dangerous discontent. On the throne
murders within the ruling family were the rule rather than
the exception. At the gates of the city was the barbarian
threat. The Turks, it is true, were still too distant to be a
menace; so far they were the terrors only of Central Asia,
sending out the fear of their name as far as India and the
Caspian, but already their ruler styled himself "Lord of
the Nations and of the Universe." In the course of their
migrations they had pushed back the Mongol tribe of the
Avars, which was now pressing more and more closely
upon the Lombards of the Danube plain. These Lombards
572 settled, finally, in Italy, while the Avars brought anxiety
to Byzantium, whose rulers bought them off.

The Avars went, but other conquerors made the Empire

tremble—Arabs, Norsemen, Bulgars. More than once Byzantium was within an ace of falling. She held out, thanks to her gold, thanks to her foreign mercenaries, thanks to her "Greek fire," a secret weapon which enabled her to set the enemy's ships ablaze; thanks, above all, to her wonderful geographical position between the open sea and the Golden Horn.

Byzantium, gnawed by an internal cancer, but strong in her Roman heritage, resisted all attacks for close on a thousand years.

WHO WAS TO BE ROME'S SUCCESSOR? THE KINGDOM OF THE FRANKS?

Who in the West would be found presumptuous enough to claim the heritage of Rome? The night of barbarism was unrelieved. The libraries, in which books of bound pages had replaced the ancient scrolls, were burned or pillaged. The schools were closed. Men could neither read nor write: the very implement of writing was forgotten—the sharpened reed or calamus, later to be replaced by the goose-quill. The rule of violence made all trade impossible. Barter took the place of money, which was ever growing scarcer. Each great estate was a closed economy, self-supporting, isolated. Towns were falling into ruin, fields running to seed. Roads were no longer kept in repair. With the disappearance of all organized taxation the very idea of the State had vanished.

Nevertheless the invaders did cease from wandering, did become sedentary. Chiefs of robber bands, elected by their men, turned themselves into makeshift heads of nations, and aimed at making their privileges hereditary. Among all the Germanic tribes now occupying the territories of the Empire, one gradually took the lead—that of the Salian Franks, which had come from the lands of salt, the area lying around the mouths of the Rhine.

Clovis, their leader, by becoming converted to Christianity, had won for himself the support of the bishops against his rivals, because most of the Germans had embraced the Arian heresy, which, by denying the divinity of the Son, eliminated a difficult mystery. Backed by the Church, the Franks took pride of place.

Gaul might have become Germany had not Clovis de495 feated the Alamanni at Tolbiac. Gaul might have become Burgundy had not Clovis driven back the Burgundians. 507 Gaul might have become Catalonia (Gotholonia) had not Clovis beaten the Visigoths at Vouille. As a result of the triumphs of the Franks she became France.

In the Frankish lands, as everywhere in the West, the name of Rome was still surrounded by a great aura of renown. It was the symbol of the order and luxury of a past age, of its grandeur and prosperity, all of them things for which the barbarians, living in conditions of anarchy, had a nostalgic longing. Except in England, where the invaders had succeeded in naturalizing a Germanic form of speech, the language of the people had remained faithful to a bastard dialect derived from the Latin. In Italy the Ostrogoths set themselves to produce a parody of the Roman Empire. Everywhere the laws of Rome remained in operation side by side with others of Germanic origin. Romans and barbarians each kept their own code, until such time as the races became so mixed that a common, or customary, law was found to be necessary.

For the races melted into one another, as did their languages and their customs. Latin literature was in its deathagony. Art had reverted to a primitive stage. The ornamentation of the weapons which the warriors used, the form of the jewels with which they adorned themselves, was closer in style to prehistory than to the perfection of the Graeco-Roman culture.

Slowly, painfully, the nations took shape. The barbarian kings devised their realms between their male children, as they might have done the booty of a pillaged city. Dynasties died. Princes murdered one another. What a

Dagobert or a Pépin d'Héristal might build was soon destroyed by recurrent schisms. But Charles, the King, after-   771
wards known as Charlemagne, succeeded in constructing a genuine empire under Frankish protection. He conquered the Lombard kingdom of Italy, annexed Germany,   774
terrorized the Saxons. He beat the Avars, who ultimately
rallied to Christianity, and made of their country an eastern borderland—Austria. His only failure was in Spain,
and the death of his nephew, Roland, in the Pass at Ron-
cesvalles, later became the theme of one of the great epic   778
poems.

In Rome, where he pledged himself to protect the Pope,   800
Charlemagne received the keys of Jerusalem and of the
Holy Sepulcher. He was saluted with the title of Emperor
of the Romans. The Pope prostrated himself before him.
Byzantium protested, but, for all that, Charles, the Emperor of the West, very nearly married Irene, the Empress
of the East. It looked, indeed, as though the world of
Christendom, welded together by the Frankish King, were
truly reviving the Empire of Rome.

Charlemagne would have liked to revive Rome's civilization, too, but in order to do that he would have needed
to be what he was not—a civilized man. He had a Court,
but it was at Aix-la-Chapelle. He claimed a Latin genea-
ology. He founded schools and had old manuscripts re-
copied. But he learned to read only with the greatest difficulty. His poets were plagiarists of Rome, but they confused the city of decadence with the classical seat of empire. Carolingian Latin was of poor quality, though, even
so, it was too scholarly for the masses. Carolingian art
could do no more than ape Byzantium.

In the sphere of economics, too, Charlemagne would
have liked to return to the ancient world. He tried to put
the old roads into a state of repair. He modified and sys-
tematized both weights and measures. He gave an impetus
to the circulation of money by minting new coins, exclusively of silver. He encouraged periodic fairs, such as

that of Saint-Denis. But the task was too great for his strength. It was not within his power to set the blood once more tingling in the veins of the exhausted West. In spite of all his efforts Carolingian economy remained primitive and rural. It could not bring into a single whole the thousands of small, self-supporting systems which the insecurity of the Dark Ages had produced.

Politically the work of Charlemagne was precarious. In vain did Louis the Pious attempt to bolster up the artificial unity of an empire constructed of a variety of peoples indifferently Romanized. His sons, in accordance with the Frankish rule, divided between them the excessive burden 843 of his heritage. The Treaty of Verdun split it into three parts, which ultimately gave birth to France, Germany, and Italy. The foundations of the nations, as well as of the languages, of modern Europe were laid. All of them were irremediably distinct from one another.

WHO WAS TO BE ROME'S HEIR? THE KINGDOM OF GERMANY?

Of these three kingdoms it was now the turn of Germany to take the lead and to claim the reversion of the Roman past. Elsewhere the feudal lords were undermining the royal authority. In France the Carolingians were in decline. Italy was divided. Beyond the Elbe, the Slav chaos was still without form. Germany alone achieved unity.

Germany. The name, with its memory of the Alamanni, was about this time beginning to appear in the writings of French and Latin authors. The Germans themselves preferred another—Deutschland, which signified the country of the Teutons. Alamanni or Teutons, both were Germanic tribes, and the peculiar vocation of each was warfare.

936   Otho the Great, elected king by the College of Nobles and Priests, turned this vocation to advantage. He imposed his authority upon the dukes, his vassals, subdued

the Slavs between the Elbe and the Oder, laid Poland and Bohemia under tribute, intervened in France, crossed the Brenner, and had himself crowned King of Italy. He en- 962 tered Rome and there compelled the Pope to anoint him "Emperor and Augustus." Like Charlemagne, he thought he could restore the Roman Empire.

What he created was, in fact, no more than the Holy German Roman Empire, a pale reflection of Rome. He too wished to bring back that civilization which the diminished West had never ceased to mourn. He summoned scholars from Italy to his Court, but, like Charlemagne before him, had himself to learn the elements of reading and writing. He had the great libraries reconstituted and old books re-copied. Such things were no more than pathetic strainings after culture. Civilization cannot be improvised.

But the German Emperors had greater difficulties still to overcome. The Papacy was an adversary well capable of matching itself with them, and ready to contest their claim to the hegemony of Christendom. The struggle be-tween the two powers, one of which combined the spiritual with the temporal, was relentless. When the Emperor, Henry IV, was brought into collision with Pope Gregory VII the duel became tragic. Excommunicated, and threatened by his own vassals, Henry drank his cup of 1077 humiliation at Canossa. Dressed as a penitent, barefooted in the snow, he implored pardon of the Pope. No doubt the incident was carefully staged to produce the maximum of effect. Certainly it was "good theater." Some years later 1084 Henry took his revenge, marching on Rome and besieging Gregory in the Castle of St. Angelo. The quarrel between Popes and Emperors flowed and ebbed endlessly, the Popes excommunicating the Emperors, the Emperors ab- 1122 ducting the Popes and raising up anti-Popes. The Con-cordat of Worms, which reached a compromise settlement in the issue of ecclesiastical investiture, did not put a stop to the struggle. But it was sufficiently clear that the Holy German Roman Empire could not seriously bring Rome back from the grave. That it was German there could be no doubt. What it failed to be was Roman. Voltaire was later to say that it was neither Holy nor Roman nor an Empire.

WHO WAS TO BE ROME'S HEIR? THE PAPACY?

The Papacy, which had stood up more or less victoriously to the Emperors, was the true heir of Rome's passion for unity, for that universality expressed in the word "catholic." Pope Gregory the Great had dreamed of an immense Christian community of federated peoples, and this ideal the Church long pursued, seeking to impose herself as guide and teacher on all the princes and all the nations of Christendom.

The Church's first temporal task had been one of self-organization. She might have been an aristocracy, with the councils wielding supreme authority. She chose instead to be a monarchy, elective but absolute, and to that end declared the Bishop of Rome to be above all other bishops. She assured the independence of the Pontiff by ordaining that he was to be elected, not by popular franchise, but by the Roman clergy. A later modification confined the vote to the College of Cardinals.

On more than one occasion the Church had to purge her own ranks. The Holy See did not always provide an edifying example. Pope John XI was the son of Pope Sergius III and a courtesan. Pope John XII—who crowned Otho—lived surrounded by concubines. Benedict IX was made Pope at the age of twelve. There were times when the tiara became the property of a single family, passing from brother to brother, from uncle to nephew; others, when it went to the highest bidder. It was in this way that Benedict IX transmitted it to Gregory VI. But even in these squalid transactions the Papacy held an echo of the Roman Empire. But more often it recalled it by its virtues.

Ever since the Emperors had moved to Byzantium the first place in Rome had been held by the Popes. They reigned over the still immature Republic of St. Peter. They wore the Imperial Purple, and in the eyes of the Christian world there could be no doubt of their pre-eminence.

Not that the Christian world always heeded the Popes' words. It frequently interpreted the Scriptures in its own fashion, which Rome condemned as heretical. The Arians refused to believe that the Son had existed from all eternity. The Manicheans explained evil by the duality of light and darkness. The Nestorians drew a distinction between the divine and the human nature of Christ. Hundreds of heresies flourished, and these had to be denounced if the unity of the Christian dogma was to be safeguarded. Battles raged around such points as Grace, Original Sin, the Holy Spirit, and the date of Easter. Rome excommunicated, thundered anathemas, and made salvation depend upon doctrinal obedience.

Arianism, the great heresy of the West, shared in the fall of the kingdoms which professed it. Another heresy arose in the East, that of the iconoclasts. The Byzantine **726** Emperors forbade all material representations of Christ, the Virgin, and the Saints. They hunted down images, destroyed icons and relics, broke or defaced the mosaics. But in the end Rome imposed her will, which was in conformity with the popular taste. Byzantium had to accept **843** the cult of images.

Several years later the East relapsed into yet another heresy. The Patriarch of Constantinople, jealous of his **880** authority, declared that Rome was no longer orthodox. The controversy died down, only to reappear in the elev- **1054** enth century. This time the breach was irreparable, and the Greek Church threw off the Roman discipline.

The Popes were called upon to fight not only for points of doctrine, but for their very existence. Rome had to defend herself against the Roman aristocrats, the Lombard

Kings, the Norse and Arab invaders, as well as the German
Emperors. On more than one occasion Popes were driven
into exile, or their persons were seized. On occasion they
were actually beaten. They appealed to the Franks or the
Italians. They fought, they negotiated, they surrendered.
But always, even after the pillaging of Rome, the Papacy
revived, restored order, and asserted its supremacy.

In the long run the Church triumphed, and Christianity
spread. One after another the princes and the peoples were
converted. St. Martin evangelized the Frankish lands; St.
Patrick preached to the Irish. The monk Augustine, later
to become St. Augustine of Canterbury, carried the gospel
into England. The monk Winfrid, afterwards St. Boniface,
led a mission into Germany. St. Cyril and St. Methodius
were spokesmen to the Slavs; St. Anscarius carried the
Word to Scandinavia. The monastic orders developed in
Italy under the auspices of St. Benedict, and grew in
France with the founding of Cluny and Citeaux. A swarm
of monks spread from Ireland into Scotland, and even as
far as Iceland. Everywhere, by their chastity, obedience,
and poverty, they offered a challenge to pagan sensuality,
barbarian indiscipline, and Oriental luxury.

It was the Church that anointed emperors and kings
"by Grace of God," thus distinguishing them from even
the mightiest of the barons. Through her, royalty tended
to become divine right. Lombard kings called themselves
"Christian and Catholic princes." Charlemagne claimed
to have been "crowned by God"; Otho proclaimed himself
the "elect of God."

"Rome," asserted one of the Lateran Councils, "is the
head of the world," and, in very fact, the Popes for a time
became the arbiters of the whole Christian community.
They threatened princes with excommunication, and compelled them to accept their decisions in matters of peace
and war. Christianity gave to the peoples rules for living.
It fixed fasts, determined feast-days, gave names at bap-
tism. In the worst period of the Dark Ages it made of the

monasteries the last refuge of ancient culture, and of its
schools the ultimate sanctuaries of enlightenment. It was   1000
Gui d'Arrezzo, the Benedictine, who invented the hori-
zontal stave and brought new life into musical notation;
formerly it had employed the letters of the alphabet. It was
from a hymn of St. John that he extracted the very name
of the seven notes of the scale. The monk Gerbert, the
future Sylvester II, brought back from Cordova the so-   970
called Arab numerals, and thereby opened unsuspected
vistas to Western mathematics. The theologian Denis the
Less proposed to reckon chronology from the date of the   980
birth of Jesus. The use of this new calendar spread over
Italy in the sixth century, over France in the eighth, and
thereafter conquered the world.

Centuries of faith, centuries of credulity. In their blind
enthusiasm for the religion of Christ the peoples could
not distinguish the true from the false. They confidently
awaited the end of the world and the Last Judgment,
which were announced, first for the year 202, then for the
year 1000. They believed that God's will could be mani-
fested by means of red-hot plowshares and boiling water.
They accused Sylvester II of holding converse with the
devil, because he was too wise. They saw Satan everywhere, burned sorcerers, and dreamed of the philosopher's
stone. They confused memories of paganism and fairy-tales
with the true faith. They adopted Merlin, the magician.
They believed, against all likelihood, that St. Mary Mag-
dalene had died in Provence, or that St. James had been
buried in a field marked by a star, *Campus stellae,* or
Compostella. Miracles surprised them not at all. It was
the absence of miracles that astonished them.

In very truth, Christianity had given them a soul.

THE ARAB CONQUEST

Meanwhile the great migrations continued. No sooner
had Christianity brought civilization to the barbarian

world than still other barbarians came upon the scene to shake the new foundations of security—this time the Arabs.

In the Arabian desert dwelt certain tribes of Semitic blood. These Bedouins (or "people of the desert") traded through the medium of caravans. For the most part they were pagan. They worshiped a white stone and a black, at Mecca.

One of them, a man called Mohammed, had, like Moses, truths revealed to him by God. These he spoke aloud, and they became the Koran (which means the "Recitation"). The inhabitants of Mecca mocked at this
622 inspired herdsman, and, since no man is a prophet in his own country, Mohammed left Mecca. This action of his was to be known as the Hegira, or "flight." He went to Yathrib, which was to become Medina, the "City of the Prophet." There he preached Islam, or submission to God, who is Allah. He taught a pure form of monotheism, forbade the worship of images, laid down a code of rules, both civil and penal, and instituted rites and fasts. He was listened to and followed. Those who rallied to his teaching were known as Mussulmans—"subjects of the divine will."

Mohammed called on them to make war against the infidels, who must be either killed or converted. The Mussulmans believed themselves to be the instruments of God. They began by making themselves masters of Mecca, where
630 they took possession of the fetishes of the sanctuary, which they annexed to their own faith. Then they set out to conquer the world.

They held several trump cards—their enthusiasm, even
632 after the death of the Prophet; their numbers, swollen by the general mass of Berbers; their military skill, which was greatly increased by the swiftness of their horses. For the Arabs, originally riders of dromedaries, took to horses when they moved into Persia, and learned from the Chinese and the Persians the use of stirrups, which were

unknown in Europe. Thus mounted, and using their bows
from the saddle, they spread terror in the ranks of their
enemies, who had never before encountered striking-
power and movement thus combined.

It seemed hopeless to think of checking the Arab flood.
Byzantium was degenerate, the kingdoms of the West were
still in the stage of growing-pains, the Christian Church
was powerless against infidels. The Arabs had only to
pounce upon the prey so temptingly offered.

They began by conquering Palestine and Syria, includ-   635
ing the cities of Jerusalem and Antioch. Next Babylonia,
Egypt, and Iran fell into their hands. Cyrenaica and Tunis,
in spite of Berber resistance, soon succumbed. Armenia
and Georgia collapsed, and Constantinople itself was
threatened. After this beginning the Arab tentacles spread   647
east, south, and west.

To the east the new conquerors found themselves in
conflict with the Turks, who at that time were still anarchic
and powerless. They took Afghanistan, overran Bokhara   705
and Samarkand, reached the Aral Sea and Ferghana, penetrated into the valley of the Indus, and absorbed large por-   712
tions of the Punjab and Sindh at a time when the rest of
India was breaking up into a scattering of small states. They
marched on Chinese Turkestan and Tarim. China at last
woke to the danger. Round Tashkent, after a series of   751
long-drawn-out battles, a condition of stalemate was
reached.

To the south Islam became firmly established along the
African coast between Abyssinia and Mozambique.

To the west the Arabs—called sometimes Moors, sometimes Saracens—got control of Africa as far as the Atlantic, and possibly as far as Senegal. Near Djebel-Tarik—   711
known later as Gibraltar—they landed in Spain. They
very soon reached Toledo and Aragon. The Visigoth
kingdom crumbled. The way was open into the territories
of the Franks. A raid into the valley of the Rhone took   721
them as far as Autun. Thrusting north from Bordeaux,

they reached a point slightly beyond Poitiers. Near Lou-
dun they were shattered by the heavy infantry of Charles
732 Martel. They were strong only in the weakness of their
enemies, and France was vigorous enough to withstand
them.

From the death of Mohammed to the so-called battle of
Poitiers a bare hundred years had elapsed. The "blitz-war"
was over. The Arabs withdrew south of the Pyrenees,
and very soon their power began to decline.

They had, in part, fulfilled their mission, since many of
the conquered peoples had accepted Islam, either because
the new religion appealed to them or because the successor of Mohammed (who was called the Caliph), enriched
by the booty of defeated empires, made generous grants
to his soldiers.

But the Arab conquests were too vast and too loosely
knit to endure for long under their new masters. The capital of Islam moved successively from Medina to Damascus,
762 and from Damascus to Bagdad, "the city given by God."
In the brilliance of the Moslem Court murders were frequent. The executioner played a part almost as important
as that of the Vizir, or First Minister. As a result of assas-
sination and revolution the Caliphate frequently changed
hands.

The provinces, governed by emirs, broke away from
756 Bagdad. The first to do so was Spain, which recognized
no authority save that of Cordova. Next came Africa with
first Fez, then Kairouan, as capital. On its own it conquered Malta and Sicily. The last to secede was Egypt,
868 which claimed Cyprus and Syria for itself, and took orders
only from Fostat and, at a later period, from Cairo. Each
of these scraps of Islam wanted its own caliph. Each of
these many sovereigns claimed to be the Vicar of the
Prophet, and fighting between them was continuous. Even
close to Bagdad a patchwork of principalities came into
existence. The Arab Empire had become no more than a
kaleidoscopic amalgam of territories.

But though its political unity was at an end, its spiritual cohesion remained, embodied in a singleness of language, since it was forbidden to translate the Koran, and in a sameness of prayers, because, in spite of schisms, the worshiper still turned his face to Mecca. Islam, which had conquered Egypt, Syria, Mesopotamia, Persia, and a part of India, later infiltrated into Madagascar, Ethiopia, the Sudan, Indo-China, Sumatra, and, at long last, Java and the Moluccas. It no longer employed the headsman, but it controlled men's minds, and Christianity could do nothing against it.

What was its legacy to mankind? To a very large extent it was a barbarian and, consequently, a negative one. The Arabs had destroyed monuments, burned libraries, cut down forests. Nowhere had they cultivated the soil. As a result of their occupation of the Levant and their capture of Sicily normal navigation in the Mediterranean had been brought to a standstill. For centuries their successors, the Barbary pirates, spread terror through what once had been a Latin sea. Their raids upon the continent of Europe disturbed the machinery of trade. They had struck at Arles and at Rome, and had closed the land routes to China. Certain texts of the Koran had a deleterious effect on agriculture and industry. Because it forbade the killing of animals, India refrained from breeding the silkworm; because the true believer must drink no wine, Egypt renounced the growing of vines. Because invasion had put a stop to the manufacture of papyrus, parchment became so dear that ancient manuscripts were scraped so that the surface might be used again. In this way many masterpieces vanished forever.

On the other hand, even when Islam separated West from East, it brought to the former something of the latter's wealth. The Huns had galloped their horses from China to Europe, but had brought with them no vestige of Oriental culture. The Arabs, on the contrary, soon achieved sufficient education to play with skill the part of middlemen. This they did the more effectively because their minds were naturally quick and lucid. They could understand and they could explain. Having no art and science of their own, they copied and assimilated to a remarkable degree. They studied not only the Chinese, but also the Hindus, the Persians, and the Greeks. Adaptive rather than creative, they revealed to the West the treasures of the East.

Having a natural gift for mathematics and astronomy, they transmitted the theory of the zero and a method of numeration. Impatient of active drama, but devotees of the spoken tale, they borrowed the substance of the *Arabian Nights* from Persia, and even from India. Natural artists, they gave birth to a mixed style in which both Persian arches and Byzantine vaulting had their place. Since the Moslem faith forbade the representation of animate objects, decoration drew inspiration from geometry, and flowered into a riot of arabesques. At Seville, at Granada, Arab architecture reached its highest point, and the richness of its decorative invention achieved astonishing triumphs.

In practical matters the Arabs played a no less important rôle as go-betweens. It is to them that Europe owes the use of stirrups, and Spain the introduction of the mule, and probably, also of smallpox. From the Arabs, ever great carriers of Chinese treasure, the West learned about sugar—which soon came to compete dangerously with honey—and about paper, which displaced papyrus. Even the vocabulary of Europe was enriched. It is from Arabic that Spanish derived much of its color, and to Arabic France owes many terms used in commerce and the sciences—from *algebra* to *magasin*. Traces of it are still to be found in the dialects of Sicily. Such are the deposits often left behind by conquerors.

THE NORSE PERIL

After the conquering horsemen came the conquering sailors, in the persons of men from the North, or Norsemen. Their own name for themselves was Vikings—the monarchs of the sea. They used narrow ships with high extremities, and these they could handle with a skill unknown to the ancients, for the Norsemen had learned the art of tacking, and could thus sail into the wind. They could turn into or away from the coast at will—landing, looting, and then taking to their ships. Alternatively, since these were of shallow draught, they would sail up the rivers, deep into the heart of the country, laying waste the banks as they moved forward. They knew nothing of fear, and were ruthless.

But, apart from their skill as sailors, these pirates were no better than savages. Their religion was primitive, and their artists confined themselves to carving weapons and jewelry. They had a form of runic writing—a distortion of the Greek and Roman alphabets—but no literature. The "Sagas," which recorded their exploits, belong to a later age.

They lacked elbow-room in the Scandinavian peninsula, where the Norwegians were settled to the west, the Swedes to the east, the Danes to the south. All three peoples carried their terror far afield.

The Norwegians already had outlying communities on the islands facing their homeland—the Shetlands and the Faroes. From them they ravaged the coasts of Scotland, descended on Ireland, and made themselves its masters. 830 One of them doubled the North Cape and sailed into the 860 White Sea. They seized Iceland, reached Greenland, and, thanks to a lucky wind, touched the American continent— somewhere in the neighborhood of Newfoundland or Labrador—an adventure that went no farther. Their discovery 999

of the unknown world was forgotten, and five centuries
had to pass before the exploit was repeated.

It was towards the Slav lands that the Swedes turned.
They began with the Baltic coast. One of their tribes—
850 Russians—were to give their name to a whole country.
Moving from lake to lake, from river to river, they reached
the Upper Dnieper and the Black Sea. At Kiev they
founded a powerful principality. On the route from Smo-
lensk to Byzantium they planted fortresses, and trading-
stations, for wherever they colonized they did business,
offering furs in exchange for textiles. They entertained the
idea of forcing the passage of the Straits, and on more than
one occasion their fleet actually threatened Constantinople.

The Danes cared neither for discoveries nor for trade
and in this they were unlike their Norwegian and Swedish neighbors. In the course of a long and epic adventure
they pillaged and terrorized the West. From their homeland they sailed to the mouths of the Rhine and the
840 Scheldt, established a foothold in the Low Countries, and
then swept up the rivers in a series of raids, carrying death
and destruction wherever they went. More than once they
sailed up the Seine, burning Rouen and Paris, pushing as
far as Melun and along the tributary streams to Meaux,
Beauvais, and Chartres. They appeared on the Loire, massacred the clergy of Nantes, and reached a point above
Orléans, on the Charente, where they sacked Saintes; on
the Garonne, where they burned Bordeaux; on the Elbe
and on the Tagus, bringing ruin to Hamburg and Lisbon.
A daring cruise took them into the Mediterranean. They
devastated Languedoc and Tuscany. They established
bases, preferably on islands in the river estuaries, from
which they moved on other expeditions. They left colonies on the Lower Seine and the Lower Loire. Then, they
866 set out to attack England, where they succeeded in driving
back the Anglo-Saxons. Everywhere they destroyed and
killed, leaving their ships only to harry the countryside.

The inhabitants trembled; the kings bought off the invaders. At long last, however, resistance became organized, and the Danes were brought to a standstill. As a result of one treaty England was divided; of another, the domain of the Norsemen in France was confined to a single province, which later took the name of Normandy. 878 885

But the Viking attack was not yet at an end. A fresh wave of Danes broke over England and won back the whole of the country. Canute the Great was recognized as King of England. Since he was also claimant to the throne of Norway, he was master of a vast realm which stretched from the Baltic to Greenland. The conquests of the Norsemen had unified the empire of the northern seas. 980 1028

Their hold, it is true, was far from permanent. Though they had begun their career as pirates, they learned wisdom at last, became sedentary, and were converted to Christianity. When they ceased to spread terror the Celts of Ireland rose, and England too tried to shake off the yoke. But she escaped the Danes only to fall into the hands of the frenchified Norsemen from Normandy. William the Conqueror landed several thousand mounted knights and archers, enough of them to beat the Saxon infantry at Hastings and to decide the fate of the island. Henceforward the old home of the Britons was to be an Anglo-Norman kingdom. William was able to make large grants of rich land to his companions-in-arms, who became the ancestors of future English barons. 1066

But the Normans were not contented to stay in the countries of the north. They hired out their services to Italian princes and Byzantine emperors. They became attached to the countries of the sun, drove the Byzantine forces from Apulia and Calabria, and captured Sicily from the Arabs. Distant though these places were from ancestral Scandinavia, they long bore the marks of their Norman conquerors. 1091

For Norman culture has its distinctive mark. It is to be found not only in the place-names of Normandy and in the syntax of the English tongue. It can be recognized in the timber-work which the Normans—former shipbuilders—put into the naves of their squat churches, from England to Sicily. It is deeply imprinted in national manners. It must, surely, have been from their Scandinavian forbears that the Normans of France got their love of quarreling, and the English their later passion for the sea.

BULGARS AND HUNGARIANS

No sooner had the Norsemen ceased from ravaging the West than a new set of nomads swept into the East—the Bulgars and the Hungarians. Their savagery so struck the imagination of Europe that their very names have passed into the vernacular as those of men who brought with them outrage and fear. From Bulgar comes *bougre* ("bugger"), from Hungarian, *hongrois* ("ogre").

Both derived more or less directly from the Huns. Scarcely a century after the Bulgars, fresh from the banks
660   of the Volga, had settled in what is now Bulgaria, they
755   were already a serious threat to Constantinople. But, for the time being, they were driven from the walls of the city, and settled down to wait until such time as the Eastern
802   Empire should grow decadent. When that moment came they swept through the Balkans, reducing to captivity a large number of Slavs, and carving for themselves a do-
927   main which stretched from the Adriatic to the gates of Byzantium. Their chief, Simon, took the title of Tsar. He too was ambitious to continue the tradition of Caesar.

Meanwhile they had lost something of their earlier savagery. They had adopted the Slav language; they had been converted to Greek Christianity. With the passage of time, and as a result of contact with Byzantine civilization, they
970   grew soft. They were no longer capable of taking the offensive. They allowed themselves to be defeated by the Princes of Kiev, and then by the Emperors of Constanti-

nople, who claimed that they had reduced them to submission.

But if the Bulgarian menace was removed the Hungarian took its place. The newcomers, who called themselves Magyars, had traveled from Siberia by the same route as that once followed by the Huns. Like them, they ate their meat raw and drank the blood of their enemies. They had shaven heads and stupid faces. Hordes of Turks had driven them from Asia, and were hard on their heels. They had crossed the Ural River and swept through Russia. They reached the Danube. The Slavs whom they there encountered were in no condition to resist. The Slovenes, Serbs, Croats, Slovaks, Czechs, Moravians, Pomeranians, and Poles were fully occupied in fighting one another or in trying to stem the ambitious moves of their German neighbors. The Hungarians had only the Moravians to defeat. That done, they settled down in the Danube Plain.

But they knew nothing about farming land, however fertile it might be. Their only skill was in horsemanship, archery, and pillage. They fell upon the provinces of Europe—on Venetia first, and the valley of the Po, then on Saxony and Swabia. Three times they devastated Lorraine. They appeared at Basle, at Bremen, before Nîmes. They threatened Rome and ravaged Tuscany. In the west they penetrated as far as Berry and Aquitaine. In the east they showed themselves in Thrace, and reached the Bosporus. Southward they traveled as far as Campania. These various expeditions lasted for more than half a century, and did not end until the German Emperor Otho finally overcame the Hungarians on the banks of the river Lech, in Bavaria.

But time had done its work. The Hungarians learned at last how to farm and plow the plain which bears their name. Their chief, Vaïk, was baptized in the name of Stephen. He transformed Hungary into a Christian state, and had the Pope bless his royal diadem, which was to remain the mascot of the Magyar nation. In return for

895

906

899

933

937

955

985

the massacre of certain pigheaded pagans he received the title of "Apostolic Majesty." He became St. Stephen, and under his aegis, Hungary entered the concert of European nations.

THE COMING OF THE TURKS

Already the Turks—their name means the "Strong"—had given men cause to talk of them. They too belonged to the same general family as the Huns, the Bulgars, the Magyars, and the Mongols. Formerly they had driven Avars and Hungarians before them towards Europe. Now it was their turn to take the same road.

For a long time their home had been in Central Asia. They would gladly have embarked upon the conquest of China, so lovely and so tempting was the prey! But China, even divided, even apathetic, was a difficult nut to crack. At any moment she might unite, whereas the West, with its nations and its faiths at perpetual loggerheads, seemed condemned to a lasting condition of discord.

Whenever China had seemed weak the Turks had turned envious eyes on her. It was the Turkish menace that finally brought the Chinese to their senses. The General, Li Shi-min, who afterwards became the Emperor 626 T'ai Tsung, defeated the Turks of Mongolia, and overcame the Turks of Turkestan. He re-established a Chinese protectorate over the valley of the Tarim, and carried its limits as far as Tibet. It was under his leadership that China renewed her contacts with Buddhist India, and received from Iran the Nestorian version of Christianity. But as soon as the Chinese showed signs of relaxing their efforts the Turks resumed their attacks. Only the presence in China of another great Emperor, Hsüan Tsung, held 751 back the assailants. But the Arabs outdid the Turks and crushed a Chinese army. Two centuries of conflict had reduced the population of China by half. A Mongol horde 936 took advantage of this weakness to capture Peking. A new

imperial dynasty, the Sung, gave all its energies to the 960
task of consolidating what still remained of China.

It was at this time that the Turks turned back towards
the West. One of their tribes crossed the Volga and the
Danube, ravaged Bulgaria, and was itself destroyed in
Greece. Another group moved on Iran, took possession 1051
of it, and pushed as far as the Caucasus. The Arab Empire, well-nigh exhausted by internal dissensions, collapsed
before them. The Turks entered Bagdad. Their leader 1055
took the title of Sultan, which means "Tyrant."

From now on the threat of them lay heavy on the
Byzantine Empire. They pillaged Asia Minor, which they
ultimately turned into a Turkish country. They appeared 1070
at Scutari. They made an Emperor prisoner. They took
Aleppo, Jerusalem, Damascus, and Antioch. They profaned the Holy Places.

There could be no hope of the Turks turning Christian,
like the Norsemen, the Bulgarians, the Hungarians. It was
Islam that caught them after they had come in contact
with the Arabs, and it was the Turks whom the Church
regarded as the enemy, the Turks whom she had to attack
when the time came for her to deliver the Holy Places.

THE FEUDAL ECONOMY

Feudalism, as all other forms of political and economic
organizations, was born of the needs of the time, for an
agricultural society. The absence of a highly organized
state, such as the Western Roman Empire had been, ne-
cessitated some form of group co-operation for mutual assistance and protection, if civilization was to endure. The
barbarian menace, the general insecurity of life and property, the cultivation of the land, the absence of trade and
of money as a medium of exchange—all were considerations.

Without pattern and without precedent (except the
little that came from isolated cases in the late Roman

Empire and in the customs of the early Germans), the feudal estate gradually evolved.

No two were alike, yet all followed the general line dictated by similar needs. Military chiefs and large landed proprietors spontaneously combined with their tenants and their small-farmer neighbors to form what may be termed small states. Each was a self-sufficient unit. Each produced its own food, supplied its own clothing, had its own court and army, and coined its own money—if it had any. The little trade that was carried on with the shrunken towns or neighboring fiefs was more likely to be a matter of barter.

Socially and economically the organization was a hierarchy. At the head was the lord. Next were his vassals and knights—his fighting men. They swore fealty to him and gave him their services in return for lands or other favors. They were of course his social equals.

Usually in each feudal manor there were some privileged tenants commonly known as freemen. They had brought their own land into the common undertaking and paid rent to the lord in exchange for the benefits the arrangement offered. They furnished also oxen and plows, but not their services, for a certain number of days each year for the cultivation of the lord's lands.

Below these were the several grades of villeins or serfs. They were not slaves, but they were bound to the land, on which their forefathers had probably lived, and they could not be separated from it. They cultivated their own strips of land, paid a certain amount of the produce to the lord, and gave him a stipulated number of days' work during the year.

The feudal régime took root in China and Japan during the centuries of anarchy, and in the parceled pattern of India, as well as in the Christian West. Only those empires which had a solid administration—as the Byzantine and the Arab—knew nothing of it.

The great barons were masters each in their own homes.

They formed, collectively, an hereditary caste whose natural function was to fight. But because they had oftener to defend themselves than to attack, they were better armed to resist than to take the offensive. The knight was equipped with coat-of-mail, helmet, and shield. He was an animated mass of iron. Against the mass of iron opposite, he had at his disposal a double-edged sword and an iron-tipped lance of ash. His castle lay behind moats and walls, and must always be prepared to stand a siege.

The castle too was heavily armored. Feudal warfare was innocent of tactics. It usually consisted of sieges or of single combat, with its own rules, its own code of honor, which, in Japan as elsewhere was inspired partly by religion, partly by chivalry. It was the expression of an age which was still barbarous, though forever trying to produce something that should be a copy of civilization.

At the peak of the hierarchy was the sovereign. But he was no more than the supreme overlord whose authority was at times more nominal than real. To the best of his ability he defended his rights against feudal encroachment —rights of justice, rights of taxation, and economic rights.

Furthermore, the Church forbade the lending of money at interest, in which she was guilty of making a deplorable confusion between illegitimate and legitimate profit, between usury and rent. As a result of this fatal prohibition, Christianity retarded the awakening of the West, which was already suffering from a cruel lack of capital. The Jews were encouraged in their banking activities, since, not having the right to own land, and finding themselves excluded from a great many occupations, they turned moneylenders and traders—at the risk of being put on the Index and of rousing anti-Semitic feeling.

In launching her anathema against loans at interest the Church had this excuse, that she was dreaming of an ideal world where men should work for the pleasure of working, where the merchant should sell without profit, and all should be honest. She would also, no doubt, in a truly

Christian world, have tried to suppress wars. But the world was not as she would have it be. The outrages committed on the Holy Sepulcher recalled her to a sense of reality. The question for her, thereafter, was not the suppression of private fighting, but the preaching of a Holy War.

THE CHRISTIAN COUNTER-OFFENSIVE

It was Spain that set the example of an attack on Islam. She wished to reconquer her native soil. The bastion of resistance in the Iberian peninsula was alive with actions and counteractions, with *castillos,* which gave to her their name. A Castilian hero, Rodriguez of Vivar, sym-
1050   bolized in his single person the whole epic struggle. The Moors called him the Sidia, and he has come down to us as the Cid. Long before Corneille, the poets of Spain commemorated him. It was many years after the exploits of the Cid that the royal house of Castile triumphed over the Moslem Caliph. The saint-king Ferdinand took Cordova and Seville. The kingdom of Granada was the last place in Europe where the Arabs maintained a footing.

But the Infidels were not confined to Spain. They held Africa; they controlled the Mediterranean; they ruled over the Holy Land. Had not one of the Caliphs destroyed the Holy Sepulcher? Were not the Turkish hordes profaning Jerusalem? Were not the Christian communities in Palestine under the Turkish yoke? Was not Byzantium appealing for help?

It is useless to try to explain the Crusades as a movement that was due merely to economic and political motives. They were primarily an act of faith—and that alone.
1095   "God has willed it," declared Pope Urban II. The kings might turn a deaf ear to the appeal, but their peoples were fired with enthusiasm. The nations of the West had not, after all, been settled communities for very long. The old instinct of the nomads awoke in them, and with it went

the hope of booty. The workless gathered to the colors.
The women and children followed the men. A fanatical
crowd set out on a march to the East—a true pilgrimage
in arms.

By way of Bavaria and Hungary this down-at-heels collection of human beings streamed to Constantinople and
into Asia Minor. They stole as they went, and left their   1096
dead upon the roads. Starvation, fever, and the Hungarians
took toll of them. The Turks had merely to exterminate
what was left. The official Crusade was more fortunate.
The propaganda of the Church gathered together four real
armies of knights who bore the Cross upon their breasts.
Frenchmen, Lorrainers, Provençals, and Normans from   1097
Italy assembled on the Asiatic side of the Bosporus. Now
that the moment had come, feeling in Byzantium, faced
with this help against the Moslem, was one of anxiety
rather than of joy.

The knights wrenched Asia Minor from the Turks,
whose power was still small. Antioch was taken. The
Christian army took Jerusalem by storm, looted it, and   1099
filled its streets with bloodshed. The West learned with
amazement of the deliverance of the Holy Places, of the
establishment of a Latin kingdom in Jerusalem.

This was the apogee of Christendom. Islam had lost the
initiative, and the Christian offensive, under the auspices
of the Holy See and the leadership of the Papal Legate,
had triumphed. Rome was once again the capital of the
world.

For centuries past Christianity alone had preserved the
buried treasures of civilization. At a time when the fields
had been relapsing into wilderness it was the monks who
had done the plowing. At a time when the schools were
closed it was the clergy who had kept alive the flame of
scholarship. At a time when the barbarians of the north,
the east, and the south had carried their destructive raids
into the heart of Europe, Christianity alone had protected
the human values.

And now Christianity was victorious. She who had once been persecuted now imposed her law (but a time would come when she too would persecute). No longer was she on the defensive, but attacking. Paganism disappeared from the West. The Infidels withdrew into the East. Even in China Christianity, in the guise of the Nestorian heresy, was gaining ground.

All this was far more than the victory of Europe over Asia. Europe, after all, is no more than a geographical expression. In the eyes of history it has no existence. Once upon a time it was no more than a scattering of races, and a time was to come when it would be no more than a scattering of nations. Only by strength or by faith has Europe ever achieved unity from the strength of Rome or the faith of Christendom.

Faced by the onward rush of the barbarians, Christendom realized her solidarity. She had been able to assimilate Norsemen and Bulgars and Hungarians. Arabs and Turks had set her shaking in her shoes. If the barrier of Byzantium cracked, fresh hordes might bring destruction. To that threat Rome replied with the Crusades; and Rome won. But, though she did not know it, by freeing the Mediterranean and the lines of communication through the Levant she had engendered an economic revolution and brought a new world to birth.

CHAPTER SIX

The Awakening
of the West

THE RESULTS OF THE CRUSADES

THE CHRISTIAN settlements in the Holy Land were far from secure. The barbarians and the evildoers had been repulsed, but not crushed. They were still on the prowl. More than one Crusade was necessary in order to protect the Kingdom of Jerusalem, or to reconquer its territories when it failed to resist attack.

The First Crusade was followed by many others, spaced across two centuries. Little purpose would be served by giving the details of them here. It is not easy to distinguish what were Crusades from what were pilgrimages, the official from the unofficial expeditions. Some were purely national affairs—German, English, French, or Catalan. Some were preached by Rome, some led by excommunicated sovereigns. There was a recrudescence of popular Crusades, one in particular, composed of children, which was without rhyme or reason. As a rule it was the kings who took responsibility for these adventures, but it is by no means certain that they always knew what precisely they were after. They would abandon their project even before they reached their goal, would quarrel in face of

the enemy, or would come to terms with the very unbe-
lievers whom they had set out to chastise.

The whole character of the Crusades changed. As the
sea-route progressively took precedence over that by land,
the Christian counter-offensive assumed the appearance of
a series of colonizing expeditions. Even when Saladin, the
1187 Sultan of Egypt, had recaptured Jerusalem the Christians
forgot their hatred of Islam. Richard, King of England,
Coeur de Lion though he was, concluded a truce. The Emperor of Germany, Frederick II, entered into negotiations
with the Moslems, as a result of which Jerusalem was neutralized, and the places sanctified by the life of Christ allowed to stand side by side with the mosques of Allah.
Nothing could have been further from such tolerance than
the spirit of the First Crusade.

Still more extraordinary was the way in which the Crusade preached by Innocent III turned away from the Holy
Places. Instead of delivering Jerusalem, it overturned the
Greek Empire of Byzantium. This curious adventure was
determined by motives more human than divine. The
Venetian shipowners, who had been hired to transport the
crusading armies, complained that they had been paid less
than the sum stipulated in their contract. They demanded
that the deficit in money should be paid in kind. The Crusaders, therefore, set themselves to capture Zara, on the
Adriatic coast, a possession of the Christian King of Hungary and commercial rival of Venice. Once they had tasted
booty, and urged on by dark intrigues, the troops marched
1203 on Constantinople, where an appalling state of anarchy
reigned. They took it, and forgot all about the Crusade
in apportioning the loot. Venice took Crete for herself,
Latin Emperors installed themselves in Byzantium, and
the evicted Greek monarchs took refuge in Asia Minor.
But no one bothered about rescuing the Holy Sepulcher
from the Infidels.

It needed St. Louis to restore to the Crusades their

Christian significance. That pious prince attempted to strike at Islam in Egypt. Then he landed in Tunis, hoping to convert the Caliph. But in everything he undertook he failed. He was made prisoner on the banks of the Nile, 1270 and died among the ruins of Carthage. His enterprises were anachronistic and out of fashion. Christians had lost their faith in the Crusades. Even in the East, so far from uniting against the barbarians, they fought among themselves, not only Latins against Greeks, but English against French, Genoese against Venetians, the Holy Roman Empire against the Holy See. National quarrels and a war of interests had taken the place of a struggle for the Cross.

The military orders, which first saw the light in the Holy Land, and had spread all over the West, lost all sense of their mission to protect the Christian states of Asia and to defend the pilgrims. The Hospitalers of St. John, who later became the Knights of Rhodes, and then of Malta, confined their service of God to the ramparts of their tiny islands. The Templars, who grew to be possessors of enormous wealth, turned into bankers. The Teutonic Knights carved out for themselves, at the expense of Poland, a domain on the Baltic coast, from which, ultimately, the Prussian state emerged. In all these operations the Faith was scarcely more than a pretext. God had become a mere flag or emblem.

THE DECLINE OF THE PAPACY

It was still Rome's ambition to rule the world, but this she was unable to do. Her reputation was still great, but it was no longer unquestioned. The Holy See proclaimed with might and main that "as sinners, all human creatures are under the jurisdiction of the Pope," but the sovereigns were breaking free of the pontifical leading-strings.

Rome could no longer ensure obedience by threatening

excommunication. Kings and peoples, conscious of their power, had ceased to be docile. Pope Innocent III was the last Pontiff who was able to impose his will upon the Christian world, and even he could not do all he wished to do. His temporal triumph was precarious. England outfaced him, and the King of France acted according to his

1216 own lights. After Innocent III a change in attitude could no longer be doubted. The Papacy was openly defied. Once again the Holy Roman Empire threw down a challenge, and the two Powers vied with one another in abuse —"False Vicar of Christ!" "Contriver of lies!" In the time of Boniface VIII the Papacy had to endure its worst affront when the envoy of the French King laid hands upon the sovereign Pontiff in his own palace. The time was not far off when the Popes, treated in their turn as naughty children, would leave Rome for Avignon.

Even the great fabric of Catholicism was showing cracks. The baptismal names which it had been in the habit of bestowing on the faithful were being superseded by surnames, which tended to become hereditary in each family. Thus was civil status born at the expense of its religious forerunner.

Not that there was any general weakening of faith in the century which produced St. Francis of Assisi, and gave birth to both the Dominican and the Franciscan orders. But Byzantium was now the home of the Orthodox Church. New heresies appeared and took root. The Patarins rejected the Old Testament; the Vaudois cast the wealth of the clergy in their teeth; the Albigenses were already foreshadowing Protestantism. Rome condemned, denounced, suppressed. The tribunals of the Inquisition began to operate. Passions grew hot, as hot as the fires of the stake. Christian men embarked on a wild orgy of killing: "Slay them all! Let God recognize His own!"

The Faith grew less rigid, less homogeneous. From Byzantium the Crusaders brought back the cult of the Virgin,

till then somewhat neglected, and there was a sudden
flowering of churches dedicated to Our Lady. Angels
brought the Virgin's house from Nazareth to Dalmatia,
and thence to Italy.

Sanctity now was less often to be found on the throne
of the Pontiff than in the palaces of temporal princes.
Very few of the Popes were canonized, but a St. Louis
reigned in France, a St. Ferdinand in Castile, as formerly
a St. Henry had ruled in Germany, a St. Edward in England, a St. Canute in Denmark, a St. Stephen in Hungary.
True, there was another side to the picture. Many sovereigns were excommunicated. The Emperors Henry V and
Frederick II, the English King John Lackland, Philip
Augustus and Philippe le Bel of. France were consigned
to Satan. But the only effect of these sentences was to
awaken in Germany, in England, and in France a feeling
of nationalism.

Indeed, the awakening of the Western countries was
closely bound up with the decline of the Papacy. If the
peoples still felt but vaguely the "differences" which separated them from their neighbors, the princes were busy
hammering out nations on the anvil and welding their
provinces together. Scholars were rediscovering Roman
Law, and in so doing, rediscovered, too, the idea of the
State. The feudal world was falling into a chaos of scraps
and patches. Now that the barbarian incursions had ceased
the middle classes no longer needed the protection of their
lords. The kings took advantage of the Crusades to assert
their authority over the barons, whom they weakened and
banished. On occasion kings and middle classes were in
league against the great lords. The commons won pre-
eminence in Flanders and in Italy. The monarchy in
France grew strong.

The solidarity of Christendom was dead. It was the time
of the hatching of the nations.

THE NATIONS TRY TO FIND THEIR FEET

But not all the nations of the West succeeded in finding their feet. Italy emerged from feudal chaos only to be swallowed up in the chaos of city rivalries. The small kingdoms of Spain were still at war—Aragon, Castile, Navarre, and the infant Portugal, against the Saracens of Granada.

Germany failed to escape permanently from the anarchy of the feudal system because of the elective character of the Holy Roman Emperor. The Emperors drained their energies in continuing the fight against Rome. In 1152 vain did Frederick Barbarossa impose silence on his barons. He wanted to be the consolidator of the Germanies, the arbiter of the West, the War Lord. He razed Milan to the ground, and put the Pope to flight. But on his way to 1190 the Crusades he was drowned in a small river of Asia Minor. With his death all hope of German unity vanished. But legend asserts that Barbarossa is not dead; that he lies sleeping in some distant cavern, and will some day awake. For this awakening of Barbarossa Germany henceforward waited. It was to be the signal of her own.

It was about this time that the epic of the Nibelungen took shape, in two thousand lines, from the old German legends. Germany was to dream of Siegfried as she dreamed of Barbarossa. The story of his fabulous treasure, drowned under the waters of the Rhine, was the symbol of her own lost greatness.

Frederick II, for all his hardihood and cunning, did not succeed in rebuilding Germany's unity. He defied three Popes in succession, only to see his authority challenged within the Empire by his feudal lords, egged on by Rome to revolt against him. Germany seemed fated to fall apart in a whirl of intrigue.

England, on the other hand, had her feet firmly set upon the road which led to territorial unity. The Anglo-

Norman monarchy rapidly became powerful. It wiped out
the last centers of Saxon resistance, which found its legendary hero in Robin Hood. Not only did it absorb Corn-
wall, Wales, and Scotland; dowry and inheritance
brought it a continental empire which added Anjou and
Aquitaine to Normandy. In Aquitaine, its most recent
"colony," it encouraged the growing of the Bordeaux
grapes which kept the English supplied with wine.

But because of its tyrannous character and its excesses
this monarchy forced into a coalition against it the clergy,
the barons, and the middle classes of England. While, on
the Continent, the house of Capet set itself to oppose
Plantagenet ambitions, public opinion in London hard-
ened. By a legal instrument King John gave up his right to   1215
levy taxes save with the approval of his Council. Actually
Magna Carta, which history has tried to represent as the
first monument of English liberties, served as a guarantee
of feudal privilege rather than of the liberty of the subject. Nevertheless as a result of it Parliament was born,
and the first steps were taken to establish a system of government which should be both representative and constitu-
tional. In spite of Rome's condemnation of these innovations, in spite of the appointment of St. Louis as arbiter
between the barons and the Crown of England, in spite
of all the attempts made by the English kings to recover
their lost authority, even at the cost of civil war, the English nation was born.

THE SUPREMACY OF FRANCE

France too found her way of destiny, or, rather, the
house of Capet found it for her. It had progressed from
humble beginnings, building up from father to son a powerful heritage. For in the law of succession lay the whole
secret of the good fortune that attended its members. It
eliminated competition and division. The Roman Empire

had never succeeded in becoming hereditary. The German Empire had never managed to free itself from the electoral system, and even England, by admitting women to the succession, was in grave danger of becoming weak. The Capet dynasty alone achieved the feat of establishing a system by which the crown descended directly in the male line by right of primogeniture. Therein lay the secret of its continuity. Therein lay the secret of France's greatness.

Thanks to a series of brilliant reigns, that greatness put out strong roots. Philip Augustus by his clear-headedness, St. Louis by his loyalty, Philippe le Bel by his shrewdness, conferred on the kingdom of France the leadership of the West. Of these three sovereigns St. Louis was undoubtedly the least skillful, the least realistic. But he compensated in prestige for what he lost in territory. In defeat he conquered. His glory shone bright even in surrender. He was a stained-glass king, a statue of nobility. He dispensed justice under an oak-tree in the Forest of Vincennes. In Egypt he tended the victims of the plague. He cured the scrofulous, and acted as arbiter in the quarrels of the European princes. He was a fairy-tale monarch, whose very faults brought splendor to the house of Capet and to France.

From reign to reign the patrimony of the French kings was rounded out. As a result of alliances and wars, of ransoms and confiscations, province was added to province. Menaced in the east by the Empire, in the north and south by the English, France managed to avert the double peril. On more than one occasion she drove back

1214 invaders from Germany. At Bouvines she won her first great national victory, and it firmly established her monarchy, and made of the king the living symbol of his country. On more than one occasion, too, she stemmed the English infiltration. She won back Anjou; she forced the Plantagenets to renounce their claim to Normandy. In the person of the Norman Pierre Dubois she sketched a dream of international arbitration, of a League of Nations under

THE AWAKENING OF THE WEST

the aegis of France. The fleur-de-lis, evolved from a lance's head, became the emblem of triumphant kingship.

Far from her frontiers, even, France was powerful and ever-present. Was not the First Crusade essentially French? Was it not on Godfrey of Bouillon, the Walloon, that the kingdom of Jerusalem was first bestowed, before passing into the hands of the Counts of Anjou, Forez, and Champagne? It was French families who ruled in Cyprus, Antioch, and Tripoli. It was Frenchmen who took root in Syria, built the arsenals of Tyre and Acre, imported their laws and their customs, and transplanted the life of France into alien lands. The Arabs were not deceived. In their eyes all the invading Christians were "Franks." Franks were the kings and princes who made of the Levant what amounted to a French colony. Franks were most of the knights who settled in Rhodes. The Mediterranean became the "Frankish Sea."

At Constantinople too the Emperors now were French. After Baudouin of Flanders it was the Lords of Courtenay and Brienne who inherited the Imperial Purple. In Rome the throne of the Popes was often occupied by Frenchmen, or by Pontiffs responsive to French influence. Naples and Sicily, which the German Emperors had inherited by **1266** marriage from the Norman kings, were conquered by Charles of Anjou, the brother of St. Louis, and it was this same Charles of Anjou, Senator at Rome and Podesta at Florence, who became, for all practical purposes, master of Italy. Even after the massacre of the Sicilian **1282** French (one Easter Sunday, at the hour of Vespers) . . . even after the appeal of the people of Palermo to the King of Aragon, who seized the island, Charles of Anjou remained king at Naples and a power throughout the peninsula.

Paris came near to being the capital of the world at a time when Rome was little more than an overgrown village. Philip Augustus ringed it with new walls, and started on the task of paving its streets. Paris fashions were copied abroad. The University of Paris had no rival. Students from all Europe, and especially from England, went thither to sit at the feet of the German Albertus Magnus or of the Italian Thomas Aquinas. It was only after living many years in Paris, and learning from her masters, that Roger Bacon set up as a teacher in Oxford.

Albertus Magnus, St. Thomas, and Roger Bacon wrote and taught in Latin. But the French language had won its spurs. The searchers out of songs, whom men called *trouvères,* or *troubadours,* told of the deeds of Roland, or the loves of Tristan and Iseult. Joinville compiled the history of his kings. Of tales of imagination the number grew in the new tongue which was known as Romance to distinguish it from Latin, and they were long known, even outside France, as *romans.* French was the official language both in London and Jerusalem. The English wrote in French. They said *"Dieu et mon droit,"* they constructed the word *parliament* out of the verb *parler,* and the Plantagenets derived their family name from the bunch of furze (*genêt*) which they wore in their caps. Italians and Germans imitated and translated the works of French writers. Crowned heads corresponded in French.

As much as, and even more than, in letters, France led the world in art. As long ago as the eleventh century the romanesque style had been peculiarly at home in France. Since the time of the Romans the West had lost the gift of building. Now it began to learn again the technique of architecture. The country south of the Loire had kept the secret of the Roman vault. Churches arose, bare and crude, but with the power to move men's hearts by their very simplicity and by a harmony of line which was effective even when it was primitive. Ornament took second place to solidity of construction. From Poitiers and Caen, from Toulouse, and then from Vézelay, romanesque art spread to St. James of Compostella, to Parma, to Durham and Lincoln, to Spires and Worms.

In the middle of the twelfth century a new means of expression arose in the Ile de France: ribbed vaulting, pointed arches, flying buttresses, transformed the craft of building. Churches soared with an upward thrust of nave and tower and steeple. The new style was primarily vertical. Stone was no more than a skyward leap lost in a luminous fairyland of glass. It was a style of excess. It turned at last to the colossal, and outsoared the puny powers of human beings. So ambitious were the schemes of building undertaken that a train of generations could not bring them to completion. The cathedrals of Rheims and Bourges were left with their towers uncrowned. Strasbourg remained with one spire only; Beauvais never progressed beyond its choir.

The art of the pointed arch was French. The Italians called it, derisively, "Gothic," because for them the word Goth stood vaguely for all foreigners from the north. But it was in France, most certainly, in the country round Paris, that the style first appeared and came to maturity. Artists traveled from abroad to learn, and showed how well they had absorbed the lesson which France had taught them by turning it to account at Cologne and Regensburg, at Toledo and Burgos. French architects were in charge of the masons and carpenters at Canterbury and Ulm, at Prague and Upsala. In Syria the castles of the Frankish knights still call to mind the walls of Aigues-Mortes or of Carcassonne.

Stone lost its coldness; sculpture became less stiff. The Angel of Rheims learned to smile, the Sainte-Chapelle grew to a wonder of lace, Mont-Saint-Michel tapered to a soaring delicacy. France, through her thinkers and her builders, set a fashion. In politics and in art the thirteenth century was the first of the great French periods.

These many marvels were, in part, no doubt due to the Christian faith. But that faith had been as lively, and less adulterated, three or four centuries earlier. Why, then, had

it been artistically sterile? Because two conditions had
been absent—a suitable soil in which to grow, the soil of
a united France, and, more especially, the provision of
those material resources which come with wealth. The
artistic revolution of the Middle Ages was the direct consequence of another revolution which was essentially economic.

THE ECONOMIC REVOLUTION

By driving the Arabs from Sicily and, later, by conquering the Levant the Western nations had succeeded in re-
opening the Mediterranean routes, and in re-establishing
the links that bound them to Byzantium and the Near
East. The Crusaders brought back with them more than
leprosy—that inexorable evil which was to lie like a blot
over Europe. In treading the road to the Cross they had
found a fortune. Setting out with the object of battling
with Islam, they had ended by trading with it. There was
contact once again between West and East.

It was the Italian cities first—Amalfi, Pisa, Genoa, and
Venice—which most benefited from the restarting of the
Mediterranean trade, and bitterly did they fight for its
mastery. But Marseilles and Barcelona were not to be excluded. There was renewed activity within the continent
of Europe. The plains of Flanders were drawn into the
orbit. The West was waking from the sleep into which it
had been plunged after the Germanic invasions.

Everywhere men began to work again. Land was
cleared. The forests yielded before the advancing plow.
The peasants learned how to alternate their crops, how to
manure and fertilize their fields. Europe came by the
knowledge of new plants—not rice alone, and sugar-cane
and cotton, but vegetables too, which could be easily naturalized—buckwheat and maize, the apricot, the saffron
(for dyeing textiles), the mulberry, which brought the
silkworm. Land-values, which had collapsed at the begin-

ning of the Crusades, shot up. In spite of a rising birth rate the demand for labor was such that wages rose. The purchasing-power of the workers increased.

The East revealed its treasures to the innocent eyes of the West. The advent of the windmill gave motive-power. The whole technique of transport was revolutionized. The wheelbarrow, first devised, perhaps, in China, made its appearance and eased the task of builder and of plowman. The use of the iron horseshoe, discovered at Byzantium, became general, and made longer journeys and heavier loads possible. Fashions in horse-furniture were changing. A long time after the Chinese (who never exploited it) the Westerners developed the rigid yoke and the breast-strap. The horse, which till then had been pre-eminently a saddle animal, could now be used for draught purposes, and men released from an age-long servitude. Byzantium, because she clung to the old methods, was compelled to retain the slave system, whereas the West, by adopting the new, could enfranchise her serfs. Economics was the parent of a social revolution.

The sea too had its novelties no less important than those of the land. Once again it was from China (unless it was Japan) that the light of knowledge came. The secret was transmitted by Arabs to Normans, and by them to the sailors of Genoa, Venice, and Majorca; and the secret was this—that a magnetized needle will point always to the north. It was mounted on a straw and set to float in a bowl of water. Contained in a little box which bore the Sicilian name of *boussole* ("compass"), this magic pointer was not yet quite at home; but the invention later showed its possibilities.

Another discovery came to aid the sailor—that of the rudder. Up till then ships had been steered by means of an oar. They now learned to respond to the movements of a vertical piece of timber turning on hinges at the stern. This invention allowed the building of heavier vessels which need no longer creep timidly along inshore. Ocean

travel became a practical possibility, and the way lay open
to the great triumphs of navigation.

The optical lens was no less fertile in possibilities.
Whether the credit for this should go to Roger Bacon is
not certain. Armed with the microscope, men were now
equipped to explore the infinitely small; with the telescope, the infinitely distant. As a result of both, philosophy and men's knowledge of the world were to undergo
great changes. The progress of astronomy helped on the
art of navigation. Future centuries were to harvest what
the Middle Ages had sown.

Within the small world of the house, too, there were
changes. They may seem insignificant, but they were to
have far-reaching effects—the chimney, the tallow candle,
the carpenter's plane, the earliest wall-hangings of paper,
the means of procuring light and warmth, the provision of
furniture and instruction. From Nuremberg came the clock
with toothed wheels. The East had shown Europe a luxury
till then undreamed of—bathing and shaving. Men began
to develop a taste for fine furnishings, for jewels, for car-
pets. (Not only the objects, but the name (*tapis*) came
from the East.) A new way of living was replacing the
discomforts of the Dark Ages.

Both revolutions, the economic and the social, were
linked with a third—that of money. The trade born of the
Crusades had set the gold of Byzantium and the Levant
flowing westward. About the same time men began again
to seek for gold in the waters of the Rhine, the Rhone,
the Po. The mines of Hungary and the Caucasus were exploited, and the yellow metal extracted from them spread
across Europe. It was many hundreds of years since gold
1232   had been minted in the West. Minting was now carried
out, first in Sicily, then in Genoa, England, France. The
first effect of this new activity was to complete the discom-
fiture of the feudal barons. They had been able to issue
silver coinage only, and this was soon eclipsed by the

output of the Royal Mints. The second effect was, by increasing the circulation of money, to make possible the substitution of wage-earners for serfs.

Increased currency issue favored the growth of banking and trade. The Church's anathemas against lending at interest were either forgotten or circumvented. Limited companies, insurance, letters of credit, all reappeared. Seas, rivers, roads, played their part in the interchange of goods. The East exported spices, perfumes, silk, cotton, and drugs. Russia sold cereals, furs, and dried fish; Scandinavia, iron and timber; England, wool, copper, and tin; France, salt, honey, and wine; Spain, leather; Germany, furs and textiles. The old system of small, self-sufficient communities gave way before a geographically arranged division of labor. A number of German ports grouped themselves about Lübeck, and organized the supply of herrings to a Christendom on which the Church enjoined the duty of eating only fish on Fridays and in Lent. This was one of the first activities of the Hanseatic League. Poitou manufactured arms; Tuscany, woven cotton goods; Flanders, cloth. Huge fairs were instituted which brought merchants and their goods together. On the route from Bruges to the Mediterranean, the Fairs of Champagne, which were held on three hundred days in each year, became the rendezvous of Europe.

Cities prospered. Merchants organized themselves in guilds, artisans in corporations. The middle class became rich and powerful, predominant in city politics. The eleventh century was the harbinger of this human spring; the twelfth saw life seething and bursting everywhere into blossom. It was the task of the thirteenth century to direct and discipline the forces thus released. Ultimately it brought to it too much organization, too much discipline, too much constraint. A time came when there was grave danger that industry and trade might be crushed under the weight of a controlled economy.

But for the moment the West was tingling with vitality. The old world of Rome was beginning to live again. There was ceaseless activity, there was abundance, there was something very like luxury. The "night" of the Middle Ages was ablaze with stars.

THE THREAT OF GENGHIS KHAN

The peoples of the West, newly awakened from sleep, and dazzled by what they saw, were, though they knew it not, living under the shadow of one of the most terrible dangers that has ever threatened civilization. A Mongol army was astir in the steppes of Asia.

Europe was almost wholly uncovered to attack. The Slav states, already in retreat under the pressure of German expansion, were too weak to put up effective resistance. Northern Russia, where Moscow had only recently been founded, was nothing but a puzzle of principalities. Kiev was a prey to quarrels of succession. Poland, menaced by the Teutonic Knights, the Lithuanians, and the Russians, was fighting for her existence. Bohemia was trembling in the balance between Poland and the Empire. Hungary was torn by the struggle between its great lords and the Crown. At Byzantium the Latin Emperors were fully occupied with the insurrections of their own subjects, the greedy ambitions of the Bulgars, and the claims of the evicted Greek dynasties, which, in the long run, were to seize once more the imperial throne. On the frontiers of Asia, Armenia and Georgia, two newly born Christian states, which, as a result of the Crusades, had freed themselves from Turkish domination, were in a very fragile condition. From Asia Minor to India the Turkish sultanates were wrapped in slumber. In Palestine and Syria Christians and Moslems were keeping wary eyes on one another, ready to take advantage of the least sign of weakness. Who, among all this scattering of Powers, would be capable of checking the new avalanche of nomads?

In the Far East the Mongols need no longer fear any adversaries in the same class as themselves. The most powerful princes were those of Cambodia, which had grown rich from the production of perfumes and precious stones, of rice and spices. In the temples and palaces of Angkor the Khmer civilization was at its highest point. But Indo-China was so remote as to be scarcely touched by the main tides of history, and its wealth lay far from the main routes of the migrations. Similarly, Sumatra and Malaya, rivals for the Empire of the South Seas, formed a world apart. Japan also was too distant. The mixed race inhabiting her islands, and worshiping the spirits of the earth and of their ancestors, had only recently been lightly touched by Buddhism, and lived under an emperor whom his military leaders had almost completely shorn of all authority. India was still in a condition of anarchy. Her peoples had got rid of the Buddhism to which they had given birth, and transformed their ancient Brahminism into a national religion. In the north, under pressure from their Moslem invaders, they had turned to Islam. Their land was covered with mosques built in a style half Hindu and half Arab.

There remained only China, and she, true as ever to herself, lay drowsing in the rank scents of her excessive civilization, much as the Roman Empire had done on the eve of the barbarian invasions. The Sung dynasty was wholly to her liking—pacifist and literate, seeking not conquest, but the exquisite life, neglecting the barbarians and encouraging the poets. In the course of two prosperous centuries her population had trebled, rising from thirty to ninety million souls. But it was apathetic and unarmed.

Kindly emperors had reorganized the free issue of corn to the needy, and the system by which cereals were bought 1057 by the State in years of plenty and stored against future failures of the harvest. One emperor, with socializing tendencies, had restored the issue of a fiduciary currency, 1069 clamped down control on all the activities of life, and fixed all prices. The experiment, however, had not lasted long.

Chinese art of the Sung period was highly sophisticated. Potters and landscape painters produced masterpiece after masterpiece. Movable type of terra-cotta made its appearance more than four centuries before Gutenberg.

1126   But already the barbarians had forced the approaches to Northern China. The earlier Mongol captors of Peking had been absorbed into the Chinese way of life. They were followed by the Manchus, who crossed the Yellow River and the Blue, before becoming assimilated in their turn. And all this while the Emperor Tsung spent his time painting birds and flowers. China, reduced to the extent of her Southern Provinces, refused to wake from her dreams. She did not want to hear the thunder of the hooves of Genghis Khan on the soil of Asia.

THE MONGOL ONRUSH

The new Mongol hordes wandered across the steppes, looking for grazing-grounds. They were complete barbarians: consummate horsemen, unerring bowmen, and clad in skins, they knew nothing of civilization, whether agricultural or urban. They ate no bread, and used no writing. It was as though they had come straight out of prehistory. Their only skill was that of seeking out their prey and striking at it like the falcon. Their strength lay in their numbers, for they were as the sands of the sea.

Their chief was called Temoudjin—a name which may
1204   possibly mean "the Smith"—and he was to hammer out an empire for himself. He had unified the tribes, beaten and incorporated the Tartar hordes, whose name the Westerners were to give to all the Mongols. He had got his
1206   men to recognize him as their chief. From now on he was the intrepid, the all-enveloping khan—Genghis Khan.

He was a man of ferocious temperament. Born in the steppe, he lived for the steppe alone. He moved in a passion of massacre and destruction. But he was as loyal as he was bold. Primitive he might be, but he knew how to govern as well as to conquer. He disciplined his armies and organized his gains. He surrounded himself with learned men who acted as his counselors, listened to their words, and understood them. This uncultured Mongol was a born ruler.

First of all he attacked eastward. He broke through the Great Wall and wrenched Northern China from the 1215 Manchus. Peking capitulated. He razed the city to the ground, merely because, as a nomad, he could see no sense in this agglomeration of houses inhabited by a sedentary population. Korea sent assurances of submission. 1218

He moved westward, spreading terror and desolation wherever he went. He took Turkestan and the Valley of the Tarim, burned Bokhara and Samarkand, overran 1220 Afghanistan and Persia. Sweeping on to the shores of the 1227 Caspian, he thrust into Russia and the Crimea. He died at the very height of his achievement.

Who was there to succeed him? In the problem of inheritance lay the weakness of the Mongol Empire, as of many of the Western nations. The question was settled in Mongolia between the descendants of Genghis. No sooner was the solution found than the Mongols took up the work of their dead leader where he had left it. They annexed Korea, completed the conquest of Persia, appeared 1237 on the Volga, sacked Moscow and Kiev, burned Cracow, crushed the Hungarians, occupied Pest, moved on to Vienna, devastated Dalmatia, and reached the Adriatic. 1242

Once more death called a halt. A successor must be found for the son of Genghis. The invaders retired towards the mouths of the Danube, laying waste the Balkans as they went. Meanwhile one of the grandsons of Genghis Khan ascended the Mongol throne.

The attack was resumed, at first against Asia Minor, where the conquering hordes swept aside the Arabs and 1242 the Turks. Erzerum succumbed. Bagdad was besieged, 1258 taken, and delivered over to the flames. Its caliph was sewn 1260 into a sack and trampled to death by horses. Next the Mongols took Aleppo and Damascus, entered Palestine, and threatened Egypt. By now their empire stretched from the Mediterranean to the China Sea, from the black soil of Russia to the yellow earth of the Far East.

Once more the Mongol "throne" became vacant. The onward sweep was halted. The Egyptians took adavantage of the pause to reoccupy Syria with an army of mercenary Turks called Mamelukes, whose leader was proclaimed caliph and sultan—in other words, political and religious chief. The Mongols fell back on Asia. Another grandson of Genghis Khan forced his followers to recognize him. 1257 He was called Kubla, and he had already given proof of his valor when, during an expedition into Southern China, he had pushed on as far as Hanoi. The Chinese had lost even the will to resist. They despised the Mongols too much to fight them. Their last emperor, aged four, was 1279 taken prisoner. He grew up and died in the peace of a Buddhist monastery. After Hangchow, Canton was taken. Kubla mounted the throne of the Sungs, and the Chinese Empire became wholly Mongol.

Kubla established himself in Peking and made it his capital. He reigned over a whole continent. His only 1281 failure was against Japan and Java, because his Mongols 1280 were less good at sailing ships than at riding horses. But the Kings of Burma, of Cambodia, and of Annam were his vassals. He was the most powerful monarch in all the world. The heir of the nomad Genghis had triumphed over the princes of the earth and the Son of Heaven.

BARBARIAN AND CIVILIZED MEET

Should not this period be named the Age of the Mongols? Were not the tiny nations of the West mere mockeries compared with the empire which had arisen in the steppe?

Militarily speaking, the Mongols were certainly superior. First, because of their numbers. One of their armies alone totaled 100 or 200,000 men, and that at a time when the fate of the nations of Europe was decided with forces infinitely smaller. The Mongols were a whole people on the move, whereas the Westerners, who had turned war into a privilege of the aristocracy, could mobilize only their élite.

Perhaps in military discipline, too, the Mongols could teach a lesson to the civilized peoples of Europe. In the hands of Genghis Khan and of his generals they had been formed into trained cohorts, admirable instruments of conquest. Pillage was organized. The Emperor was the unquestioned master of all.

In matters of tactics the West was weak. The Mongol horsemen could move with disconcerting rapidity. The knights of Europe, on the contrary, were cumbered by their armor. The attackers could loose a storm of arrows, disappear, return, ever elusive. The attacked could neither hit back nor flee.

Above all, the Mongols were united, while their enemies were divided. The Pope might preach a Holy War, but in vain. The kingdoms of Europe continued to fight one another, with never a thought for the common danger. If they could be brought to sink their differences it would be against Islam, the traditional foe, and not against the Mongols, to whom they gave scarcely a serious thought. Indeed, they rejoiced to learn that the "Tartars" had won a victory over the Saracens. They regarded it as divine vengeance. The triumph of the Tartars was their own.

The West went so far as to indulge the illusory hope of an alliance with the Mongols for the reconquest of the Holy Land. Pope Innocent IV even sent missionaries for their conversion. The Mongol Emperor replied with insolence, demanding that the Pope come to his Court in the guise of a humble vassal, and render homage with all the kings of Christendom. St. Louis, in his turn, sent him a Franciscan, and a number of sacred gifts.

1254   The grandson of Genghis answered: "There is but one God in Heaven, and, on the earth, one king—Genghis Khan, the son of God." St. Louis was bidden to pay tribute.

Nevertheless the Mongols soon lost their insolence. Perhaps they had been dazzled by their contact with civilization. Some of them had come across the Nestorian version of Christianity in China, and had adopted it. Accustomed to destroy everything, they respected the churches. They slaughtered Moslems, but not Christians. For a brief space in Syria there was even a genuine Franco-Mongol alliance. Later they sent an embassy to Rome, and to Paris a Nestorian priest to whom Philippe le Bel accorded the honors of the Sainte-Chapelle. They asked for military cooperation. "O King of France, if you will send us troops we will take Jerusalem and give it back to you." But Philippe le Bel had other matters to worry him, and declined the offer.

The proud Mongols were now sufficiently civilized to know that, in the long run, it was beyond their power to be truly strong. They could conquer and kill, they could spread terror and bloodshed, but they could build no durable monument. History was to remember the name of St. Louis far longer than that of Genghis. The Cathedral of Chartres and the *Summa* of St. Thomas Aquinas were to count for more than the sack of Peking or Bagdad. Tiny Europe was richer in promise for the future than all the Empire of the Steppes. The Mongol peril did not prevent—indeed, it scarcely troubled—the awakening of the West.

Meanwhile the Mongol conquerors suffered the same fate as do all barbarians when brought in contact with civilized peoples. Civilization conquered them. They might reduce China to slavery, but it was not the Chinese who became Mongol, but the Mongols who became Chinese. The Emperor Kubla, surrounded by Chinese officials, behaved like a true Son of Heaven. He restored the roads and the canals; he created a postal service; he held all religions in respect, honored the descendants of Confucius, and looked with a favorable eye on Taoism and the doctrines of the Buddha. His successors were fervent Buddhists. He controlled prices and organized the distribution of rice and millet. Under the Mongol Emperors China remained China still.

Of all the things that civilization revealed to them it was paper-money that most intrigued the Mongols. They showed a strong tendency to abuse it. In Persia they had recourse to inflation, at the risk of provoking civil discord. Even in China they so increased the issue of paper that devaluation set in, and they were compelled to return to a metal currency. They were like new-born babes seeing the world for the first time.

The Mongol Empire reopened the trade routes of Asia which Islam had closed. A few Western travelers even ventured into this unknown world. One of them, who took the ancient silk route, wrote the story of his residence 1271 in China, and of all the wonderful things he had seen. He found cause for astonishment in everything—in the rivers, where jasper was found; in the lakes, where men fished for pearls; in the crowded cities; in the ports seething with ships; in the grandiose palaces. He made notes about the 1292 monetary system and the postal services. He wondered and he remembered.

This traveler who discovered the Far East was representative of the new appetites of which the West was growing conscious. His name was Marco Polo, and he wrote in French. But he was a merchant of Venice, and the forerunner of the Age of Italy.

CHAPTER SEVEN

The Age of Italy

TWO CENTURIES OF DECLINE

THE HISTORY of mankind is made up of alternating periods of progress and decline. After the century of Pericles, after the century of Augustus, Greece and Rome became decadent. Similarly, after the thirteenth century, which marked the high point of the Middle Ages, the fourteenth and fifteenth centuries ushered in an age of regression. In Western Europe, as in China, civilization began to flow backward, or, at least, ceased to be productive. Only a few islands of prosperity carried on the work of creation. Italy, in particular, found in her Roman past a solid basis for new greatness.

That China should withdraw into slumber was a natural consequence of the Mongol conquest. Genghis Khan had foreseen, not without a sense of melancholy, that his descendants would enjoy to excess the easy satisfactions of civilized living. "When this generation is no more," he had said, "the men of our race will wear garments of gold, eat rich, sweet foods, and clasp in their arms the most beautiful women of the world. And they will forget that they owe it all to us!" What contempt and bitterness there is in those words! But they were true. The Mongols caught the Chinese infection, and lost the power to maintain their conquests. The genuine Chinese, who had never for

a moment forgotten their hatred of the invaders, overturned the usurping dynasty, and replaced nationalist
Mings upon the throne. But, in their aversion for their
conquerors, they wanted to destroy all that might keep
their memory green. They turned the clock back a hundred years and sank once more into the tradition of a
philosophic softness. They made up their minds to ignore
the foreigner, to live isolated from the rest of the world,
and in thus turning inward on themselves they caused the
spring of their genius to dry up. Thereafter, instead of out-
distancing the West, China let Europe catch up with her
and pass her in the race. She was never again to emerge
from her own Middle Ages.

But the West was trampling her own fields to mud. The
younger nations were at one another's throat, and constant
fighting left them exhausted. Civil wars and social upheavals came thick and fast, following hard on the heels
of foreign strife. The wars of religion were born. Population dwindled and the value of land fell. As though all
these scourges were not sufficient to ruin economic activity, men vied with one another to strangle it with their own
hands. By absurd regulations they multiplied their prison-
bars and increased the number of their fetters, reducing to
vanishing-point the liberties thanks to which Europe and
trade had both been showing signs of reawakening. They
killed the spirit of enterprise and invention.

The different Governments took in hand the direction
of economy. They taxed the export of raw materials and
the import of manufactured goods in such a way as to buttress their own national industries. The first effect of this
policy of tariffs was to ruin the Fairs of Champagne,
where all the currents of the West had met.

The corporations strove to defend the "rights which
they had won" against all risk of competition. They fixed
prices, forbade advertising, determined and "froze" the
quality of the articles produced by their members. Certain

of their rules did, it is true, operate in favor of the artisan, in that they regulated hours of labor, and of the consumer, in so far as they combated fraudulent procedure and the high cost of living. But, for the most part, these corporative enactments merely sanctioned the privileges of the employer by making it impossible for the journeyman to become a master, or of the big cities, by protecting their monopolies against the products of the smaller towns and of the countryside.

Such self-centered conservatism was fatal to all progress in technical methods. If inventiveness did still raise its head it was in spite of the corporative system, and at the risk of finding itself opposed by established prejudice, of overturning custom, and of breaking through the organized discipline within each trade.

The most sensational of the new inventions was that of printing. Long after China, Europe discovered how to reproduce pictures and writing. The Low Countries introduced a method of wood-engraving. At Mainz Gutenberg invented movable types. But for a long time to come this astonishing discovery served only to multiply the number of Bibles, devotional manuals, and formularies of procedure. It was as though the world had grown timid of innovation.

1418
1438

But Italy, at least, realized the implications of what had happened. Not only did she carry the art of typography to a high level of perfection, fixing for centuries to come the roman and italic alphabets. In every domain of human activity she blazed new trails. It was her turn now, as it had been France's in the thirteenth century, to give an example of productivity to the world. France had been rich then; Italy was rich now, and from her commercial prosperity she drew the sap of growth and of an ultimate flowering.

ITALIAN POLITICS

From the purely political point of view the position of Italy was not reassuring. Where was her splendid Roman unity? From end to end of the peninsula the foreigner was in control. The house of Savoy, which was of Burgundian origin and had vast domains beyond the Alps, reigned in Piedmont. The house of Aragon, which already owned Sicily, had taken Sardinia, and ended by evicting the house

1442 of Anjou from Naples. In Rome the Pope was no more than one prince among many, always at odds with his neighbors. The Papal States were made up of disparate scraps. The North of Italy was a puzzle of rival communities, dominated by a few opulent cities.

Even within each of these tiny states there was a war of factions. Formerly the supporters of the Papacy had been at daggers drawn with those of the Empire, Guelphs against Ghibellines. Now it was the middle classes who fought the feudal nobility, or the plebs who rose against the middle class. To check disorder recourse had constantly to be had to some soldier of fortune, who made himself into a temporary dictator, somewhat on the model of the Greek tyrants. The powers of the podesta became hereditary, and the Commune tended to become a Seigniory. In this way did the great families establish themselves—the d'Este at Ferrara, the Scaliger at Verona, the Visconti and, after them, the Sforza at Milan. The lords took the title of princes, and the Italian cities became absolute monarchies.

Some of them, however, evolved in a slightly different way. Florence and Venice preferred the reign of plutocrats to that of adventurers. At Florence it was the upper middle class that got control of the government, though at the cost of handing it over, for all practical purposes, to a dynasty of bankers—the Medicis. At Venice it was the oligarchy of rich merchants that won the day. There was

an elected doge, but he was under the control of the Great
Council of Notables, until such time as the Tribunal of
the Ten seized power. The dictatorship there was of wealth.

Italy, broken into tiny pieces, was at the mercy of anyone who could establish his supremacy. The cities waged
incessant warfare. Florence shook off Pisa; Milan absorbed
Genoa; Venice took possession of Verona and Padua.
Rome fought against Florence. The ambitious and the
greedy crossed constant swords. Alliances were formed
and dissolved.

But the Italians liked fighting no more than the Romans
of the decadence had done. The art of war interested them
as an art, but not at all as war. Rather than get themselves killed, they preferred to rely for protection on soldiers of fortune who hired them troops. These were the
condottieri and their mercenaries. It was a good deal
cheaper to pay these auxiliaries than to run the risk of
pillage. The *condottieri* laid down the law to Italy. Occasionally they assumed the government of the cities. They
too were frequently more merchants than soldiers. A time
came when they learned to regard war—that dangerous
game—as no more than a species of deal.

It was at this period that the Italian language exported
military terms. The words *brigade* and *bastion* are derived from Italian roots (as is also *poltroon*). Others
are *camp, ambuscade, squadron, soldier,* and *sentinel.*
But it was also the period at which the vocabulary of
plotting developed in the peninsula: *brigue* ("intrigue")
is Italian—and its derivative, *brigand.*

For Italy was the teacher of diplomacy to an even
greater extent than of war. She was the land of broken
alliances and unspecified understandings and complicated
knavery. The word *imbroglio* is hers. There treason
flourished. Machiavelli was born in an atmosphere of cunning perfidy. His name has given us the adjective Machia-
vellian. Italy had found her path of destiny.

THE ECONOMIC PROGRESS
OF THE PENINSULA

Neither the quarrels settled by armies of mercenaries nor the plotting controlled by a few great families much bothered the inhabitants of the peninsula. Though they might have no great political stability, they benefited from a solid economic continuity. Their strength lay in industry, commerce, and banking. Venice received raw sugar from the Levant and refined it for the whole of Europe.

The cloth trade was prosperous at Florence and Venice. Silk was one of the mainstays of the same two cities, as well as of Genoa, Pisa, and Lucca. The manufacture of wall-hangings flourished at Mantua, Ferrara, Siena, Florence, and Rome. Glass-making and lace were predominant occupations in Venice. Ships were built at Pisa, Venice, and Genoa.

The Italian shipowners were masters of the Mediterranean, of which the Crusades had given them the freedom. The Venetians, who had begun by being no more than fishermen, the Pisans, and the Genoese, freed from the competition of the sailors of Catalonia and Provence, were in fierce competition for the trade with the East. They brought to Europe the products of China, India, Persia, Arabia, and Russia. Pisa and Genoa instituted a Council of the Sea which controlled commerce and subsidized naval dockyards. At Venice the doge cast a ring, each year, into the Adriatic in token of espousal. Each spring six squadrons, more than three thousand ships and thirty-six thousand seamen, set off on journeys that brought them perfumes and spices.

The trading cities were forever increasing the number of their "factories" and colonies. Pisa acquired concessions at Tyre and Constantinople. Genoa had her foot firmly set at Galata and in many of the Aegean islands, in Asia

Minor, and as far as the Crimea. Florentines took possession of Corinth and Athens. Venice possessed Istria, Dalmatia, and a number of Greek cities. In the very teeth of
the Pope, who had forbidden all trading with Islam, she
entered into a commercial treaty with the Moslems of
Egypt. She had her representatives in Persia and sent her
commercial travelers to China.

But in Italy, as elsewhere, the public authorities and corporations laid a heavy, and an increasingly effective, hand
on economic activity. A hierarchy of workers took
shape, the purchase of raw materials became a monopoly,
the secrets of manufacturing procedure were jealously
guarded, certain sea-routes were made obligatory. At Pisa
and at Venice strict laws regulated the size of ships, the
number of their anchors, the set of their rigging, the com-
position of their crews. Not a single vessel could sail before a fixed date. At Florence the great corporations ener-
getically defended their interests, controlled prices, and
established customs rates. Genoa fell from prosperity because she had been too liberal in a world where liberal was
a dead term.

Banking, however, managed to evade the dead hand of
control. It was by banking that Italy extended her influence. The very word came into existence in the peninsula, together with others, such as *agio* ("stock-jobbing"),
credit, cambistes ("dealers in bills"), and *bankruptcy*.
Siena and Lucca specialized in the handling of silver. One
of the first limited liability companies was born at Genoa
—the bank of St. George. The Venetians boasted of be-   1407
ing the Lords of Gold and of Christendom. At Florence
the fortune of the Medici family was built on banking.
Its members were the greatest bankers in the world. Italian gold currency, florins and ducats, were at a premium.
From Italy Europe learned about bills of exchange, ac-
counting, marine loans. In Italy originated the pawnshop,
which was instituted by the city authorities as a means of
combating the excessive interest charged on loans issued

on security. Everywhere the Italian financiers ruled as
kings. After the suppression of the Templars the Lombards, or men of the peninsula, covered Europe with the
network of their agencies. They advanced money to monarchs and cities. To them, in England and in France, was
farmed the collection of taxes and the minting of money.
The foreigner could do no more than limp after them in
imitation. In Germany the Fuggers of Augsburg loaned
money to emperors and princes. In France a man like
Jacques Coeur symbolized the rise of commercial and
banking capitalism.

LITERATURE AND THE ARTS

Because of her wealth Italy became the home of literature and the arts. Florence, more than any other city, was
the center of this renaissance.

Dante, born at Florence, wrote his *Divine Comedy,*
Boccaccio, who had learned at Florence the arts of trade
and banking, countered him with a "Human Comedy."
Petrarch, the Tuscan, was at once poet, scholar, geographer, and historian. All three wrote in that Tuscan tongue
which was to become the standard of Italian. But once
the young horse of literature had started on this race of
masterpieces it soon lost its wind. In the course of the
fifteenth century Italian suffered a setback. The scholars
and the humanists almost ceased to write in any language
other than Greek and Latin. They had found the lost
manuscripts of Cicero and Lucretius, and set themselves
the task of Christianizing Plato. The Turkish menace,
lowering over the Balkans, had started a tide of literate
refugees flowing from Byzantium towards Italy, where
they were made welcome, and acted as propagandists for
Hellenism. The Academies of Florence and Rome played
at reviving Athens.

In the visual arts too the Italians sought inspiration in a
deliberate return to antiquity. There is a Graeco-Roman

sobriety in Giotto's frescoes; Ghiberti's bronze doors are, in strict fact, a species of goldsmith's work; Donatello's statues are a lesson in the application of classical canons; the Cathedral at Florence, built by Brunelleschi, shows a conscious break with the pointed style of the north. The artists of the other Italian cities followed their Florentine brothers in freely copying from the antique. They restored the round-headed arch and the domed roof to a place of honor, disdained the flying buttress, and rehabilitated the Ionic and Corinthian orders. Though in Venice the palaces still showed a mixed style of Gothic and Oriental, in Rome Bramante was beginning the building of St. Peter's, and in Milan Leonardo da Vinci was starting his extraordinary career. The Quattrocento struck the first note in the symphony of the Renaissance. In the vicinity of Naples a marble was dug up which came later to be known as the *Apollo Belvedere*. Reverence was paid to it   1496 as to a messenger from the Ancient World.

Beyond the frontiers of Italy the old formulae were beginning to degenerate. The building of cathedrals was continuing, but at a slower tempo. The imaginative daring which might have produced something new was lacking. Non-ecclesiastical buildings began to be planned on a less ambitious scale. Cities were sprouting houses with pointed gables. In England the Gothic style developed into a system of rigid lines, while in France it had lost its earlier freshness and spontaneity and was becoming confused in a riot of flamboyance and masons' lacework. Wars are not a good seeding-ground for art.

Flanders and the Low Countries, which were spared such miseries, enjoyed sufficient prosperity to erect great belfry-towers, market buildings, and town halls. It was there that easel-painting made its appearance with the brothers Van Eyck, a form of art more intimate than fresco, less sketchy than illumination. It developed a new technique which, thanks to the discovery of a drying medium, could make use of oil for the glazing of pictures, with the result that colors acquired a freshness till then unknown, and, with Memling, a quality of harmonious smoothness. But it was Italy that saw the beginnings of painting on canvas, a form of picture-making which had been forgotten since the passing of the Romans. It very soon displaced the older methods of working on walls or panels. The use of canvas bestowed on painted master-pieces the gift of eternity.

Though the influence of Italian art was not everywhere predominant, the lessons of the Florentine sculptors had already traveled as far as Hungary, and Italian architects were in demand as far away as Russia, where Ivan III rebuilt the Kremlin. At about the same time the human-ism of Italy was sweeping over the foreign universities, the Sorbonne and Oxford, Heidelberg and Nuremberg, Cracow and Prague. The Dutchman Erasmus studied at Bologna, and lived for a while in Venice. The Pole Coper-nicus was a student in Padua and taught in Rome. In France and in Spain the Italian authors were translated, and sonnet-making on the Italian model was widely prac-ticed.

For the fashions of the peninsula were conquering the world. Playing-cards, for instance, which had originated in China, or, perhaps, among the Arabs, made their first appearance in Europe at Viterbo. The weaving of silk sent Italian workmen to Lyon. The art of faïence, brought from the East by the Arabs, was perfected at Faenza. The filling of teeth was invented by a professor of

1450 Bologna. The use of table-forks, the improvements in cookery, the introduction of Italian ices and pastries, these, as well as modes in dresses and adornment, we owe to the Medicis, who took them to the Court of France. It is to the Italian language that we owe such words as *pantaloon, pantoufle* ("slipper"), *escarpin* ("dancing-shoes"), *umbrella, perfume, pomade.* The characters of the *commedia dell' arte,* born of popular improvi-sation, and later to enjoy a world-wide fame as figures in marionette plays, pantomimes, and at masked balls, were native Italian. Harlequin haled from Bergamo, Scapin from Milan, Pantaloon from Venice, Punch and Scaramouche from Naples.

It is by the legacy of such things, trivial though they may seem, that the lasting influence of a country and a century is to be measured.

RETREAT OF THE WEST

The dominance of Italy was to some extent a result of the general decline of the West. France, in particular, which had early assumed the leadership of the nations, had suffered an eclipse. She had had to brace herself to meet an attack from England, and this attack had lasted for over a hundred and ten years.

Some such conflict was inevitable so long as the kings of England were also rulers of Aquitaine. They had either too much or too little. When the direct line of the house of Capet died out both Valois and Plantagenets claimed   1328
the succession of the French throne. Brittany and Flanders provided additional causes of strife. English merchants   1340
were in need of a Continental market. They wished to sell wool to the Flemings and to buy wine from the growers of Bordeaux. War broke out.

The English had wanted it and prepared for it. They were fewer in numbers than the French, but better equipped. Their bowmen could put three arrows into the air at one time. Enforced military service made it possible for them to throw a unified mass of infantry into the field against the antiquated levy of French knights. At Crécy, at Poitiers, at Agincourt, they won the day. The French kings moved from surrender to surrender. One of them died in captivity. Another was compelled to agree that after his death the two countries should be unified under the scepter of England, and Henry VI of the island realm was actually proclaimed King of France in Paris.   1421

There is no knowing what would have happened had the two countries really become one, or what then would have been the course of world history. It was a young girl of Lorraine who settled that question once and for all. To Jeanne d'Arc was given the miraculous intuition that France could be saved only by her legitimate kings. Obe-
1429 dient to her Voices, she relieved Orléans, and had the Dauphin Charles crowned at Rheims. She was taken prisoner and burned alive. But France gathered round Charles
1453 VII, regained her unity, and chased the English from the national soil. But the struggle had exhausted her. There was scarcely a misfortune that did not come her way. She was burdened with one king who was mad and with several who were minors. She suffered at first hand ruin, pillage, and treason. Her money lost its value. Prices rose. There were riots in her cities, uprisings in her countryside. Bands of brigands roamed her provinces. The feudal lords rebelled, and it needed all the subtle patience of a Louis XI to get the better of the Dukes of Burgundy.

England was no better off. She too saw the value of her money dwindle. She too saw prices rise and trade going to ruin. As in France, the barons rose in rebellion. Foreign war was followed by civil war. For more than thirty years the white rose of York fought for the throne with the red rose of Lancaster. Parliament played a waiting game, ready to give its support to the victor.

In all these annals of distress one page especially stands out. An epidemic plague, originating in the Levant, spread
1350 terror through the West. The Black Death swept away a third of the population of France, two-fifths of the population of England. In the space of a few years the numbers of men and women living in Europe dropped from seventy-five million to fifty million. Everywhere the wolves prowled round unburied bodies.

The destiny of Flanders, for long an appanage of Burgundy, was more brilliant. That happy province lived prosperously on the wool trade. Bruges, center of art and industry, was the metropolis of the north. But periodic waves of unemployment broke, at times, in bloody uprisings. By degrees Flanders lost many of her markets to Florence, and much of her capital in raw material when England began to weave her own wool. In an effort to defend her prerogatives Bruges plunged obstinately into the pathless wilderness of extraordinary trade regulations. To make matters worse, her harbor silted up. Her activity declined, to the advantage of the newer city of Antwerp, which was careful not to put obstacles in the way of free trade, and opened the first commercial Exchange. **1460**

Germany remained divided and impotent. National feeling, so far as she was concerned, was dead. Though the house of Hapsburg—to which the Dukes of Austria belonged—had seized the crown of the Holy Roman Empire, the imperial idea was now little more than a memory. The only prosperous community was the Hanseatic League, which grouped a number of German cities for purposes of commerce. It ruled over the northern seas, set up agencies at Stockholm, Bergen, and London, and traded with the East by way of the Vistula, and with Italy by the Atlantic route, which was safer than the overland lines of communication. It could fight as well as bargain. It imposed its will on Denmark, and forced her to give it access to the Baltic. The fairs of the German cities became **1370** the successors of those of Champagne. But already the days of the Hanseatic League were numbered. In many of its cities the people rose against the dictatorship of the merchant-princes. Disagreement increased in the very heart of the League. Soon its powers crumbled, and its last adherents, brandishing out-of-date title-deeds, claimed their privileges in vain. The Dutch and English merchants were waiting to step into its shoes.

On every side of Germany the nations were growing more self-conscious and more strong. On the north Denmark succeeded, for a time, in grouping under one sovereign all three Scandinavian countries. In the east the Lith- **1397**

uanian family of Jagellon managed to unite Lithuania and
Poland, countries which till then had been rivals. As a result of its enterprise the threat of Germanism was kept at
bay. At Tannenberg the order of the Teutonic Knights
was defeated. Poland strengthened her hold on the mouths
1410   of the Vistula, and even managed for a time to make
Hungary and Bohemia her satellites. Still farther to the
1480   east, Russia cast off the Mongol yoke, and Ivan III,
that great collector of territories, reviving in his own interest the traditions of Byzantium mixed with a dash of
Asiatic influence, proclaimed himself Tsar of all the Rus-
sias. Thus while France and England remained at daggers
drawn, the Slav world was erecting a strong defense
against the world of Germanism. Not from those still bar-
baric distances was to shine the light of a new civilization.

Salvation might have come from the Church had it not
been for the fact that Christendom was cruelly divided,
and remained divided for as long as the status of the
Papacy was in a condition of degradation. Rome even
ceased for a while to be the capital of the Catholic world,
1308   and the sovereign Pontiffs held their Court at Avignon. A
French Pope set himself up in opposition to an Italian,
and the College of Cardinals, in order to cut the Gordian
1378   knot, elected a third Pontiff. The different nations rallied
1409   round the Holy Father of their choice. The scandal was
great, and so was the ensuing state of anarchy.

The Papacy emerged much weakened from this period
of schism. Its authority was eclipsed by that of the councils. Its ambitions were centered on temporal ends. The
Popes thought less about directing the consciences of men
than about disputing with Florence or with Naples over
scraps of territory. Their religious mission was the least of
their concerns. Their only passion was for politics. All of
them took delight in luxury, several lived far from edifying
lives, and Dante, the Ghibelline, does not hesitate to place
the simoniac Pontiffs in the fifth circle of his Inferno. But
Dante had lived at a time that knew nothing of the orgies

of Alexander Borgia, orgies more suited to a period of
pagan license than to Christian morals.

But the Church was now threatened by a still more
serious crisis. New heresies began to show their heads,
not among the illiterate many, but among the doctors of
theology. At Oxford the Englishman Wyclif was teaching   1376
that authority belonged to God alone. In Bohemia John
Huss was preaching the Gospel and denouncing the vices
of the clergy. He attacked the cult of images, of the Virgin, and of the Saints. Excommunicated and delivered over
to the flames, he died with great serenity at the stake. But   1415
the people of Bohemia broke into the churches and drove
out the Catholic priests. The religious disturbance went
hand in hand with a national insurrection in which the
Czechs were brought into opposition with the German
princes. Finally the Catholics had to come to terms with
the heretics and agree to tolerate the Church of Bohemia.   1433
They found some compensation for their defeat in a widespread burning of witches. This first rebellion was a forerunner of others. Rome, because she had not put in mo-
tion the necessary reforms, was no longer capable of maintaining the unity of the Faith.

DANGER FROM THE EAST: THE TURKS

Just at this time, when the West was in retreat, a new
danger was taking shape in the East. The Turks burst into
Europe.

They were no longer the earlier Turks whose arrival in
Asia Minor had stimulated the Crusades. The Mongol adventure had spelt almost complete eclipse for them. The
Moslems of Egypt, torn by palace revolutions, were similarly in a state of decline. The Mongols themselves, even,
were no more than a shadow of what they once had been
under Genghis Khan. Their empire was in pieces. They
had been driven from China and Northern Russia, and

were soon to suffer the same fate in Southern Russia and in Persia.

Two new Turkish tribes sprouted on the soil of Asia, which produced nomads as other countries produce crops. These two tribes were only distantly related. They knew nothing of one another, and were to be involved in bitter fighting. They were the Turks of Othman and the Turks of Tamerlane. The former had led a wandering life to the north of Afghanistan before migrating in the general direction of Asia Minor. Their leader, whose name they took, calling themselves "Ottomans," attacked the Greeks

1340 of Byzantium, took Broussa, and made it his capital. The invaders crossed the Dardanelles, defeated the Bulgars and the Serbs, crushed the allied forces which took the field against them, and captured both Adrianople and Salonica. They were now masters of the Balkans from the Adriatic to the Black Sea. The wretched Emperor at Byzantium, whose territory was now shrunk to scarcely more than the extent of his city, recognized the Ottomans as his overlords, and surrendered his sons as hostages.

Europe trembled. This time the danger was not merely at her gates, but within her walls. The barbarians were treading her native soil, and the barbarians, on this occasion, were Moslems. They seemed to be determined to make an end, once and for all, of that insolent Constantinople which had so obstinately outlived Rome by almost a thousand years. Their chief, Bajazet, besieged the last stronghold of the Byzantine Emperors. He broke up a

1396 Christian Crusade and enlarged his Asiatic possessions. It looked as though Constantinople were at his mercy.

But at this precise moment another body of Turks put in an appearance and, unaware of what they were doing, saved Constantinople for a further half-century. These Turkomans had emerged from the steppe, as the Huns, their fathers, had done before them, and the Mongols, their cousins. At their head was a man of blood, Timour the Lame (Timour-lenk) whom Europe was to know as Tamerlane.

This ruthless conqueror set himself up to be the heir of Genghis Khan, but he lacked the Mongol's gifts. He could fight, murder, pillage, and burn, but he knew nothing of organizing an empire or of assimilating the conquered. His expeditions were no more than raids which led to nothing.

Tamerlane, maybe, prided himself on living again the epic career of Genghis. He began by liberating Transoxiana and Samarkand from the Mongol yoke, and made the latter place his capital. He might, when it suited his purpose, invoke the Koran and declare a Holy War in the name of Islam, but that did not prevent him from attacking and laying waste the Moslem states. When he gave orders that great mounds of human heads should be raised, when he filled the lands through which he marched with slaughter, it was less from motives of religious fanaticism than because he felt an itch to kill and to spread terror.

His campaigns through the length and breadth of Asia were conducted with lightning speed. But, since he never occupied the countries which he devastated, the enemy were forever reorganizing in his rear, so that he was frequently compelled to begin his work over again. Three times he had to stop in mid-career to crush the Persians. Twice he galloped across the Russian steppes. Six times did he return to the banks of the river Ili, in Siberia. His enterprises were without shape or form, determined only by his personal whim. He moved on from Tiflis to Ispahan, where he massacred 70,000 men, appeared before Bagdad, crossed the Ural and the Volga. He took possession of Azov, and had the Genoese and Venetian traders, who had sent him presents, butchered in cold blood. He made a headlong dash on India, where the Sultanate was in a state of complete decadence. The defenders' elephants were no match for the Turkish cavalry. He cut down 100,000 prisoners, took and looted Delhi, the treasure

1387
1395

1398

from which made Samarkand a city of wealth, and had the Hindu partisans of Meerut flayed alive.

It may be that from this period dates the migration of a poor caste of non-Aryan Hindus, who were driven from their homes by the Turkish terror. Be that as it may, a nomad people seems, about then, to have spread across the continent and reached the nations of Europe, where they lived on, wandering from place to place, existing on petty thievery and hedge-trades, singing, dancing, and telling fortunes. A false origin was assigned to these vagabonds. They were called Bohemians in France, Egyptians (gypsies) in England. The Italians named them Zingari, the Spanish, Gitanes, or Tziganes. They themselves said that they were Rouman-chal, the wandering men, a word that later became *romanichels*.

Tamerlane took little account of these swirls and eddies of humanity. Leaving India behind him, he marched against the Mamelukes of Egypt, took Aleppo and Damascus, and ruined Syria.

1400

It had been inevitable that sooner or later the two Turkish clans should come face to face, and this they now did —the followers of Tamerlane and those of Bajazet; on the one side Ottomans, on the other Turkomans. The gauntlet was thrown down. Tamerlane, proud of the extent of his empire, was insistent that he be named the one and only chief of the Turkish race. But Bajazet stood firm. On the outskirts of Ancyra—the future Ankara—a gigantic battle was joined, involving close on a million men. The Ottomans collapsed. Bajazet fell into the hands of Tamerlane's soldiers, and died a prisoner. The victors had merely to continue their triumphal march. They pillaged Broussa, took Smyrna by storm, reached the Sea of Marmora, and tore the Ottoman Empire to shreds.

1402

The Christians of Europe showed as much delight as though they themselves had defeated Bajazet. The Christians of Asia were less well pleased, because Tamerlane had buried four thousand of their number alive. But he

cared little about the West. It was China that tempted
him, as it had tempted Genghis in an earlier age. Why,
under the pretext of converting it to Islam, should he not
take it in his stride and amass a vast hoard of booty? He
gathered a powerful army all agog for conquest. But death
put a stop to his plans. China and the world found them-   1405
selves freed from the threat of Tamerlane.

With dramatic suddenness the whole Turkoman menace
crumbled into nothing. With Tamerlane dead, nothing
was left of his fragile empire. The Mamelukes reoccupied
Syria; the Turks of Persia turned Persian; the Sultans of
India recovered their domains; the Mongols of Siberia and
Russia settled down once more in their territories.

But the most important event of all was that the Ottomans resumed their offensive.

This time no diversion came to the help of Europe. The
Ottomans reconquered the Balkans as far as the Danube.
The time had come to make an end of Constantinople. The
last defenders of the city were Italian adventurers, and
Venice, waking at last to what was at stake, resolved to
intervene. But it was too late. The Turks entered the old   1453
capital of the Eastern Empire as conquerors. It became
Istamboul.

But the capture of Constantinople had no more than a
symbolic significance. It marked neither the beginning nor
the end of conquest. The Ottomans became masters of the
Aegean, failing only to overcome the Knights of Rhodes.
They occupied Athens and Corinth, reduced Albania,
Serbia, Bosnia, Herzogovina, and took the Crimea. They
were content to wait until the Moslem states of Arabia
and Africa should collapse as a result of internal weakness.

The administration of their empire was as firm as that
of Tamerlane's had been non-existent. The Sultan was an
absolute monarch, the unquestioned master of the lives of
all his subjects. In one thing only did he fail—to acquire
the religious as well as the political headship. The Holy
Cities and the Caliphate escaped his clutches. But he could

dispose of vast financial resources thanks to the revenues flowing in from his territories and to the tribute paid him by the conquered peoples. His army, a model of disciplined force, was to keep Europe trembling for many years to come.

THE ART OF WAR

It was by the use of his cavalry that Tamerlane had conquered, and the Ottomans took much pride in the spahis who acted as the Sultan's bodyguard. For all that, the age of the mounted warrior was drawing to a close.

The Czechs, during the Hussite wars, had developed a new system of defensive tactics. They had improvised field-works with combat vehicles. By means of these wheeled centers of resistance, which they surrounded with hastily constructed ramparts of earth, they organized strong-points. This meant that cavalry was reduced to play a purely passive rôle.

The heyday of the knight was over. The French, with conservative obstinacy, still clung to him, and paid heavily for their foolishness. The English, the Germans, and the Italians were learning to pin their faith to the infantry, which, preponderant in the ages of Greece and Rome, had latterly played only a secondary part. The footmen, armed with bow and crossbow, mowed down the advancing horses, and forced the knights, encumbered by their heavy armor, to fight dismounted. "Infantry," *fantassin,* are both words of Italian origin. The *fante,* like the German *lansquenet* (*Landsknecht*), was the squire who fought on foot. But it was the squires now who won battles.

The new military technique was brought to perfection by a young nation which had only recently emerged in its alpine fastness. Three forest cantons had freed themselves from Austrian overlordship, and concluded a "pact in perpetuity." Round this kernel grew the Swiss Confederation, whose independence Austria was forced to recog-

1291

1394

THE AGE OF ITALY

nize. Legend attributes to William Tell the first act of liberation. This hypothetical hero was a bowman, and the
Swiss never forgot it.

Swiss tactics, which quickly came to maturity, consisted
in forming infantry into a compact square, pikes pointing
outward, halberds ready, crossbows loaded. This "hedge-
hog" reintroduced into military history, though with a difference, the ancient phalanx of the Greeks.

From now on the individual fighter was a figure of the
past. The "square," on the Swiss model, became the tactical unit. It was adopted by the Germans and the Spaniards; later, by the French and the Italians. The Turks,
too, made good use of compact masses of dismounted
archers. These constituted their "new militia," the "Yen-
itcheris," to whom Europe gave the name of Janissaries.

Another military revolution went logically hand in hand
with this resurrection of the infantry. The feudal levy
tended to disappear. Military service was no longer a privilege reserved exclusively for the aristocracy. Certain nations—England, for instance, and the Swiss cantons—had
recourse to mass enlistment. Conscription gave numer-
ical superiority. But, in general, it was to the mercenaries that the princes looked for their main support—to the
German *Landsknechtens,* the French "free-archers," the
Italian *condottieri.* For a long time to come the Swiss hired
out their man-power to foreign nations. This reappearance
of the mercenary also implied a return to antiquity.

In order to pay these auxiliaries the princes of Europe
needed regular supplies of money on which to draw. The
period which saw the rise of standing armies saw also the
organization of a system of regular taxes, payable in cash.
In France Charles VII established, at one and the same
time, an annual poll-tax and a professional fighting force.   1445
It was now, for the first time, that the fighter became a
"soldier."

The feudal levy, already undermined by the double
recrudescence of the infantry and the mercenary, was to

receive an even more shattering blow, though it took longer to develop. Sooner or later the invention of firearms made body-armor useless.

Both the Chinese and the Hindus had used gunpowder, but only for the manufacture of fireworks. In European 1300 hands the dangerous mixture became a fighting weapon. It may have been, as is sometimes stated, a Franciscan monk of Germany who, seeking the secret of making gold, had realized the explosive properties of gunpowder. It may have been in Upper Italy that the first "thunder-tube" was constructed. Be that as it may, it was early in the four-teenth century that the invention gained currency, and that a primitive form of artillery was used in the siege of 1330 fortified places.

The denunciation leveled at this diabolical invention by the nobles of Europe was far from being disinterested. It was called immoral and disloyal. Could a great lord bring himself, in honor, to fall before a discharge of fire manip-ulated by a mere peasant? To revenge themselves on this outrage against the code of war they caused all captured canoneers to be mutilated. In spite of this, however, gun-powder continued to work its ravages.

The effects of the early mortars were relatively mild. Their range was less than that of the plebeian crossbow; their aim was far from accurate; their rate of fire was low, and the material efficacy of their discharge doubtful. At 1346 Crécy the English cannon caused more noise and dismay than damage. But balls of iron soon replaced their stone prototypes, and tubes of cast bronze replaced those of wrought-iron. Artillery became a formidable weapon.

Very soon the idea occurred to somebody to construct movable firearms. Culverins were mounted on carriages. 1380 Next the tube was inserted in a wooden shaft ending in a butt. The arquebus (another Italian word) was cumber-some, but it could throw a projectile twice the distance of a crossbow. The infantry "squares," equipped with this weapon, more than ever asserted their superiority over horsemen.

In all these ways the art of war was undergoing a profound change. Methods of recruiting, tactical handling, armament—in every sphere there was alteration and renewal. In the course of ages these revolutionary developments were to have incalculable consequences, abolishing private wars, which were a legacy of the feudal system, reducing the importance of the nobility and enhancing that of the common people by raising them to the perilous dignity of combatants, increasing the sense of national solidarity. Finally, by transferring to firearms the power which till then had been wielded by rapidity of movement, they eliminated for all time that menace of the nomad which had recurred again and again to trouble the peace of the civilized world. Never, now, would there be another Attila, another Genghis Khan, another Tamerlane. Europe, with its fire-spitting jaws, was henceforward to control the destinies of the world.

THE END OF AN AGE

The Turks were no longer nomads. They were merely the enemies of Christendom. They turned the new technique of war to their own advantage. Their armies could draw on an inexhaustible reserve of man-power. Their fleet, mistress of the Black Sea, was modeled on that of Venice.

As formerly the Arabs, so now the Turks, barred the trade routes of Asia. It was their presence in the southeast of Europe which forced back Poland towards the north, and compelled her to seek an outlet on the Vistula. It was their appearance in the Mediterranean which hastened the decline of Italy.

Naples felt the danger when the Ottomans landed at Otranto and stayed there for a full year. Venice suffered a more permanent hurt, for she was driven from the   1480

Aegean and from Greece. She was even threatened on
the Adriatic coast.

By what routes now were the dwellers in the West to
reach India and China and obtain the spices and rare
fabrics of the Far East? The Mediterranean, from being
a highway, had become a dead-end. Other itineraries must
be discovered. An attempt must be made to round the
continent of Africa, perhaps to circle the world, and so
reach India from behind. No doubt the discovery of new
routes hastened the decline of the Mediterranean ports;
but it was also this decline, the result of the Turkish invasion, which drove the sailors of Europe to seek their
fortune farther afield. Proof of this, if proof be needed,
can be found in the fact that the greatest of all the discoverers was by birth a man of Genoa.

With the shift in the axis of trade the great period of
Italian prosperity came to an end. But that was not the
only reason. The cities of the peninsula had failed to
adapt themselves to a rapid change in conditions. Like
many other elements of the old life, they had come to
believe that their privileges were permanent, and had clung
firmly to the old routines of life. They died from protection
carried to excess, and from a system of municipal socialism.

Nor had they long remained without competitors in the
West. Both France and England, once they had recovered
from the consequences of a quarrel that had lasted far too
long, had begun slowly to rebuild their industries. Instead
of buying from Italy they produced what they needed themselves, and no longer exported their raw materials. Finally,
Spain and Portugal, situated between the Mediterranean
and the Atlantic, and thus magnificently placed to undertake the conquest of new worlds, were making ready to
outdistance Italy.

Save in terms of trade, the Italians were ill-equipped to
fight. Politically the peninsula was so hopelessly fragmented that it was out of the running in the race for dominance. It was not long before her military power began to

decline. Her noble families took more readily to speculation and art patronage than to war. The Swiss might be
willing to fight to the last man, but the Italian mercenaries
were sparing of their blood, and preferred to settle quarrels by the easier method of discussion. When two armies
of *condottieri* met they estimated one another's numbers
instead of joining battle, and the less numerous surrendered to the stronger. Such scheming may be suited to the
mood of highly civilized communities, but in a bellicose
world it was bound to lead to national decline. Italy the
fair was a tempting prey to the first adventurer who might
choose to attack her.

All that was left to her was to shine with a bright brilliance in the dilettante pursuits. She inspired the greatest
writers of all countries. A third of Shakespeare's plays
have Italy as background—Venice or Mantua, Messina or
Verona. Inventor of instruments, the native home of
Stradivarius, she established the standard of musical notation for the rest of the world. She still was, and would
long remain, the cradle of the arts and sciences. At the end
of this same fifteenth century Leonardo da Vinci was at
the height of his glory, committing to canvas the features
of Mona Lisa, inventing the earliest sluices, designing
flying-machines. Michelangelo, Raphael, and Titian were
achieving fame, and the language of Petrarch lived again
in the writings of Ariosto. Since, too, Machiavelli was pre-
paring to instruct princes and peoples in the subtleties of
government, Italy was to find herself giving to the nations
of the West their best and craftiest practitioners of politics
—men like Mazarin, families like the Medicis.

But her greatness and prosperity were of the past. The
heyday of Florence and of Venice was over. The leadership of the world was passing into other hands.

CHAPTER EIGHT

The Age of Spain

A NEW WORLD

THE EARTH is round. Beyond the oceans lay a world of which history, as yet, knew nothing, for history, so far, had been confined to the nations of the old hemisphere, from the Atlantic to the China Sea, from the coasts of the Far North to the approaches of the African desert. If peoples living elsewhere could be said to have had any history at all, it must bear a strong resemblance to prehistory.

It seems certain that the world which was later to be known as America had, in the dawn of the human race, received as immigrants men traveling from Asia across the Behring Strait, and from Oceania by way of the various groups of islands which studded the Pacific. They had scattered across the continent, settling here and there in small, isolated clans. Almost everywhere their way of life had remained extremely primitive. Only a few sketchy attempts at civilization had prospered between the tropics, in spots where height above sea-level had served to moderate the prevailing heat.

In Mexico a race of hunters, coming from the north, had mingled with the aboriginal inhabitants, who were agriculturists. From this fusion sprang the Toltec nation, whose remains take the form of finely painted pottery and

500

high pyramids topped by temples. Several centuries later 1000
a fresh wave of warlike intruders, also from the north,
settled down on the Mexican plateau. These were the
Aztecs, who conquered the Toltecs. They founded Tenoch- 1324
titlan (the Cactus of the Rock), which afterwards became
Mexico City (the Home of the War-god). They had the
secret of working gold and copper, a vigesimal system of
numbers, a calendar, and hieroglyphic writing. They were
ruled by an elected king assisted by a council, also elected.
The land was divided between the Crown, the nobility, and
the people, each "lot" being indivisible. They were active
in trade, using as currency many devices, from gold-dust
packed in tubes made of the bones of birds to cocoa-beans
and small squares of cloth.

In Yucatan, opposite the Antilles, these same Aztecs
had overcome the civilization of the Mayas, who had
known how to build cities of stone and have left the remains of colonnaded temples reminiscent of those of
Egypt. The Mayas could write and were skillful farmers.

In what was afterwards known as Colombia the Chib-
chas also practiced agriculture, and the working of metals. But their monarchy had long been decadent.

Finally, in Peru the original settlers, whose architects,
sculptors, and potters have left noble traces of themselves,
had been supplanted by the Quichuas, whose civilization, 1100
at once crude and sophisticated, was based upon a system
which combined despotism with communism in the interest of a single family, that of the Incas.

The Great Inca was the offspring of the sun. As such,
he was absolute master and sole landowner—much in the
manner of the Pharaohs. From his family were drawn the
State officials and the priests. The Incas had a special language which was used by nobody else, and practiced polygamy. The people were no more than a herd of animals,
to be used for labor and for war. They owned neither
land nor its products, which were gathered into store-
houses and doled out. They could not save or bequeath.

Their state was one of complete equality but no liberty. They could not travel unless they obtained authority to do so, and were forbidden to have more than one wife apiece. Military service was compulsory, as was labor, which took the form of fertilizing the fields with guano, irrigating, breeding the llamas held in common, dyeing textiles, exploiting the mineral resources of the country, maintaining the roads (which were metaled), and building palaces and temples.

This socialist community, governed by statisticians, was warlike. In order to bring production to the level of their needs, and to find new land for clearing, they fought and conquered their neighbors. From the Peruvian plateaus they overflowed east of the Andes, and southward as far as Bolivia and the Argentine. War was a permanent institution of Quichua communism.

1350

The other scattered agglomerations of the American continent were all both communist and warlike. In the vast forests which stretched from the St. Lawrence to the Rio de la Plata the clans everywhere formed savage communities, knowing nothing of private property and living by fishing, hunting, and war.

This huge new world was nothing but barbary on a gigantic scale. In later ages the philosophers of Europe made it fashionable to admire the sagacity of the Iroquois or the architectural daring of the Incas. Actually these transatlantic civilizations were all in the period of infancy and far behind the countries of the Old World.

Their backwardness was due, in the first place, to certain natural lacks. The American continent had none of the vegetable and animal wealth which goes to the making of civilized living. There was no wheat, barley, or oats. There was no rye, nor were there vines. The horse and the ox were unknown. Because there was a complete absence of draught animals, no one had thought of inventing the wheel or the plow. The American peoples, because they had never known how to extract or work iron ore, failed to emerge from the Bronze Age.

Even the most advanced tribes were still primitive. The Aztecs owed their victories to the superiority of their armament, which consisted of sticks studded with chips of flint. The Quichuas could reckon the years only by means of knotted cords. They were ignorant both of writing and of money. In varying degrees these savages everywhere made human sacrifices to their gods, and habitually ate human flesh. Their "civilization" was no more than cannibalism.

Fetishists or polytheists, they worshiped animal totems, the spirits of their ancestors, the stars, or the forces of Nature. The Aztecs had spread the belief in a bearded god with a white skin who, once upon a time, after dwelling among his brown-skinned people, had departed to the east across the limitless seas. This god had promised to re- 1492 turn. And return he did. Three miraculous vessels, fitted with sails, made a landfall in the tropical isles. They carried men whose skin was white, and had voyaged from the horizons of the rising sun.

THE DISCOVERIES

The men of Europe had now the means of adventuring across oceans. All the inventions which, in the thirteenth century, had revolutionized the technique of navigation had now been brought to perfection—the fixed rudder, at first secured with thongs, now mounted on iron hooks, and the compass, which had long passed the stage in which it had been no more than a shallow vessel filled with water on which a straw had been set to float. The magnetic needle was now fitted with a pivot. The use of lateen sails made it possible to move close in to the wind. Hulls were more solid, and ships heavier. The four-masted type could venture far from land.

But the mere ability to make discoveries was not

enough: the will was needed, too. The reasons had to be
very strong before men would willingly face the storms
of unknown seas. The reasons which produced this result
were at the same time nobly spiritual and crudely ma-
terialistic.

God played His part in this new movement of adventure. It was Europe's intention to resume the Crusades,
and perhaps to deliver the Holy Places by taking them in
the rear. There was an ancient tradition to the effect that
India had been Christianized. Might it not be possible to
make common cause with her against Islam and the
Turks? The discoverers were the new champions of the
Faith.

But next to God came spices. The aromatics of the
East, which for so long the Venetians had brought to
Europe, were objects of worth: pepper, cloves, ginger
played not only a part in domestic economy, but in the
pharmacopoeia as well. Sugar too came from the East.
How could these valuable commodities be secured for
Europe as long as the Turks barred the way? The discoverers who tried to round the African continent, or who
sailed blindly westward, were in search of a new spice
route.

Next to spices came gold—gold for which Europe was
starving, without which the economic life of the West
would be faced with a cruel shortage of money. In a developing world the means of payment were lamentably
insufficient. If new money was to be minted there must be
gold, and again more gold. Men were dreaming of an
Eldorado whose mountains were of pure gold, whose
houses were adorned with it, where it served to pave the
roads. The alchemists had failed to find the philosopher's
stone, and so it was that the discoverers became seekers
after gold. They found it, and in so doing grew forgetful
of their service to God.

The enterprise was far from simple. At sea there were
rocks and tempests ever in wait for the adventurous who

sailed without the help of charts, and in complete ignorance of depths, winds, and currents. Whole fleets disappeared without leaving a trace. On land the men had to
contend with mosquitoes, snakes, and poisoned arrows.
The ships' crews and the tiny forces of armed soldiers
were decimated by hunger, thirst, and fever. A handful
of intrepid adventurers set out to find and annex territories more vast than the lands from which they came.
They had to subdue whole peoples whose warriors could
sometimes be counted by the million. Success could be attained only by enthusiasm and indomitable perseverance.
Those who could bring such ventures to completion must
be possessed of a passion for God and a fury for gain.

Private enterprise achieved the miracle. For these conquerors were not only the lieutenants of kings and the
builders of empires. Primarily, they were simple-minded
men guided by faith and intent on making their fortunes.
They were not always in the service of their own country.
Columbus of Genoa and the Portuguese Magellan made
their discoveries in the interest of Castile. The Venetian
Verrazano was employed by France; the Genoese Caboto,
or Cabot, by England. The shipbuilders who fitted out the
fleets of the conquistadors at their own expense were often
quite modest men. Humble captains appropriated whole
provinces. To consolidate their powers and secure their
title-deeds they chose to serve great sovereigns. A notary
would gravely draw up a legal instrument of possession in
the name of some distant monarch.

Not infrequently these pioneers fought at odds of one
against two hundred, and emerged victorious. With mi-
nute armies they captured capitals. Their triumph was
made possible by the technical equipment of Europe—
horses, firearms, sailing-vessels. The natives of the New
World were at the mercy of these astonishing beings who
could gallop, spit thunder, and force the winds to do their
will. They received them as devils, or as the gods foretold by Aztec prophecy.

TWO EMPIRES

The Portugese set the example. Living, as they did, on the balcony of Europe, they were better situated than anyone to sail the Atlantic. Their ambition at first was to drive the Arabs from Morocco, and then to reach India and the
1417   land of spices by circling the African continent. They annexed Ceuta, reconnoitered Madeira, occupied the Azores, doubled Cape Verde, and reached Guinea. Dias discovered
1486   the Cape of Storms, later renamed the Cape of Good Hope. Vasco da Gama, whose exploits were sung by the poet Camöens, penetrated into the Indian Ocean. This was the
1510   highway to India, and there Albuquerque took Goa and laid the foundations of the Portuguese Empire.

But India was only a stage on the spice route. In order to reach the fountain-head of these treasures the Portuguese made an alliance with the Chinese against the Mos-
1511   lems, and occupied Malacca, which gave them command of the passage to the Isles. In China itself they established themselves at Macao. They pushed as far as Nagasaki, on the very threshold of Japan. In the Moluccas they obtained the monopoly of the trade in aromatics. Before their coming Arabs and Jews had long been trafficking in the Red Sea and as far as Japan. With the advent of the Portuguese, West and East again made contact.

The Portuguese Empire was little more than a shop-front. Its "factories" lay thick over Africa, on the littoral of Asia, over the Sunda Archipelago. Its aims were purely commercial. Each spring, a fleet sailed from Lisbon loaded with the manufactured products of Europe—glass, textiles, wines—and made for Malabar. It returned eighteen months, or two years, later, carrying treasures gathered from Malacca, Macao, and Goa, with the addition of contributions from Persia and Mozambique. Lisbon acted as a clearing-house for pepper, cinnamon, nutmeg, cloves, lacquer, silk, pearls, and diamonds. She took the place of

Venice as the refinery of Europe, and kept the Continent supplied with sugar.

The aim of the Spaniards was to reach the same goal by different means. Everything was now encouraging them to undertake great enterprises. Long divided between two kingdoms, they had at last achieved unity in the peninsula.

The marriage of Isabella of Castile with Ferdinand of Aragon had paved the way for a unification of the realms, 1470 and their joint territories were further enlarged by the accession of Navarre. The Moslem enclave of Granada, last tottering vestige of Islam's greatness, capitulated. At last the Arabs had been driven from Europe. Spain, having achieved political unity, sought a religious equivalent. She forced conversion on the Moors, expelled the Jews, and seized their property. This latter operation gave her the means to finance great naval expeditions.

She set herself to find a westward passage to the Indies. The learned had asserted that the earth was a sphere, and that only a single ocean separated Asia from the Iberian coast. In the same year that Granada fell 1492 Christopher Columbus set sail westward with his caravels and fetched up in the Antilles. Until the day of his death he believed that he had set foot in Asia, and that the savages whom he had seen were Indians. He was given the title of Admiral of the Indies. There was a feeling almost of disappointment when the error was realized— when it was discovered that what he had found was a New World—for Columbus had come on little gold and on no spices of any kind.

At length the geographers decided to inscribe on their 1503 maps the words "Mundo Nuevo." A printer of Lorraine 1507 baptized this land with the name of a Florentine who had explored it, Amerigo Vespucci. America had made her entry on the stage of history. Six years later the Spaniard Balboa caught sight, across the American isthmus, of a 1513 second ocean. Spain, whose object it had been to reach the Spice Islands, sent Magellan to sail this new sea. So 1520

easy was its crossing that he called it Pacific. He reached
the Moluccas. Man had succeeded in making the circuit
of his planet.

But America was a country worthy of the most careful
attention. It contained pagans ripe for conversion, and a
rich subsoil ripe for exploitation. Cortez conquered
Mexico; Pizarro, Peru. To the first of these the Aztec ruler
gave gold-dust in the vain hope of getting rid of him. To
the second the Inca paid a golden ransom as the price of
his freedom. There, at last, was the precious metal so
long and so eagerly desired. Spain was not likely to let
the prey escape.

Methodically she proceeded to appropriate all this
wealth. As Portugal had her annual spice fleet, so had
Spain her gold one, which sailed from Seville (and, later,
from Cadiz). At Martinique or San Domingo it split into
two separate squadrons, one making for the Antilles and
the Gulf of Mexico, the other calling at Panama for the
cargoes from the southern provinces. They joined forces
again at Cuba, and returned to Seville after an absence of
eight months. Throughout each crossing, which lasted
from fifty to sixty days, they were escorted by ships of
war to protect them against privateers (English, French, or
others). For the nations of Europe were casting jealous
eyes on the treasures of New Spain, and seeking to get hold
of them by piracy.

Portugal in the Spice Islands, Castile in the Land of
Gold, had each taken the lion's share. But their ambitions
came into conflict, and, in order to assign to each its proper
and legitimate field of activity, the Pope laid down a line
of demarcation between the two empires. It ran straight
from pole to pole, passing one hundred leagues (later, in
consequence of protests from Lisbon and a convention between Portugal and Spain, three hundred and seventy) to
the west of the Azores. Everything beyond this boundary
was to belong to Spain—that is to say, practically the
whole of the American continents—all to east of it was to

1525
1533

1493

be Portugal's—namely, the Indies, Africa, and a small portion of America which the Portuguese sailor Cabral had   1506
discovered by chance during a storm. Brazil-wood grew
there, from which vegetable dye could be made, and it gave
its name to the country.

In this way was the world revealed by discoverers parceled out between the two Powers of the Iberian peninsula.
Henceforward, and in their interests, the balance of power
was dislocated.

THE CONSEQUENCES OF DISCOVERY

By their finding of the New World the discoverers had
brought a whole hemisphere into history. As a result of
their endeavors fresh blood was set flowing in American
Barbary. The old continent too was metamorphosed. The
upheaval, as it affected America, was radical and complete.
To the new lands Columbus took horses, pigs, poultry,
rabbits, sugar-cane, and cereals. Horses were imported in
such great numbers that eventually they wandered wild
over the prairies. Sugar-cane made the fortune of the Antilles. The Indians learned to eat beef instead of their
fellow-men, and to cultivate the soil instead of spending
their time in hunting.

It was not only draught-animals that America, in her
state of nature, had lacked, but man-power too, and much
man-power was needed for the exploitation of her mineral
resources. The work was too hard for the natives, whom
the missionaries and the ordinances of the King of Spain
tried to protect from ill-treatment. These savages, after
all, had souls, and were fit material for conversion. It
would have been in the highest degree improper to teach
them the catechism and to treat them with brutality, at one
and the same time.

Men, therefore, must be imported as well as foreign
fauna and flora. Since Africa was a land of slaves, it was
in Africa that the labor must be found for the working of

the mines. Portugal extracted Negroes from her colonies
in Africa to the end that Spain might be able to extract
gold from hers in America. For centuries to come man-
hunting was to empty the one continent in order to pop-
ulate the other. As a result of the slave trade millions of
black men were transplanted.

Meanwhile a new race was emerging from the inter-
marriage of Spaniards and American natives. A new culture was coming into being on the ruins of the pre-Colum-
bian pseudo-civilizations. Castile created an extension of
herself in America, much as Rome had reproduced her
own way of life in her colonies, and France hers in the
Levant. From California to Rio de la Plata—with the
single exception of Brazil, which was Portuguese—the
current language was the Spanish of Castile. Two
Viceroys represented the Crown, one in Mexico, the other
in Lima. To both these cities universities brought an echo
of Salamanca. Learning was pursued and books were
printed. Hundreds of cities arose in the Castilian style.
Archbishops shared between them the empire of men's
souls. The Cathedral at Mexico was the largest built anywhere in that century.

Faults there were bound to be in the carrying-through
of so vast a task. The Spanish conquerors did not always
treat the conquered with gentleness. From the Arabs they
had inherited a cruel rapacity. To the debit side of the
undertaking must be placed many bloody episodes and
much frightful torture. The Spaniards destroyed and
decimated. But at least they acted in good faith. If they
took the gold they were convinced that they brought
more than a *quid pro quo* in their gift of Christianity to
a world of idolaters. There was a spirit of brotherhood
even in their atrocities, and so rich was their positive
achievement that the errors of their imperialism may well
be overlooked.

To Europe the Spanish conquests gave in return the
dowry of new lands: syphilis, in all probability, which

spread through the continent after the return of the first
caravels, but also products hitherto undreamed of, which   1519
were to change man's whole conception of living—potatoes, imported from Peru into Spain and destined to conquer the world; tomatoes and the cassava plant and the   1540
cocoa-berry, all three originally native to South America;
Peruvian bark used by the Jesuits in cases of fever, from
which quinine was extracted; tobacco, first valued as a
specific against headaches, but soon smoked after the
fashion of the Redskins.

But the gift of all gifts, the essential commodity, was
gold—paid in ransom, acquired by pillage, or mined from
the earth. The wave of American gold broke over Spain,
and from Spain drained into Europe. In the space of a
hundred and fifty years 176 tons of the precious metal
made the passage of the Atlantic.

Hard on the heels of gold, silver began to cross the
ocean. The discovery of mines in upper Peru, and the in-   1545
vention of a low-temperature amalgam caused a sharp   1554
rise in the production figures. Within the same hundred and
fifty years immediately subsequent to the discovery of
America, Spain received nearly sixteen thousand tons of
silver. Between the beginning and the end of the sixteenth
century the quantity of precious metals at the disposal of
Europe increased ten times. Shortage had been turned into
saturation. The world had known no such revolution
since money had first been invented in Lydia.

Inflation of metal currency led to an inevitable rise in
prices. In Castile they quadrupled in the course of the
century. In France the cost of wheat went up ten times.
But rates of interest diminished and credit developed.
Government stocks made their first appearance, and the
number of joint-stock companies increased. Men began
to look to salaried employment for their means of liveli-
hood, rather than to the wealth derived from land. But if
the rich grew richer the poor grew poorer. The two movements were inseparable. Wages rose more slowly than

prices. In Castile they trebled in the course of the century, but even that advance was attained only by gradual and difficult degrees. The proletariat of the cities reacted with strikes and riots. As the difference between social conditions became more marked, the class struggle grew more bitter.

These phenomena were most noticeable in the great centers of finance and industry, and these were not situated in the Iberian peninsula. It was Flanders that was cast for the rôle of splendor and peril. Though the prosperity of Bruges was on the decline, she gave to the world a word which was to make the fortunes of many. The hereditary home of the Van der Burse family, where business-men **1549** and bankers met together, was the first Bourse, or Stock Exchange, on record. Lisbon being too proud to shoulder the task of distributing center for the spice trade, it was on Antwerp that the duty devolved. That city became the greatest clearing-house that Europe had known since Venice had slipped out of the main current of international trade. Its port handled more of the Atlantic traffic than London, Liverpool, Hamburg, Amsterdam, Nantes, Bordeaux, or any other port in the West. Its Bourse took precedence of those at Frankfurt and Lyon. It was towards her that the great tide of precious metals flowed, for Spain had no desire to amass great reserves of gold and silver. Naturally lazy, she preferred to exchange her wealth for foreign goods at the expense of her trade balance.

Economic activity, proudly sailing under the banner of individualism, became frantic. In order to increase the output of the transatlantic mines the Spanish Crown had vested their ownership in her colonial settlers, taking for herself no more than a half, then a fifth, and finally a tenth, of their output. As consumption grew, a system of free trade developed between the nations. The Low Countries and Spain bought wheat, France sold salt, Naples alum, Sicily and the Baltic countries cereals. The German and Flemish bankers made capital advances to the shipowners of Spain and Portugal. The family of Thurn and Taxis organized the first European postal service. Employments born of the many new inventions caused the rigid framework of the old corporations to crack. There were newcomers to the world of handicrafts—printers and publishers, paper-makers and book-sellers, founders of ordnance and speculators in the slave trade. New materials brought about a change in technical methods. Cotton made its appearance among the older textiles; chocolate entered on the social scene. New needs were born. The world was living at a quicker tempo.

THE POLITICAL LEADERSHIP OF SPAIN

The consequences of the great discoveries were not only economic. On the political level they had promoted Spain to the first rank among the nations. What would have happened had the New World been found by the subjects of some other Power, had the Japanese, for instance, who were good sailors, beaten the white men in the race for America, or had the English colonized the southern part of the continent? Then, indeed, the balance of the world would have been upset.

On the grandson of Ferdinand and Isabella, Don Carlos, afterwards to be known as Charles V, was heaped the burden of an astonishing legacy. From his maternal grand-   1516
mother, Isabella, he inherited Castile; from his maternal grandfather, Ferdinand, Aragon, Naples, and Sicily. As the descendant of his paternal grandmother, Mary of Burgundy, he held the Low Countries, Flanders, Artois, and Franche-Comté. As the heir of his paternal grandfather, Maximilian, he possessed Austria and the Hapsburg claim, consecrated by long tradition, to the throne of the Holy Roman Empire. Elected Emperor, he became master of a   1519
world on which the sun never set. In his name Mendoza   1535
founded Buenos Aires, Valdivia conquered Chile, and De   1541
Soto discovered the Mississippi. When, at the end of a

proud reign, Charles retired to a monastery, the better to
1555 prepare for death, it was he alone who abdicated. Spain
continued.

In the person of his son, Philip II, the Spanish monarchy
grew even greater. Though Spain and Austria were now
two distinct countries, they were closely linked by a family
pact. Philip, a headstrong sovereign, crafty and careful,
clung resolutely to his paternal legacy, and even increased
it. Heir to the throne of Portugal through his mother, he
1581 conquered that country, and annexed it to the Spanish
Crown. The two transatlantic empires were now fused in
one, and Philip's name was given to an archipelago in the
land of spices, the Philippines. Seville and Lisbon were the
two leading cities of the world. Spain had a footing in
Oran and Tunis. Almost the whole of Italy was under
Spanish influence, from Naples to Milan, from Palermo to
Genoa. For a short while Philip could call even England
his home, when he married Mary Tudor. Later, when he
took Elizabeth of Valois to wife, he dreamed of becoming
the master of France.

Spain was in evidence everywhere. For almost a century she struggled with France on the battlefields of Italy.
Naples and Milan were states in a struggle for the hegemony of Europe. In spite of Charles VIII's artillery, in spite
of the alliances of Louis XII, in spite of the victories of
Francis I, it was Spain who emerged victorious. Except
in Venice, Rome, and Piedmont, she reigned over Italy.

The scene of the fighting changed, moving from Italy
to France. Spain intervened in French affairs, subsidized
supporters, maintained garrisons. For a brief while there
were Spanish troops billeted in Paris. It was questionable
whether France would be able to hold out against the
powerful neighbors who threatened her from north, east,
and south, from Flanders, Milan, and the Pyrenees. She
was weakened by quarrels of succession, impoverished by
civil war. She had no national army. Not until the coming

of Henri IV, of Richelieu, and of Mazarin were the fortunes of France restored. But Ravaillac's dagger and the 1610 convulsions of the Fronde served the Spanish cause well by 1642 putting off the moment of France's rise to greatness.

Against England Spain had at first an easy task. England had a small population; her sovereigns sat uneasily on their throne, and Parliament was grudging of military subsidies. The English were a race of sheep-breeders and agriculturists; not yet had they heard the call of the sea. They would have counted for little in the politics of Europe had not a queen of unusual vision and enthusiasm opened their eyes to their true mission. Elizabeth boldly fronted Philip II. She imprisoned and executed Mary Stuart, whom Philip wished to place upon the English throne. She challenged the leadership of Spain upon the high seas, and dispersed a fleet which the Spaniards had believed to be "invincible." Whether Britain's naval supremacy should be 1587 dated from this victory is open to question. Actually it was no more than a local success, and the English were still only serving their apprenticeship upon the seas. Elizabeth's fleet failed at the Azores and in the Tagus. Spain remained still powerful afloat.

Elizabeth's true successor was Cromwell. The Stuarts —those "stewards" (or seneschals) who came from Scotland—were no more than a decorative interlude in the political history of the island. They tilted against the already liberal traditions of the British people and broke their heads against the opposition of Parliament. Kingship was abolished, Charles I beheaded. Charles II wished 1649 to call in Spanish help. It was the Protector, Oliver Cromwell, who really pursued the policy laid down by Elizabeth.

But these internal disturbances kept London for a while a stranger to the affairs of Europe. England, divided, lacked the means seriously to challenge Spain, which, even after the death of Philip II, remained the leading Power of the world.

The influence of the Castilian throne spread far afield.

It served as a model to all the absolute monarchies of Europe, to the Bourbons as well as to the Stuarts. The king decided on all matters of peace and war. His word was law in home affairs and foreign. His councils were there only to be consulted. The proud landed nobility, ruined by monetary inflation, became the lackeys of the Court. When its members came into the presence of their sovereign they approached him on their knees. The Escorial, that gloomy combination of palace and Pantheon which Philip had built in the volcanic wastes of Castile, was the center of the universe.

CULTURAL LEADERSHIP OF SPAIN

The first meridian by which navigators fixed their position passed through Cape Verde. In the course of time it shifted to Paris, and then to London. For the moment of history which we have reached the Hispano-Portuguese reference was in the ascendant.

That first meridian has the value of a symbol. Not only marine bearings, but other things as well, used the Iberian peninsula as a touchstone. Castilian fashions were the rage. Well-bred men in every country piqued themselves on following the Spanish mode. Coquettes everywhere found their inspiration in Madrid. The pavan was a favorite dance. Other countries were quick to adopt for their windows the particular form of hasp known as *espagnolette*. Spanish coins were much sought after, silver douros and pistoles of gold. The very name *pistole* was retained in France to designate the ten-livre piece in the currency of Tours. The influence of the Spanish language was no less widespread than that of Spanish money. From it we derive not only words like *guitar, matamore* ("braggart"), and *serenade,* but a number of terms belonging to the military art and to literature—*adjutant, aviso* ("dispatch-boat"), *parade, fanfaron* ("boaster"), *romance,* and *fabulist,* while it was by way of Spain that the very

names of the new foodstuffs from across the Atlantic
reached Europe—cocoa, chocolate, tomato. From that
time on more than half of the New World was to speak the
language of Castile.

For good or for ill Spanish literature set the tone. It
started a mania among the precious for affectations and
euphuisms, and made popular the reading of tales, first of
chivalry, and then of pastoral artificiality. In Hispanicized
Italy Tasso was influenced by both. But Spain also took
pride in Cervantes, whose legacy to the world was his story   1605
of the exploits of Don Quixote.

The Spanish theater not only produced Lope de Vega
and his 1800 plays—*es de Lope* ("it's one of Lope's") was
the slogan of perfection—but created an immortal type,
Don Juan. It served as a guide to Shakespeare, teaching
him how to mingle the sublime and the comic, and it
inspired Corneille, providing him with the material for
the two greatest tragedies and comedies in the whole of the
French repertory.

In the visual arts the prestige of Italy was still para-
mount. The French built their chateaus on Italian lines,
bringing them into conformity with their own taste. There
was no longer a Michelangelo in Rome, but in Venice
there were Tintoretto and Veronese, who celebrated with
the brush the splendors and the glories of the city of the
Doges. In other ways Italy was now scarcely more than a
Spanish colony, and, though it was she who gave birth to
the Baroque, Spain soon made the new style her own, finding completely to her taste its spectacular flamboyance of
form, and a self-conscious theatricality to effect which was
wholly in keeping with her own genius. This voluptuous
development in the arts of painting and architecture came
to its fullest flower in Vienna and Madrid, and soon spread
to the young continent of America.

Flanders was another Spanish outpost. It was in the
school of Antwerp that the Bavarian Albrecht Dürer   1520
formed his style. Flemish art, proceeding from the gro-

tesque inventions of Hieronimo Bosch and the Breughels, found in Rubens its most luminous expression. But
1628 Rubens was not ignorant of Madrid, where, indeed, he worked for several years. The Spanish churches were adorned with Flemish paintings.

But Spain possessed geniuses of her own. The Cretan Theocopuli, known as El Greco, gave miraculous form to the burning fanaticism of the Iberian race. Three men of Seville—Zurbarán, Murillo, and Velásquez—carried Spanish painting to the heights, and their influence was felt even by the Persian miniaturists and the Mogul artists. So full of masterpieces did the Royal Collection become, later known as the Museum of the Prado, that for all the painters of the world a visit to Madrid was considered to be of more importance than a trip to Rome.

The sciences were making great strides along the road to truth. Had not the discovery of the New World taught men to distrust the Ancients? Aristotle had not so much as suspected the existence of America, and for that reason he lost much of his authority. The Fathers of the Church had been deceived. Consequently men ceased to accept their statements at face-value. Factual observation became the fashion. Experimental science was on the way.

The Pole Copernicus had explained the "movement of the celestial bodies." The Dane Tycho Brahe and the
1543 Swabian Kepler carried on his work. Galileo of Pisa, armed
1616 with the earliest telescope, conquered planetary space. Of what use was it to condemn him? Whatever the Holy Office might say, the earth *did* turn.

The knowledge of mankind advanced step by step with
1542 that of the universe. Vesalius, who was doctor to both Charles V and Philip II, opened a new chapter in anatomy. Servetus of Aragon established the lesser circulation of the
1622 blood; Harvey, the Englishman, the greater.

Meanwhile the exact sciences found the instrument they needed when François Viète of Poitou perfected the alge-
1579 braic method.

Not everything was of Spanish origin in this great leap forward of the intellect. But the part played in it by the Hispanic Empire was preponderant. The cultural capitals of the world were Madrid and Antwerp, Seville and Brussels, Salamanca and Mexico. The century of gold was also the Golden Age of Spain.

THE REFORMATION

In the religious life of Europe, too, Spain was prominent. But now men were beginning to take sides in religion, and she was the champion of only one of them. Against the Catholics were ranged the Huguenots.

Renaissance implied Reformation: not Renaissance in the Italian sense, which was no more than a glorification of Greek and Roman antiquity, but Renaissance as Spain had understood it—an adventuring along new roads and a widening of the human understanding. It is no paradox to say that Protestantism was brought into existence by what, originally, had been a purely Catholic enterprise.

Rome, there could be no doubt about it, had roused discontent in the minds of the faithful. As Christians, they were shocked by the decadence of the Popes and by the general laxity of the clergy. As taxpayers, they found the financial demands of the Holy See excessive. As patriots, they felt outraged by the political encroachments of the Papacy. A wind was rising—that same wind of individualism which had already shaken the fabric of the corporative economy, and blown great gaps in the old ways of living. The Catholic discipline was beginning to feel its effects.

Voices had already been raised against Rome, some of them violent, like that of John Huss, others prudent, like that of Erasmus. A Saxon priest, Martin Luther, made a   **1517** clean break with the Catholic Church. His excommunication served only to popularize his cause. But, all things considered, Luther was a timid rebel. He did no more than proclaim the rights of the individual conscience. Others among the Reformers showed a greater revolutionary zeal. Some preached the burning of images; others wanted to set up a form of worship without priests. The Spaniard Servetus denied the Trinity. Zwingli rejected, at one and the same **1523** time, both Pope and councils, both Mass and Sacraments. In Alsace there were extremists who were out for the abolition of property. Taking the Old Testament as their authority, they wanted to establish polygamy.

John Cauvin of Picardy, known to history as Calvin, refused the compromise accepted by Luther. At Geneva he **1536** taught that men must take only the Gospel as their guide. The Genevese Pope threw down a challenge to the Pope at Rome, and rivaled him in intolerance.

How did the people react to all these new doctrines? The southern countries of Europe maintained an attitude of reserve. In Italy the Pope maintained the sense of unity. In Spain Catholicism, with its saints of both sexes, its images, and its pomps, was too much in tune with popular aspirations ever to be seriously in danger. But elsewhere there were convulsions and civil wars, as a result of which the Protestants infiltrated and established themselves firmly.

So far as Germany was concerned, it was of little use for Charles V to condemn Luther. It was the princes he had to bring to heel, and they were inclined to declare them- **1555** selves in favor of the reformed religion. The whole of Northern Germany became Lutheran, and all Western Germany Calvinist. Only in the south did the influence of Rome remain unshaken—in Austria and in Bohemia, where scenes of bloody repression took place. As a consequence of the religious schism, the Holy Roman Empire fell to pieces. In spite of the fact that Luther gave to Germany not only a matured and common language, but also a number of patriotic phrases ("Deutschland über alles," "Gott mit uns"), the people of that country definitely lost the sense of nationality. Their only function now was to serve foreign princes as mercenaries.

England at first hesitated on the threshold of the Refor-

mation. The Anglican Church broke with Rome, but not
with the majority of Catholic practices. It was the struggle
with Spain for the control of the seas that pushed Elizabeth   1588
into the arms of Protestantism. It was the quarrel of the
Catholic Stuarts with the Puritan Cromwell that finally   1649
estranged the English people from Roman Popery.

In France the battle was fierce and indecisive. Most of
the French remained Catholics, but their sovereigns frequently veered towards Protestantism, less from religious
conviction than from political expediency. Their main object was to ensure themselves against the Spanish peril by
any means that might come to hand, and this they could
best do by supporting the Reforming Princes of Germany
against the Emperor, or by helping the Flemish rebels. The
Massacre of St. Bartholomew, which the Escorial hailed as
a victory for Spain, was, in fact, no more than an accident   1572
of French politics. On the other side of the account must
be placed the fact that Catherine de Medici was willing to
treat with the Reformed religionists of La Rochelle, that   1593
Henri III took arms against the Guises and the League,
that Henri IV reconquered his kingdom with the help of
Protestant England. If the policy of the French kings turned
out, in the long run, to be favorable to the Catholics (was
not Paris "worth a Mass"?) the reason was that the unity
of the country must be preserved. So far as foreign affairs
went, their attitude was, as ever, mainly anti-Spanish, and,
therefore, anti-Catholic.

In the name of Christ men embarked upon an orgy of
mutual excommunication and slaughter. The ideological
duel between Rome and Geneva, which became a struggle
for leadership between Madrid and London, was transformed, without much difficulty, into an international war.
The fight raged not only between brothers, families, and
cities, but also between peoples and groups of peoples.
Against the threat of Austro-Spanish encirclement, France
sought an alliance with the Turks. Against the Turkish
menace, Austria turned to Persia for help. The elective

throne of Poland became the stake in a long battle between religious denominations. The Swede, Gustavus Adolphus, firmly installed in Riga and Finland and strong in the possession of a national army, became a great Lutheran power fighting in the interest of religious faith. The repercussions of the war were felt even across the Atlantic. And so it came about that almost the whole world was involved in the struggle.

THE COUNTER-REFORMATION

In the normal course of events it was from Rome that a lead in the counter-offensive should have come. The Church, however, was finding considerable difficulty in establishing a doctrine on the basis of which she could take her stand and strike back. The theologians strove laboriously to confute the heretics, but it took the Council of Trent twenty-five sessions and eighteen years before a satis-

1563   factory definition of the Catholic Faith was found.

It was not that Rome was adamant against all innovation. What she wished to do, and succeeded after long deliberation in doing, was to restore the dignity of the Church. Pope Gregory XIII went so far in modernism as to authorize a change in the calendar, which, since the days of Caesar, had been at variance with the movement of the sun. The Julian year had consisted of 365 days and one-quarter. In this calculation there was an error of eleven minutes. These minutes had gradually accumulated until

1581   they had become a day. The Pope, in order to remedy this state of affairs, suggested the suppression of three bissextiles every 400 years. To rectify the fault already committed it was proposed to annihilate ten days. Thus the 5th

1582   of December, 1582, became the 15th. The Catholic countries corrected their calendar in accordance with Papal instructions, but others remained loyal to the Julian system. Protestant Germany ultimately rallied to the solar reckoning, but not until 1700; England not until 1742; and

Sweden in 1753. Orthodox Russia, however, was still clinging to her chronological error in 1920. In this matter it
was the Catholics who first took notice of the lessons of
science.

But the schism of the calendar counted for little in the
greater schism of the Faith. Who was to lead the movement
of the Counter-Reformation? The King of Spain bore the
title of Catholic Majesty. The Holy See had delegated to
him the spiritual sovereignty of the New World. It was
Spain that now became the champion of the Roman religion, not only within the framework of her own empire,
but in countries too beyond its frontiers. The means she
employed were at first pacific. She had her great mystics—
St. Theresa and St. John of the Cross—and her great missionaries as well, men of the stamp of St. Francis Xavier.
She had her tribunals, those of the Inquisition, which had
been created for the purpose of deciding on the sincerity
of converted Jews and Moors, and now, by bringing a ruthless ferocity to the condemnation of Protestant heretics,
saved Spain from the horrors of a civil war and the perils
of dissension.

But above all Spain had a Catholic "militia" in the Society of Jesus, which had been founded by Ignatius Loyola,
a soldier turned monk. It was an organization which com-   1537
bined the characteristics of piety and military training, and
it gave its discipline to the service of Rome. Ignatius became the first General of the Jesuits. His two immediate
successors were Spaniards, and most of those who later
held the office, whether Belgian, Neapolitan, or Florentine
by birth, were vassals of the Spanish king.

By means of propaganda, education, and intrigue, the
Jesuits worked for the Catholic Faith. They helped in the
spiritual reconquest of the Rhineland and of Poland. They
evangelized the heathen of America and the Indies. They
showed in the councils of the princes of the world a zeal,
sometimes open, sometimes concealed. They increased
the number of missions and colleges in all the countries of

the earth. The Church of Jesus which they built in Rome served as an architectural model in a style which rapidly spread everywhere. Its distinguishing mark was a glorification of the Virgin and the Angels, of the Immaculate Conception and the Child Jesus. To the austerity of Puritan art it opposed a system of decoration both ostentatious and flamboyant.

But Spain also served Catholicism sword in hand. Not only did she war in Europe against all the reformed sects and the countries which adopted them, but undertook in Africa and the Mediterranean a new Crusade against the Infidels. The task was one of reconquest. The Moors had been driven from Granada and the African littoral from 1541 Melilla to Tripoli. Later they had reoccupied Algiers, from which Charles V failed to expel them. They put themselves under the protection of the Turks, who were rich and well armed, and, as masters of Alexandria and Rhodes, of Chios and Cyprus—places taken either from the Genoese or the Venetians—in a position to command the whole of the Eastern Mediterranean. Suleiman the Magnificent had defeated the Hungarians and laid siege to Vienna. The Spaniards, driven back on Oran and threatened on the high seas by the Barbary pirates, rallied in defense of their own territories, while proclaiming themselves the defenders of Christendom. Their fleet, in conjunction with that of Venice, crushed a Turkish squadron off Lepanto, in 1571 the Gulf of Corinth. More than one hundred Turkish ships were taken, and thousands of Christian captives were released. Cervantes, serving as an obscure soldier, celebrated this spectacular victory of the Cross over the Crescent. Nevertheless the Turks were still dangerous. They reorganized their fleet, managed to maintain their hold on Cyprus, and still exercised domination over their North African possessions—Tripoli, Tunis, and Algiers. Morocco carved for herself an independent empire from the sands of the Sahara.

On the northern marches of her territories Spain had another duty to perform. There, too, as guardian of the

Catholic Faith, she had to defend her position inch by inch against the aggressive intentions of the Reformation and the nationalist uprisings of the occupied provinces. On the shores of the North Sea, as in the Mediterranean, she was forced to uphold a conservative policy. She had opened her jaws too wide, and was embarrassed by the size of the mouthful. She had too much on her hands in the world at large to put up a successful resistance anywhere.

The small community of the Low Countries was the first to shake the Iberian colossus on its pedestal.

THE BIRTH OF THE LOW COUNTRIES

The provinces grouped round the mouths of the Scheldt, the Maas, and the Rhine had the inestimable advantage of being both opulent and magnificently placed. For a long time now Flanders had been the main center of the textile industry, and Antwerp was the leading port of Europe. These northern plains were designed by destiny to be the battlefield of Europe. From her point of vantage in Brussels Spain was well placed to intervene in Germany, to make her voice heard in the Baltic, and to invade a France caught between two fires. Nothing in the world would induce her to abandon an advanced post which guaranteed her the hegemony of the Continent.

Calvinism had made rapid progress in those lands. Was Philip II to let Satan triumph? He knew that if he were to allow the Flemings liberty of conscience he would very soon have to concede political independence, and that, in the long run, he would lose the precious provinces altogether. The insurgents, so said the proud Spaniards, were nothing but a handful of "scamps" (*gueux*). "Up the Scamps!" was 1566 the reply of the rebels; and they gloried in the name.

Philip tried to establish the Inquisition in Flanders. This led to a popular uprising. Mobs broke into the churches and profaned the altars. The Spaniards applied the harshest measures of repression, but the revolt, supported by the

English and financed by the French, kept breaking out again. The Northern Provinces declared themselves to be "United," and the euphemism made it quite clear that they would soon announce their independence. A Prince of the Empire, William of Nassau, Lord of Orange, assumed the headship of the "Scamps." Would he dare back their claims? To this question he replied, "I will maintain" **1573** ("Je maintiendrai")—a phrase which became the motto of the Low Countries.

The Spanish Government, always impecunious, lacked the wherewithal to pay its troops. The "Scamps" triumphed. Holland and Zeeland became federated, and The Hague issued a proclamation to the effect that Philip II was no **1581** longer their king. Only the Belgian provinces, where most of the people were Catholic, kept their Spanish garrisons.

From now on the United Provinces were to become a Great Power, not by reason of numbers, but because of the quality of their effort, of their army, which was magnificently disciplined and carefully trained, and of their school of painting, made famous by Franz Hals and Rembrandt, portraitists of genius who took the rich bourgeois as their sitters; of their philosophers, among whom was Spinoza; of their men of science, among whom were Zacharias Jansen, the inventor of the microscope, and a certain Van Helmont, who created the word "gas," and, above all, of their financial and economic enterprise.

Spain had herself built the fortunes of The Netherlands. By closing her harbors to Dutch tonnage she had forced the Low Countries to find markets elsewhere. By bringing ruin to Antwerp as a result of her repressive measures she had made it possible for Amsterdam to grow great. By expelling the Jews from the peninsula and the Protestants from Flanders she had provided the United Provinces with both capital and capitalists. Since neither Jews nor Protestants took any account of the canonical ban on lending at interest, they became the kings of the banking world.

Amsterdam, with its girdle of canals, was, in some sort, a new Venice. Once the Dutch had closed the approaches of the Scheldt it no longer had to fear the competition of Antwerp, and became the successor of that city both as port and banking center. It was towards her that the tide of precious metals now set, thanks to the balance of trade which The Netherlands could show. Her Bourse prospered. Her joint-stock companies and commercial enterprises grew in number. Speculation became a national industry, and included in its activities even such things as rare tulip-bulbs.

The City of Amsterdam created a bank which became the clearing-house for all traders. It held the monopoly of all exchange operations. To its depositors it offered a low **1609** rate of interest, but complete security. It placed no difficulty in the way of the movement of capital, and that is the surest way of attracting money. It soon became the commercial center of the whole of the Low Countries and the cashier of the West. The metal florins which it minted were at a premium. The success of Amsterdam led to much envy among her neighbors. Hamburg and Nuremberg did their best to be her imitators.

But the Dutch did not confine their activities to banking. They sold their cheeses, their herrings, and their tulips. They printed and published a large number of books: the Elzevir family became famous in the world of literature. Following the example of Venice, they issued a gazette which served as inspiration, in France, to Théophraste Renaudot. Dutch dockyards covered the seas with ships.

For the true glory of the Low Countries lay in the seas and beyond them. The geographer Mercator developed a new system of map-making. The physicist Van Drebbel made submarine navigation a practical proposition. The Dutch explorers sought out a new route to the Spice Islands, which they tried to reach either by working round the north of Asia (Barents discovered Spitzbergen), or the **1596**

1616 south of America (Schouten rounded a cape to which he
gave the name of his native city, Horn). While plowing
1606 the Southern Seas the navigators of the United Provinces
came across a continent which they called New Holland
(later to become Australia), and a land which still retains
1642 the name they gave it—New Zealand.

The Low Countries blamed the Iberian Empire for the
fact that they were at war with Spain. When an effort was
made to keep them from trading with the Indies they inaugurated a clandestine traffic in spices, gold, and slaves, and
took no account of Cadiz and Lisbon. When they were shut
out from America they set themselves methodically to
1609 pillage the Hispano-Portuguese colonies, and to smuggle
their produce. The jurist Grotius proclaimed the doctrine
of the Freedom of the Seas, and the seas became their
home. The ancient Portuguese Empire, which Spain found
the utmost difficulty in protecting, was their natural prey.
1621 They seized the Sunda Islands, and founded Batavia, the
city of the Batavians. Their companies, which controlled
the spice trade, set up factories in India, Ceylon, and
Malaya. They ventured even as far as Japan, where, the
only Europeans to be treated with toleration, they acquired
the right to land at will on an island near Nagasaki. In
1652 Africa they took from the Portuguese the harbor of the
Cape, and established an agricultural colony there. In
America they established themselves at Surinam, at Cura-
çao, on the coast of Guiana, and in Brazil. They bought
from the Indians the island of Manhattan, on which
1626 they built the city of New Amsterdam, the future New
York.

This new empire claimed to be nothing but a trading
concern. The Low Countries colonized, not in order to
impose a religious faith, but for the sole purpose of earn-
ing big dividends. Under pressure from their European
rivals they were prepared to ally themselves with the Infidels, as the French had done with the Turks, and the

English with the Persians. The Reformation had broken down the solid Western front. The Spaniards might claim that their colonial enterprises were in the nature of a Crusade. The Dutch regarded theirs only in the light of a financial operation.

THE NEW EMPIRES OF THE WEST

Spain was no longer the sole World Power. The Dutch Empire, and others like it, were coming into existence beyond the oceans.

England became conscious of her vocation as a seagoing and colonizing nation. In her case Puritanism was the leaven of capitalism. It opened the way to a fiduciary currency (with warrants issued by her goldsmiths and notaries). Navigation under the British flag, protected by Cromwell, developed at a prodigious rate. By the beginning of the seventeenth century the Port of London surpassed even Amsterdam in importance.

For a long time, no doubt, the English sailors operated mainly as pirates, and their exploits consisted, for the most part, in seizing the gold-laden galleons of Spain, and in developing a hit-and-run technique suitable to the numerically weaker side. But there were other Englishmen who set out to explore the oceans. In their search for a North- 1553 east Passage to the Indies they found how to reach Russia by way of the White Sea. In attempting to find a similar route by the northwest, they happened on the land of the Eskimo. In the course of his journey to the Pole, Baffin 1615 reached the 78th degree of latitude. Cabot had discovered Labrador, and Gilbert had annexed a portion of New- 1497 foundland. English emigrants settled on the coast of Amer- 1583 ica, fleeing from economic difficulties or religious persecution at home. Between the St. Lawrence and the Hudson 1620 they founded New England. Farther to the south Maryland came into existence, named by the Catholic colonists 1634

after the wife of Charles I, and Virginia, which the Puritans
1584 christened in honor of Queen Elizabeth. These settlements
were widely scattered, often at odds with one another,
and without contact with the motherland. But their population grew, and prosperity was not slow in coming. For
the English, as practical folk, learned to adapt themselves
to local conditions. They did not concentrate their efforts
on searching for gold or converting the natives. They
found it more profitable to fish for cod or to grow tobacco.

The French too were anxious to get their share of the
New World. They had captured Spanish ships, it is true,
1514 but they had also explored the Newfoundland Banks.
1534 Cartier discovered Canada (which, like Columbus, he be-
1603 lieved to be in Asia), and Champlain succeeded in founding a precarious colony there. In spite of the daring of the
discoverers, in spite of the perseverance shown by the pioneers of New France, the enterprise proved to be laborious.
The climate was harsh; the Iroquois were hostile. Paris
did not always give sufficient support to the Canadian effort. In any case, the French colonists were not numerous,
and the few thousand men who were willing to face exile
in the land of furs were too often preachers, too seldom
1620 farmers. It needed a Richelieu to organize systematic colonization on the Dutch model, with commercial companies
having a stake in success.

The Swedes, in their turn, tried their luck on the banks
of the Delaware. But New Sweden was eliminated by the
1638 Dutch of New Amsterdam, who, in the course of time,
were evicted by the English. That was the law of the New
World. The Europeans who settled there fought one another, Dutch against English, English against French,
English and French against Spaniards. Nevertheless it was
the destiny of the continent to become Europeanized. The
farthest provinces, the remotest islands, even if they yielded
neither gold nor spices, became the prey of those in search
of colonies. Their people farmed and administered the

land. The Colonial Period, now opening, set the political
ambitions of Europe by the ears.

THE OLD EMPIRES OF THE EAST

Meanwhile, beyond the boundaries of Europe, the East
was continuing to live its separate and peculiar life, indifferent to the religious controversies which were shaking
the Christian peoples to their foundations, and hardly at all
susceptible to that appetite for trade which was felt so
strongly in the West.

Russia, though not really so very far away in actual distance, seemed to belong to another world. She looked on
the Europe of the Reformation as a place of lunatics, while
Europe, in return, regarded Russia as a nation of barbarians. Their ignorance of one another was abysmal,
though contact was not altogether lacking, since there
were outbreaks of fighting between Russia and her western
neighbors. The Swedes pushed the Muscovites back from
the Gulf of Finland; the Poles drove them from the Baltic
provinces. The Tartars settled in the Crimea, carried out a   1571
raid on Moscow, which they burned, and another on the
Ukraine, which they pillaged. The Russians found compensation for these losses by moving east and peopling the
Siberian wastes. They adventured on to the White Sea   1618
and reached the Pacific.   •   1648

Their Emperor was all-powerful. When the Russian
Church broke with the Patriarch of Constantinople, whom
it suspected of wishing to come to terms with Rome, he
became the religious head of his people. He owned enormous tracts of territory, on which the peasants worked as
serfs.

Turkey was at once threatening and fragile. She had devoured Hungary, reduced North Africa, and successfully
resisted Spain. But her power was undermined by a suc-   1526
cession of domestic revolutions, intrigues of the harem,

and treacheries on the part of the Viziers. In Constantinople hangings and stranglings merely served to delay, by
a reign of terror, the day of Turkey's inevitable decadence.
The time had gone by when the Ottoman hordes could
keep Europe in a constant state of nervousness.

A sophisticated civilization held sway in Persia, where
the influences of Islam, China, and Venice met. In Ispahan,
its new capital, the Court had elaborated a luxurious routine of manners and procedure. It was a country of exquisite miniature-painting, and, at times, of extravagant
cruelties. One of the Shahs had the eyes of two of his sons
put out. The third he murdered.

India, the mere name of which threw Europe into an
ecstasy though it remained an almost completely unknown
land to the majority of Europeans, was emerging from her
long anarchy. A descendant of Tamerlane, Akbar, King
1556   of Delhi and Agra, conquered and unified the provinces of
the north and center, building them into one of the richest
empires in the whole world—the Empire of the "Grand
Mogul." Under his patronage Indo-Moslem art flourished.
He amassed vast hoards of those precious metals for which
India has always had a passion.

China of the Mings was living on its past, lost in a cloud
of ancestor-worship. The great period of Chinese culture
was over. Artistic genius was slumbering. Military enthusiasm had declined. The attitude of China towards Europeans was one rather of apathy than of tolerance—and
she readily acquiesced in the presence within her borders
of both missionaries and traders. There was very little, if
it came to that, in which she was not prepared to acquiesce.
She allowed a Manchu horde to gain a footing in Mukden,
and even went so far as to call upon its warriors to help
1621   her settle one of her own internal quarrels. Of this incident
the Manchus took full advantage. They drove the Ming
dynasty from the throne, and became the masters of all
China. The country made no attempt to react violently
against this offensive. True to itself, it assimilated the con-

querors. In course of time the Manchus became more 1651
Chinese than the Chinese themselves. They abandoned
their nomad ways and settled down. The Manchurian forest disappeared, and, in its place, appeared fields of rice
and soya.

In Japan the situation was very different. After centuries
of feudal warfare and anarchy a centralized state was taking shape, elaborately organized into a hierarchy, and
strongly nationalist in feeling. All foreigners were kept
strictly at bay. The Portuguese had been allowed to carry
on trade with the Southern Islands. Francis Xavier had
been able to preach in Nippon. But all that was over.
From now on the Japanese closed their harbors, refused
to admit foreigners into their territories, and forbade 1638
their people to travel beyond the borders of their own
island empire. For more than two centuries Japan remained a world apart.

But, whether accessible or closed, these various Eastern
empires had now ceased to count in the history of the
world. What happened to them was of purely local significance. Not from them was light to come. They no longer
created, no longer invented. They had ceased to weigh de-
cisively in the destiny of mankind. The etiquette of their
Courts might, here and there, be brilliant, the legacy of
their art might still be exquisite, and their peoples prolific.
Irremediably, they had fallen behind in the race. Europe,
with her caravels and guns, with her telescopes and
printing-presses, had finally taken the lead, and it was impossible now to put the clock back.

THE DECLINE OF SPAIN

But the time had come when in that Europe which was
the world's center of gravity Spain was to lose her position
of leadership. The fault was to some extent her own. She
was paying for her laziness, which had always inclined her
to despise hard work and turn up her nose at trade. It was

not permitted for her noblemen to work, and who is there in Spain that does not regard himself to some extent as noble? She was paying for her all-absorbing love of gold, because it had helped to make her soft, and to turn her young people from the fields and the workshops. She was paying for her demographic impoverishment, which had been brought on by colonial emigration and aggravated **1609** by the mass expulsion of imperfectly converted Moors.

The Spanish edifice was cracking. Her empire was too vast and too loosely knit. Alone, the determination of Madrid bound together Flanders and Naples, Portugal and Milan, Mexico and the Moluccas. The colonies became animated by a jealous spirit of particularism, and this, in the long run, led to their breaking away from the mother country. Madrid believed that she could safeguard the unity of the imperial territories by turning her colonies into a preserve. Foreigners were forbidden to trade with them, or they with foreigners. Customs dues and rigorous import regulations penalized the transference to Spain of products from abroad and the re-exportation of goods coming from the Spanish overseas possessions. The royal ships claimed the monopoly of the carrying trade. This policy of mercantilism broke the back of vigorous enterprise and provoked a series of economic crises. Worst of all, it set an example. England and France sought to preserve their trade balances by restricting and prohibiting the entry of all objects of foreign manufacture, by favoring the export of goods from their own factories, by insisting that their cargoes be carried only in bottoms flying the national flag. There was a war of tariffs. One system of autarchy vied with another, and because, in the long run, Spain could not do without foreign wheat and foreign manufactures she became the first victim of her own economic nationalism.

If Spain was to retain her political and military pre-eminence she needed an energetic sovereign, an unrivaled fleet, an invincible army. But after Philip II the Catholic kings,

too young or too weak to carry the weight of their responsi-
bilities, delegated their power to favorites. Faced by the
English and Dutch squadrons, the Spanish fleet found it
impossible to remain mistress of the seas. The Dutch took   1655
the Moluccas, the English Jamaica, and even the French
were able to get a footing in the Antilles. Last tragedy of
all, the Spanish army began to fall off in quality. Because
of a lack of Castilian troops it took to absorbing more
and more foreign soldiers into its ranks. Its generals were
often Belgians or Italians. Its enemies found a way of
countering its tactics. The Spanish infantry, bristling with
muskets, excelled in defense, but, where possible, refused
to be drawn into pitched battles. For Spain the whole art
of war consisted in laying siege to fortified cities. The
Swedish school of fighting introduced dangerous innovations and developed open fighting. Gustavus Adolphus
and Condé together reinstated the offensive.

For thirty years the Powers of Europe were involved
in a war which spread across the Continent. In appearance,
it was a war of religion. It began as an uprising of Calvinist Bohemia and the Reformed Princes of Germany against   1618
the Austrian Emperor. In fact, what was at stake was the
whole system of the Austro-Spanish hegemony. The Em-   1620
peror crushed Bohemia. But France, wholly Catholic
though she was, was too much concerned in breaking her
encirclement to let such an opportunity slip. Richelieu sent,
first Danish, then Swedish, troops to fight the imperial
armies of Wallenstein. The Danes were beaten; the Swedes
would have been victorious had not Gustavus Adolphus   1632
been killed in the very moment of success. France had to
enter the lists against Spain. She was menaced with invasion by way of the Oise and through Roussillon. She held   1635
firm. It was Spain who faltered. Catalonia revolted, quickly 1636
followed by Portugal, where a member of the house of   1640
Braganza was proclaimed king. At Naples a fisherman
roused the populace. At Rocroi, at Fribourg, at Lens, the   1643

1648   Spanish army was overcome. The old empire was everywhere cracking.

The Age of Spain was at an end. Preponderance passed, on land to France, on sea to England. Each of these two Powers, in turn, was henceforward to lead the world.

CHAPTER NINE

The Centuries of France

FRANCE AND THE WORLD

FOR AT least one hundred and fifty years it was to be France that would be the leading Power in the world. There were moments during that period when her position of political supremacy was menaced, and even shaken, but she retained unquestioned, and at a very high level, her cultural domination. This she kept for a very long time, even after her military might had foundered.

France's position of leadership during the seventeenth and eighteenth centuries was more firmly established than that of Spain had been in the sixteenth, or that of Italy in the fourteenth. Not unless we go back to Rome shall we find such another example of absolute preponderance. But Rome had stood almost without a competitor against a world of barbarism, whereas France imposed herself on a Europe where there was no lack of rivals.

How was it that she attained to this position? First, by reason of her own natural advantages. She lay, geographically, at the point where all the great lines of Western communication met. She looked out on the Mediterranean, which was the great artery of civilization, and also on the Atlantic, which had become the highway of the new merchant fleets. She possessed a far larger population than any other country of Europe. In the middle of the seventeenth

century, when the whole world contained no more than
five hundred million inhabitants, France numbered nineteen million. England and Scotland together maintained
no more than six, and Spain in her decadence had suffered
a fall from eight to less than five million. Neither the German Empire nor even Russia in her vastness could count
on any comparable demographic wealth.

But this was not all. France's political institutions were
a guarantee of that internal order and stability without
which no country can be great. The old monarchy of the
Capets, which had become that of the Bourbons, was then
at its apogee. The Fronde, a still-born revolution modeled
on that of England, had had little more than a nuisance
value, and had opened men's eyes to the need for a strong
central authority. Two reigns, covering between them a
period of one hundred and thirty years, were acclaimed by
the hopes and enthusiasm of the whole nation.

The idea of absolute monarchy by no means outraged
the public opinion of a country which infinitely preferred
an all-powerful sovereign to an all-powerful Prime Minister. It wasn't, if it came to that, strictly accurate to say
that the king *was* absolute. His powers were limited by the
existence of many privileges and immunities granted to
provinces, cities, and trades, and these combined into a
rich and varied pattern of public liberties. Some of these
were frequently abusive and anachronistic, and those who
derived benefit from them were violently opposed to even
the most needed reforms. The Parliament of Paris, after
being ridden on a tight reign by Louis XIV, took advantage
of the regency to reassert its right of remonstrance. Louis
XV, who was nothing if not clear-sighted, dissolved it; but
the timid Louis XVI reversed his decision, and by so doing sounded the death-knell of the monarchy.

The French kings worked unceasingly to build up the
country's strength. They gave her an administration; they
organized an army which, equipped and disciplined by

Louvois, served as a model for all the armies of Europe. They labored to make France united.

The kingdom of France was the fruit of long cultivation. It had been necessary to build it piece by piece, at the expense both of intractable feudal barons and greedy neighbors. Violence and cunning had each played a part in achieving the final result. Local loyalties had to be overcome as well as rebellious individuals. Religious conformity, without which Protestantism, a state within a state, would have undermined the stability of the whole, was attained only after many cruelties had been committed and much shrewdness employed. Henri IV had granted an Edict favorable to the Huguenots, because at that time the most dangerous enemy was Spain, a Catholic Power. Louis **1685** XIV revoked it, realizing that the greatest threat would henceforward come from England, a Protestant country. It was essential that no foreigner should ever be in a position to call upon sympathizers and accomplices within the realm.

The territorial unity for which generations of kings had worked was now well on the way to being realized. The great lords, brought to heel by Richelieu, were finally tamed for good and all by Louis XIV. Their function at Versailles was no more than that of inoffensive courtiers. The last islands of alien influence were, one by one, eliminated. France enlarged her frontiers by taking occasional bites out of German-speaking or Flemish-speaking countries in such a way as to increase her own security. By war **1659** Louis XIV appropriated the province of Roussillon, part **1678** of Flanders, Franche-Comté, and Alsace. By peaceful means, as a result of "conversations" which not infrequently ended in the issue of an ultimatum, he annexed Montbéliard and Strasbourg. He bought Dunkirk for five **1681** million francs. His apt pupil, Louis XV, absorbed Lorraine and purchased Corsica from the Genoese. The **1766** shape of France was being rounded out. **1768**

It was not always ambition, the passion for conquest,

that urged the kings thus to enlarge their domains. Far more often it was a desire to give to France those favorable frontiers behind which she could live in peace—the Pyrenees, the Alps, the Jura, the Rhine. The whole foreign policy of France was built on two wise axioms: she must never be called upon to wage simultaneous war on two fronts; she must never allow her neighbors to become too strong.

Spain had for many years based her continental supremacy on her possession of the Low Countries. First, she was driven from Holland by the revolution of the "Scamps," and then from Belgium, as from all the rest of her Burgundian heritage. On the day when the throne of Madrid fell vacant Louis XIV claimed it for his grandson. Rather than not see him safely installed on it, he braved the Austrian Emperor, who wanted the succession for himself, and a coalition of all Europe. The matter was one of prime importance, not less than that of preventing the reconstruction of the Empire of Charles V and breaking the encirclement of France. The war lasted for fifteen years, and cost a great deal of money, but Louis got from it all that he really needed. Austria received the Flemish and Italian heritage; England took Gibraltar, which she wanted as a post of observation. But the grandson of the Roi Soleil reigned in Madrid, and Spain, with her immense American empire, reverted to the Bourbons. "The Pyrenees have ceased to exist," said the *Mercure de France,* if not Louis XIV in person. It is well that we should be quite clear about the extent of the French gain. There was no longer a hostile Spain, no longer any danger of a concerted attack from north and south. Bourbon Spain could be counted upon to act as an ally of France in most of her conflicts, and the Pyrenean frontier would never again be violated.

1713

Meanwhile the whole of the French ring-fence had been strengthened. Vauban had carried out the work of fortification with skill. For a century and a half France was to experience no war on her own soil, and no revolution. The battlefields of Europe would lie elsewhere.

THE WORLD AND FRANCE

Spain, from now on, had to be content with a secondary rôle. The Empire, the old Holy Roman Empire, the control of which the Hapsburgs had always kept in their own hands, was no more than a scatter of principalities. The Treaties of Westphalia, conceived by Richelieu, delivered by Mazarin, and confirmed by all the subsequent treaties made by Louis XIV and Louis XV, had been carefully designed to keep Germany fragmented. Over some three hundred and fifty sovereign states the Emperor had a merely nominal authority. He was the impotent President of a federation of autonomous territories. Within the principalities of Germany philosophers and musicians might dream in peace. So far as that quarter was concerned, France could be easy in her mind, and she remained so until the last days of the monarchy.

1648

True, Austria was still strong, but her strength was dispersed. The rich lands of Flanders, the key position of Europe, and the meeting-point of French, English, and German aspirations, were far away and difficult to defend. Naples had freed herself from Vienna, and was ruled by a Bourbon. There remained, besides the Duchy of Austria, Tuscany, Lombardy, Bohemia, and Hungary. Within this latter France was generous with subsidies, and was careful to foment trouble whenever the opportunity arose.

1735

It soon became apparent that Austria need no longer be feared. A new Power was growing up in Central Europe, a Power whom it would now be necessary to contain. The Prussian star was in the ascendant. The Electors of Brandenburg had built themselves a kingdom from a number of fiefs scattered between Poland and Frisia. It lacked cohesion. It was poor. Its population was small. But in the hearts of its kings the old German lust for war had reawakened. They imposed upon their army a ferocious discipline. Beatings and blows played no small part in its training. They forged it into an instrument of conquest. Frederick II, breaking with the slow-moving tactics of the day, made remarkable use of it. His method was to seek his enemy out and bring him to battle. His favorite ma-

1745 neuver was flank envelopment. He won Silesia from Austria, and patiently nibbled away at Poland. The bare, waterless, melancholy heaths of Prussia were systematically colonized. Peasants were settled on them, where necessary by employing a system of forced transferences of population. Industries were built up. The voice of the new kingdom began to make itself heard in the concert of Europe. France, at least, was fully aware of the growing peril. To Louis XV must go the credit of realizing that Prussia seemed likely to occupy the place formerly held by Austria on the Continent. Logically, therefore, Austria must henceforward be the ally, Prussia the enemy.

Against Prussia, as once against Austria, Poland was the natural associate of France. But she was a liability rather than an asset. Her anarchic constitution, which turned her king into the servant of the Diet and left the country in the hands of the great landowners, made it impossible for her to establish her independence. Her elective throne was a prize for which battles were fought. The Saxon kings, who

1709 won it, were more concerned about Saxony than about Poland. The Prussians, the Austrians, the Russians, did their best to meddle in the affairs of the unfortunate country. They were all of them reckoning on its almost certain extinction. In vain did French philosophers publish *Considérations sur le Royaume de Pologne*. The carnivorous nations were intent on dividing up the prey. Dismembered

1773 Poland saved herself ultimately from Russia only by dint of seeking protection in the arms of Prussia. And those arms crushed the life out of her.

Russia had only just begun to loom over the European horizon. Previously she had been looked upon as an Asiatic

Power, and one that was exclusively rural in character.
Peter I wished to give her some degree of polish. Not only
did he set his face against the wearing of beards and robes;   1699
not only did he reform the calendar, substituting the era of
Christendom for that of Constantinople. He set himself to
bring about a complete renovation of Muscovy. In the
marshes of the Neva he built a new capital called after his   1703
patron, St. Peter. He made the Tsars the spiritual as well
as the political heads of the nation. He disciplined his
army after the German fashion, began the creation of a
fleet on the Dutch model, and completely overhauled the
fiscal system. He founded universities, libraries, observa-
tories. But the old savage Adam sometimes looked through
the mask of the civilized gentleman. He had his brother-in-
law beheaded and his own son condemned to death. With
his own hand, at a banquet, he cut off a number of heads.
Though a man of gigantic stature, he was not unlike Alexander of Macedon, a mixture of the brute and the genius.

After his death Catherine II carried on the work he had
begun. She was a woman of strong passions. She gave to
Russia an autocratic and bureaucratic administration,
which made of that vast and primitive country a piece of
complicated machinery. She had to face revolts among the
Cossacks and the serfs, both of which she repressed with
much bloodshed. Russia was still, as it had always been, a   1774
nation of slaves. Almost all the inhabitants were peasants,
and almost all the peasants the personal property of the
great lords, the monasteries, or the churches. But it had
now become a huge and overgrown empire. Peter the Great
had presented it with Riga. Catherine founded Odessa.
The Tsars reigned from the Baltic to the Pacific, from the
White Sea to the Black. They dreamed of Byzantium.

To resist it adequately Poland was no longer, Prussia not
yet, sufficiently strong. But two traditional allies of France,
Sweden and Turkey, had their eyes firmly fixed upon it.
Sweden, stretching from Bremen to Stralsund, was well
placed to play an important part in history—too important

a part, maybe, seeing that her king, Charles XII, lacked
the means to carry out his daring schemes. This monarch's
thirst for glory—he loved war as passionately as he loved
hunting—lost him the control of the Baltic and the posses-
1715   sion of a number of German cities. In the hands of sovereigns whom a weak constitution had stripped of all real
1719   power Sweden declined. Civil strife broke out between the
pro-Russian and the pro-French factions, between the
"Bonnets" and the "Hats." But Gustavus III put an end to
this anarchic state of affairs, restored the royal authority,
and reorganized the army. He served France as a loyal
1772   ally in the north.

In the south Turkey set herself to resist all Russian attempts at expansion. She was no longer that nomad empire whose appearance in the Levant had set the Christian
world trembling. She had grown sage, urbanized, and effeminate. She was well on the road to decadence. Turkish
motifs furnished the setting for the ballets in *Le Bourgeois*
1683   *Gentilhomme*. But though, generally, the Turks might be
treated as a joke they were still capable of action. They
laid siege to Vienna and abandoned it only after a coalition had taken the field against them. It was in celebra-
1687   tion of this defeat that bakers first produced "crescents."
Austria stripped them of Hungary and Transylvania; Venice of Dalmatia and the Morea; Russia, first of Azov, then
of the Crimea. The Greeks were undermining the Turkish
power from within. The spirit of its enterprise was broken.

Farther to the east Persia lay in a condition of apathy.
She very nearly succumbed to an attack from Afghanistan,
1710   and was being subjected to growing Russian pressure on
1723   the shores of the Caspian. She was finally torn to pieces
by internal discontents.

India, on the other hand, was prospering. After a succession of Court intrigues the Empire of Akbar devolved on
Aurangzeb, who resembled Louis XIV in magnificence,
1690   Genghis Khan in cruelty. This bloodthirsty conqueror
made himself master of Tibet, of the Deccan, and of the

kingdom of Golconda, which enjoyed a fabulous reputation for wealth. He pillaged and slaughtered. But he could also govern. During his reign Indo-Persian art reached its highest point. Delhi rivaled Versailles. Aurangzeb was tolerant. He admitted Christians into his realm, granted Pondicherry to the French, and confirmed the rights which the English had acquired in Madras and Bombay. Little did he realize that his imprudence had let the wolf into the fold! His successors, incapable of resisting the local nabobs, were still less suited to put up any sort of effective defense against the greedy Westerners, in whose eyes India was the paradise of big business. The European trading companies multiplied the number of their "factories," and were in violent competition with one another. The "Ile de France" and the "Ile Bourbon," afterwards renamed Mauritius and Réunion, were French steppingstones on the way to Chandernagore. The Cape and Ceylon similarly served the Dutch. The English were in Calcutta. India was the stake, and even the battleground, of Western ambitions.

China at least escaped the attentions of the greedy. Not that they had forgotten her, but the Manchu emperors had made her strong enough to stave off foreign outrage. They even extended their domain over Central Asia, from Mongolia to Nepal, and went so far as to impose their suzerainty on the Annamites, who were masters in Indo-China. Meanwhile the Dane, Behring, in the service of Russia,   1725 discovered Kamchatka and the sea which separates the north of Asia from the north of America. The Russians established themselves in the Kurile Islands. Europe was stretching her tentacles widely.

Japan remained impenetrable.

ENGLAND, MOTHER OF COALITIONS

Of all these countries, near or far, none was in a position to dispute the leadership of France. But one nation

there was which did not fear to challenge her. England
might be small, but her voice was loud, and the whole
history of this period is filled with the coalitions which she
set on foot in Europe, and by the battles which she waged
at sea with the object of bringing down the power of
France.

It might seem at first sight that the project was beyond
her capacity. England was still an agricultural country
with a small population and a small army. Not seldom her
representative institutions stood in the way of her political
ambitions. Even her dynasty was not firmly established or
secure. After the Cromwells, father and son, had come
the Stuarts, who were financed by Louis XIV and supported by the Tories. These were followed by William of
Orange, who was backed by the Whigs, and, finally, by
the Hanoverians, who oscillated between the two parties.
Her unity was far from complete. Catholic Ireland was no
better than a colony in a constant state of rebellion, to
which, finally, London had to grant an independent Parliament. Scotland, even after the Act of Union which
changed the name of the island kingdom from England to
Great Britain, fought for the Stuart pretenders against the
Hanoverians.

But England was mistress of the seas. Her commerce
had outdistanced, first, that of Spain, then, that of Holland. The French, too much occupied on the Continent,
could put up no effective opposition to the English in their
chosen element. Besides, they were not natural sailors.
The ambition of French fathers of families has always
been to buy for their sons employments of profit. Englishmen preferred to send their children to sea or to the colonies. The British flag, properly protected, moved freely
everywhere. From the moment that England captured the
monopoly of the slave trade from the Spanish settlers her
economic victory was assured. London, Bristol, South-
ampton, and Plymouth flooded black Africa with hardware,
glass beads, and alcohol. The same ships which carried

these goods sailed back from Africa loaded with "Ebony," which they bartered in America for the sugar, the rum, the tobacco, and the cotton of the New World. In the sixty years that followed the death of Louis XIV English trade trebled in value. But, since exports were always in excess of imports, England grew rich. The Bank of England, in spite of an early sequence of crises, became a model for the whole world.

It was not only because of her fleet that England was mistress of the seas, but also because of the various vantage-points which she had succeeded in acquiring at the intersections of all the great maritime routes. From Gibraltar and Minorca she could keep an eye on the Mediterranean. By entering into an alliance with Denmark she was in a position to guard the approaches to the Baltic. She obtained a monopoly of trade in the Arctic, and supplied Russia through Archangel. She held scattered posts all over the Atlantic, secure in the loyal support of Portugal, who sold her wine in exchange for wool.

England's most valuable auxiliary was Holland. From the moment William of Orange united the two nations in his person it became obvious that war between England 1688 and France for supremacy would have to be fought out to its bitter end. It was to be a new Hundred Years' War. It lasted, in fact, for even longer. From battle to battle it went on, from truce to truce, until it ended on the field of Waterloo.

What France lost at La Hogue was not so much a fleet as her taste for seafaring. She never again launched better battle squadrons than those given her by Colbert. Only 1690 her privateers carried on the naval struggle with some degree of success, and more than once gave the English a rough handling. Duguay-Trouin even succeeded in carrying 1711 out an astonishing raid on Rio de Janeiro.

On land France kept the Powers of Europe at a respectful distance, and broke up more than one coalition. But London succeeded in putting the pieces together again.

Religion had ceased to play any part in the wars of the
Continent. Catholic France was as ready to join hands with
the Protestants of Sweden or Germany as with Islam. Nor
was the issue one of political ideology. Louis XIV supported the Dutch Republicans against the house of Orange.
What, fundamentally, was at stake was the hegemony of
Europe. London, traditionally hostile to the strongest nation across the Channel, sought to re-establish the balance
of power by setting the countries of Europe by the ears.
Since the greatest threat came from France, it was against
France that England roused all the countries she could
manage to seduce. Diplomacy or corruption, all was grist
to her mill. Anything was good enough to furnish a *casus
belli,* beginning with the question of succession to the
thrones of Spain, Poland, and Austria. France was sometimes beaten, but never crushed. The armies of this period,
recruited and paid with much difficulty, and often supple-
mented with foreign mercenaries, never exceeded two hundred thousand men. Financial considerations made it impossible to mobilize whole nations. Owing to the tactics
employed, success could never be fully exploited. Fear of
desertion led generals to keep their men in as compact
masses as possible. They would not risk the pursuit of a
defeated enemy, and never embarked upon a winter campaign. For these reasons wars were apt to drag on without
ever being brought to a definite conclusion. Treaties of
peace were signed as a result of weariness.

In the colonies, however, England took a number of
guarantees which she would not willingly abandon. One
1713 of her constant causes of nervousness was the possibility
that the French of the St. Lawrence might join hands with
their countrymen at the mouth of the Mississippi and overrun her American settlements. Louis XIV had to hand over
1763 to her Newfoundland, Nova Scotia, and Hudson Bay.
Louis XV gave her a free hand in India and in that part
of Canada which had been civilized with such pains and
was so dear to French sentiment. The Spaniards, in alliance

with France, had, similarly, to surrender Florida to the English. It began to look as though North America would become entirely British.

Despite her successes, England could not really shake the preponderance of France. Her greatest advances were made in the fields of economics and politics. In the realm of intellect she had, no doubt, men of genius. Newton completed and corrected the work of Descartes. Locke prepared the way for Rousseau. The Royal Society of London came into existence before the Académie des Sciences. English freemasonry spawned all over the Continent. But these successes were not enough to disturb the supremacy of French thought. Even in matters of intellectual speculation the English were always English, whereas the French spoke and thought for the whole human race. France of the seventeenth century sang the praises of reason. France of the eighteenth century extolled the glories of sentiment. England was less concerned with ideas than with material conquests. That is why, in the end, she won the day. Her national egotism got the better of the altruism of a France who never identified her culture with her nationalism.

GOLD IS STILL KING

The economic battle went hand in hand with the political. As formerly, as always, gold enjoyed a prestige in the world which nothing else could equal. At that period it was still believed that wealth consisted in the amassing of yellow metal. It was important, therefore, to have more of it than anybody else.

Colbert formulated a doctrine of pure and unadulterated mercantilism. His whole policy was directed to attracting gold into the country, and preventing it from going out again. In order to carry out this plan it was necessary to sell and, consequently, to produce. Industry was encouraged, manufactures created, canals dug: one such, a triumph of technical accomplishment, was designed to link the Atlantic with the Mediterranean. Regular road services were instituted, bonuses were given to naval dockyards, types and standards of textiles were regulated. It was made easy for commercial enterprises to get loans and fiscal adjustments. Colbert fully realized the limits of State intervention. He showed trade the way it ought to go, but put no obstacles in the path of private initiative. This was the great period of French economic life.

To keep gold from leaving the country the level of imports had to be kept below that of exports, and this was done by checking the inward flow of foreign goods by means of a customs tariff. But the foreigners followed suit, and a tariff war ensued. Holland levied a surtax on French luxury goods, and prohibited the importation of brandy from France. France retaliated against herrings and Dutch textiles. The affair created a *casus belli*.

France nevertheless grew rich. Her ports prospered. Her cloth finally displaced that of Holland and England. The full flow of business was, however, impeded by the multiplicity of her internal tolls, and by the diversity of her weights and measures, an outworn relic of ancient local tradition. The circulation of money, too, was made difficult because France lacked adequate supplies of currency. How was this state of affairs to be remedied? Russia had tried, without success, to substitute copper for silver. Might not paper money be used to make up the deficiency in metal coinage? Following examples once set in China and in Persia, a number of bankers in the northern countries had experimented in this direction. The Bank of England was issuing notes. France, taking advantage of the reform in her monetary system, took, if rather timidly, the plunge.

Gradually she grew more daring. A Scotsman named Law had a wonderful scheme to offer which would turn all this paper into wealth and power. Paris went wild with enthusiasm. There was an enormous run on banknotes, and these were used by their possessors to buy shares in the

1716

marvelous Mississippi Company. Everyone started to speculate. Inflation set in. The heady wine of gambling achieved 1720 miracles. But then came disappointment. Enthusiasm turned to panic. The system collapsed.

But Paris had set an example. In Amsterdam and London shares in a variety of colonial companies were eagerly bought up. So great became the abuse of credit that it 1720 almost died of the treatment. A revival, however, set in. Very slowly men began to realize the true virtues of investment. The financiers had a clear road.

Gold was still king, but with the coming of paper there were other things to dazzle men's eyes. Certain French economists laid it down that land was the only real source 1755 of wealth. In England Adam Smith was teaching that only 1775 by working can nations grow great. In the dusk of a setting mercantilism the liberal star was shining.

The passion for voyages and discovery revived, now that octants and sextants were in common use. Thanks to these instruments, it was now possible to calculate degrees of latitude, while the improvement of marine chronometers enabled sailors to reckon longitude as well. The English, great readers of *Gulliver* and *Robinson Crusoe,* plowed the South Seas. Cook visited New Zealand and Australia. The 1770 French too sailed their great carved vessels into unknown seas. Bougainville reached Tahiti. La Pérouse disappeared in Polynesia.

In the New World a group of Franciscans had carried Spanish colonization to the shores of the Pacific, and built a village which was to grow into San Francisco. But it was still French pioneers who opened the great land routes. 1673 Father Marquette had sailed down the Mississippi, and Cavalier de la Salle had explored its mouths. The names 1682 "Louisiana" (rich with echoes of Louis XIV), and "Nouvelle Orléans" (with its memories of the Regent) brought to America the very vocables of France.

THE CLASSIC AGE

Louis XIV, Louis XV—the words designate styles and centuries even more than kings. To say so is not mere flattery, for Versailles, in very truth, ushered in the Classic Age.

Le Roi Soleil loved order and symmetry. He inspired Mansart and Lenôtre and the parks and palaces designed by them. His influence is to be traced no less in the solidity of Le Brun, in the coldness of Boileau, in the stateliness of Bossuet, and in the rigorous architecture of Racine. He was Reason crowned and throned. Conscious of the grandeur of the Ancient World, he sought to revive it. Conscious of his own grandeur, he had his praises sung and the magnificence of his reign extolled in marble and in verse. He did not limit his trade of kingship to the administration of public affairs, but saw that it should play its part in the great spectacle of intellectual activity. He gave his patronage to the Académie Française, which codified the language, to the Académie des Sciences and the Académies des Beaux Arts. He imposed Molière on French taste. With the same lofty pride which claimed to settle the affairs of Europe, pointing to himself as the protector of the Hungarians, the peacemaker between Sweden and Denmark, the man who alone could master the Pope or the Doge of Genoa, and distributing his subsidies among the German princelings, he dictated standards to the Court of France, which, in turn, dictated fashions to all the Courts of the world.

Louis XIV might die—but not his prestige. The Classic Age continued, if by classic we understand a striving after perfection. It was still from Paris and Versailles that orders were issued to the forces of art and letters. The architecture of Gabriel recaptured something of Greek purity—with a French complexion. Under Louis XIV and Louis

XV the makers of furniture produced their masterpieces. The century was lacking in poets, but it had Watteau.

It was the Age of Philosophers. Is it true to say that there was divorce between the Court and the world of letters? Saint-Simon, that embittered champion of the feudal idea, represented at once Versailles and anti-Versailles. Fénelon, the forerunner of much Utopianism, was tutor to the Dauphin. The Regent, eager for popularity, played at liberalism. Choiseul expelled the Jesuits. Voltaire might be occasionally imprisoned, but, for all that, he was the King's historiographer. Rousseau was invited to Court. The *Encyclopaedia* found admirers among members of the Government. Louis XVI was a freemason.

It was also the Age of Scientific Marvels. Descartes invented analytical geometry; Fermat, the differential calculus. Pascal established the groundwork for a calculation of probability. Following on the heels of Newton and Leibnitz, who devised the infinitesimal calculus, Lagrange and Legendre developed mathematics into a marvelously efficient tool.

The applied sciences benefited from these various discoveries. Descartes had explained the mechanism of the celestial bodies by a theory of vortices. Newton successfully countered him with his Law of Universal Attraction. The French astronomers verified his findings. In physics, Pascal checked Torricelli, and Mariotte completed the work of Boyle. In biology Linnaeus got on the track of the transformation of species. La Condamine revealed the existence 1736 of the rubber-tree. The chemists discovered cobalt, nickel, platinum, manganese, hydrogen, oxygen, nitrogen, and chlorine. Lavoisier was the father of modern chemistry.

The world learned with amazement of unsuspected forces. Denis Papin foresaw in steam vapor a new motive-power, which was developed by the Scotsman Watt. Cugnot 1698 constructed the first steam car, the Marquis de Jouffroy 1769 the first steamship. The conquest of the air was exclusively 1776 a French affair. Montgolfier got the first hot-air balloon

off the ground, and Charles produced the first practical
1783 balloon filled with hydrogen. Pilâtre de Rozier was the
first man to leave the ground. Blanchard, together with
1785 the Englishman Jeffries, made the first aerial journey over
the Pas de Calais.

Another of the many marvels was electricity. At first, it
was no more than a curiosity, in Court and city alike.
Watching the discharges of Leyden jars became a favorite
1749 amusement. But Franklin conceived the idea of the lightning conductor, which was tried out in France on the
advice of Buffon. Romas, a new Prometheus, made a kite
1753 with which to accumulate electricity from the air.

A German charlatan called Mesmer claimed to be able
to cure illness by means of magnetism. Paris, where reputa-
tions are made or lost, crowded round his magic tub. A
Sicilian adventurer, Cagliostro, became the rage of the
capital. He claimed the power to call up spirits. People
became as much excited about the bogus as about the true.
Sects of credulous adepts frequented the magnetizers. Thus
not only did advances in the sciences and in their practical
application seem to prove the Progress (with a capital P)
lauded by philosophers, but they drew after them all the
mounting idiocy of the human race. The decline of Christianity appeared to be moving hand in hand with a riot
of superstitions masquerading under the name of science.

Such was the atmosphere of the last years of the French
monarchy. Montgolfier balloons and the study of electrical
phenomena seemed, in their own way, to be the prelude
to a new world for all mankind.

THE INFLUENCE OF FRANCE

Centuries of France; centuries of a Gallicized Europe.
By her intellectual vitality and by her language Paris ruled
the world. Ideas were circulating more effectively now,
and more quickly than in past ages. Men of letters and
scholars were corresponding with one another across the

frontiers. Without wishing to, and even against the grain, Louis XIV found that he was sending abroad some two hundred thousand ambassadors, all representative of the French way of life. For such were the Protestants who fled from repression. They settled in Switzerland, in Prussia, in England, and in Holland. They wandered as far afield as Boston, Charleston and the Cape. By their departure France lost subjects, but she made up for her deprivation in acquired influence.

But even without this emigration the example of France would have prevailed both in the high reaches of science and in the world of ephemeral fashion. From Sweden to Portugal, by way of Russia, Prussia, and Austria, the despots were learning the lessons of the new enlightenment. All the Courts of Europe wanted to dress in the French mode, cook like the French, dance the minuet and the gavotte as they were danced at Versailles. The meridian of Paris had dethroned that of Cape Verde. In England and in Holland type-faces on the Latin—that is to say, the French—model were superseding the Gothic. London, Leipzig, Amsterdam, aped the *Journal des Savants*. Everywhere gardens were being designed in accordance with French taste. For better or for worse, foreign princes were reproducing Versailles in miniature for their own use. The French style was everywhere being copied, ranging according to the whims of the French sovereigns, from Louis XIV to Louis XVI, over many varieties from the solemn to the gay.

England, though hostile, could not escape the prevailing infection. The monarchy of the Stuarts imitated that of the Bourbons. The theaters of London produced plays by French authors. The historian Gibbon wrote in French; the Minister Walpole corresponded in French. Even in wartime many Englishmen traveled in France.

In Sweden the Chancellor, De la Gardie, was French by extraction. Descartes was summoned to Stockholm, where he ended his days. Gustavus III read Voltaire and frequented the salon of Mme. du Deffand. He created a Swedish Academy on the French model.

In Denmark the Minister Griffenfeld wrote French fluently. The King, Christian V, invited French artists to Copenhagen. The works of the dramatist Holberg are studded with Gallicisms.

The culture of Frederick II's Prussia was wholly French. The Frenchman De Launay reorganized his finances. French manners and French gallantry were all the rage at Sans-Souci and Potsdam, where reproductions of Marly and of the statues of Pigalle were to be found. Frederick himself had a passion for all things French. He could scarcely speak German. He refused even to take notice of the young Goethe. It was in French that he sent his orders to his generals and his ministers. He wrote verses in French. He imposed the French language on the Academy of Berlin, and made the scholar Maupertuis its President. He corresponded with Voltaire, and invited him, with d'Alembert, Diderot, and Rousseau, to visit him.

All the Courts of Germany were minor French colonies. Dresden imitated Paris. Leibnitz wrote in French. Lessing, though he liked to be thought restive under French influence, submitted to it entirely. In Vienna Francis of Lorraine, who had married the Empress Maria Theresa, transplanted French customs. Their son, Joesph II, adored Paris. He too wrote to his generals in French. The whole Court of Austria spoke French.

In Poland two queens, Maria de Gonzaga and Maria d'Arquien, introduced the modes and manners of Versailles into Court circles. Louis XIV even dreamed for a moment of founding a French dynasty in Poland. The Lesczinskis and the Bourbons were blood relations. When Stanislaus Poniatowski was elected to the Polish throne he wrote to Mme. Geoffrin: "Mamma, your son is king." This monarch, the elected choice of Russia and Prussia, spoke almost nothing but French.

Russia came late under French influence, because she

was a latecomer to Europe. But she made up for lost time. Peter the Great took a citizen of Geneva, Lefèvre, to be his counselor, and got a French architect to draw up plans for St. Petersburg. When he visited Paris and was shown the city by a son of Jean Bart, he embraced the statue of Richelieu. He modeled his system of taxation on that of France. Catherine II employed Falconet to design a bronze statue in memory of the reforming Tsar. Though she was German by birth, she corresponded with Voltaire and Buffon, read Bayle and Montesquieu, received Diderot at her Court, invited d'Alembert to superintend the education of the Grand Duke, and wrote bad plays in good French. At Petersburg the French theater became a State institution.

France was everywhere—even in the Turkish Empire, where the Comte de Bonneval reorganized the artillery, and where French influences were powerful, notably at Constantinople, Cairo, and Smyrna; even in China, where Père Gerbillon acted as tutor, doctor, and adviser to the Emperor; even in India, where all Westerners were known as "Franguis," as, once, in the Levant they had been called "Franks"; even in Spanish America, where echoes of the *Encyclopaedia* were to be heard.

From all countries visitors flocked to Paris to absorb knowledge, to learn good manners and good speech. The children of the Royal House of Denmark went there to complete their education. Aristocrats from Sweden took service in the Regiment of Royal Suédois. Foreign men of learning were invited there. The Dutchman Huyghens introduced his pendulum clocks into the city, and dedicated a work to Louis XIV. Cassini of Nice organized the Observatory; Roemer, the Dane, worked there at determining the speed of light. Franklin lived at Passy. Volta worked in Paris with Lavoisier and Laplace.

1676

Music felt the influence of France less than did pure learning. Opera was born in Italy, and the great composers—Bach and Beethoven—were either German or

Austrian. Nevertheless even in this field France had a part to play and a style to impose, from Couperin to Rameau. Lulli lived at the Court of Louis XIV, Mozart visited Louis XV.

In short, the fame of Paris haunted all the capitals of Europe, as the example of Louis XIV haunted all its sovereigns. They, like him, wanted to be called "The Great"— Peter the Great, Frederick the Great, Catherine the Great. Not one of all these "Greatnesses" but was an imitator of the Roi Soleil.

THE TRIUMPH OF THE
FRENCH LANGUAGE

It is not enough to say that the language of Racine and Voltaire, of Colbert and Choiseul, was, outside France, the favorite of Courts and of the circles of the élite. In many cases it supplanted foreign languages altogether, and it influenced all of them permanently. Even when the prestige of France began to decline the speech of all the great peoples of the world remained impregnated with French expressions and French turns of phrase.

Almost everywhere in Europe in the seventeenth and eighteenth centuries it became the fashion to mix with the native speech words imported from France. Conversation and books were streaked with them, and these borrowings, becoming naturalized, garnished every vocabulary.

The English acquired the habit of saying *à la mode, apropos, badinage, gallery, bas-relief*. They adopted the term *civilization*, which was more or less of a newcomer.

The Dutch said: *theater, republikein, soevereiniteit, general, admiraal*.

The Germans said: *blond* and *brunett, Mode, Dame, Delikatesse, Toilett;* also, *Armee, Marschall, Marine, Kavallerie, Politik;* even *Konzert, Romanze, Melodie*.

The Danes said: *papier, komedi, melancoli.* The Swedes, *adjo, byra* ("bureau"), *etikett, parfym, toilett.*

The Russians had many French importations—*kourtisany, tseremonia, equipage, soldaty, batailly.*

The Hungarians said, *ombrelle, alamode, billet, artillerie.*

The Italians said, *tolette;* the Spaniards, *libertinage* and *etiquetta;* the Portuguese, *dessert* and *belas letras.*

All used the term *fricandeau.*

These are but a few examples among thousands. There was a regular invasion of Gallicisms. They cropped up in the language of the kitchen, in the language of the army, in the language of gallantry, in the language of politics.

But the real triumph of the French tongue lay elsewhere. It won the day over what had hitherto been the universal language used formerly by all the men of letters or of science, and by all diplomats. By substituting French for Latin, which itself had been substituted for Greek, Paris conquered Rome and avenged Athens.

Latin, though a dead language, had taken its time in dying. The Church clung to it obstinately. For centuries it had remained the language of the Law and the universities. It had held pride of place over every form of national speech. It was the international tongue. But it found great difficulty in adapting itself to modern conditions. How could it possibly stand out against the youthful vigor of French?

Diplomatic usage set the seal on the victory of French. The Treaties of Nymegen and Utrecht had been drafted in Latin. But the reign of Louis XIV ended with a linguistic victory. It was in French that the Treaty of Rastadt was **1714** drawn up, when Austria recognized the cession of Strasbourg.

From then on, *de facto* if not *de jure,* French became progressively the language of international courtesies. It was in French that England and Russia concluded their pact of alliance. It was French that provided a medium of communication between Hungary and Poland, Prussia and Sweden, the Two Sicilies and Turkey. All treaties of peace, all commercial agreements, were in French. When England wished to announce to the Diet of the Empire that a new king had come to the throne it was in French that she did so. When the ambassador of the Tsar had audience of the Sultan he addressed him in French. When Catherine II gave notice to the world of the treaty which established Russia on the shores of the Black Sea she used French.

"What is it that has made French the universal language of Europe?" It was the Academy of Berlin that proposed **1782** this question for competitive debate. Rivarol, who carried off one of the prizes, gave only a partial answer when he extolled the "admirable clarity" of the French language. Other answers are that it is more accurate and richer. The triumph was that of France herself even more than that of her tongue, of Louis XIV even more than of Voltaire, the incomparable Voltaire. The French language became universal only because France was, or had been, the greatest Power in the whole world.

Contrary to appearances, France was not in her decline during the last years of the monarchy. She was still the most highly populated country of Europe, with her twenty-five million inhabitants. Austria came next with twenty-two, then Russia with eighteen, Poland, with eleven, Spain with ten, England with nine, Naples with six, Prussia with five, Sardinia with three, Sweden with two. Paris was the third largest city of Europe, ranking after London and Constantinople. But no European state outside France had three cities of more than a hundred thousand each— Paris, Marseilles, and Lyon. Russia had only two—Moscow and Petersburg; Austria two also—Vienna and Milan; Spain two—Madrid and Barcelona. England had only London, the Low Countries only Amsterdam, Prussia only Berlin, the Pope only Rome, Venice only Venice.

At this same moment of history the foreign trade of France, then at its highest point, far exceeded that of

Great Britain. The French Empire produced, in San Domingo, more sugar than the whole of the rest of the world (Bordeaux was now the chief refinery of Europe); France was, too, the largest grower of wheat. That fact was not without its importance. France was the most thickly populated and the most productive of all countries. Her language had the widest currency and was the best beloved of all verbal means of communication.

And, at the same moment of history, France won a great battle. With the coming of the American Revolution she dealt a shrewd blow at her enemy across the Channel.

THE AMERICAN REVOLUTION

After the loss of Canada the French possessions in America were reduced to two islets off the coast of Newfoundland and the rich sugar islands of the Antilles. England ruled from the St. Lawrence to Florida. Beyond the Mississippi began the empire of Spain.

The old English colonies of the Atlantic seaboard had increased in size as a result of immigration. They offered a home to men who came to trade in furs, to clear the forests, to cultivate the soil. Their population had now reached the three-million figure. So long as they had feared the possibility of French envelopment from Canada and Louisiana they had remained loyal to the motherland. But that particular danger had disappeared and the American colonials began to realize their own strength.

For them liberty was an old love. Not seldom it had been to safeguard their religious liberty that they had fled from Europe. The teachings of the French philosophers had found in them a promising soil, and in Franklin a responsive voice. It was well that London should be on her guard!

The British Parliament piled tactlessness on tactlessness. Hard pressed for money, it claimed the right to levy taxes on the Americans without consulting them. The colonials   1767

reacted violently, and Choiseul poured oil on the flames.
London at first withdrew, and then returned to the charge.
1774 The Americans struck back. They refused to buy English
goods. The English retaliated. American ships were seized
1775 on the high seas. This led to armed rebellion. The Congress
of Philadelphia proclaimed the Union of the American
1776 States and their independence.

"All men are created equal," announced Jefferson in the
Declaration of Independence. But what equality of strength
could there be between mighty England and the infant nation of America? The United States had neither an army
nor credit. They improvised a paper currency which rapidly
collapsed. They mobilized a militia which with difficulty
1776 put up a fight. In spite of General Washington the English
appeared in New York.

The only country on which the Americans could rely
for help was France. From her alone could the United
States hope to receive financial and military aid. The writer
Beaumarchais, a man who lived by his wits, turned his
hand to selling guns. The Marquis de Lafayette came forward with the offer of his sword. The Comte de Rocham-
1780 beau sailed with a small army.

It was greatly to the interest of France to seize this opportunity of revenging herself upon England. Her navy had
been reorganized by Suffren, de Frasse, Borda, and La
Motte-Picquet. Her military schools were the finest in
Europe. Her artillery was better than that of any foreign
army.

Spain, at first hesitant, joined France. The neutrals had
little love for the "Tyrant of the Seas." The English, already held in check by the Americans unaided, reeled
1781 under the blows of the coalition. In the Mediterranean
French and Spanish forces took Minorca. In the New
World French and Americans were victorious at York-
town. In London the Whigs were ready to negotiate. They
bought peace at a price.

The Treaty of Versailles restored Minorca and Florida

to Spain, five factories in India, together with Senegal, to   1783
France. It recognized the independence of the United
States.

From then on free America had leisure to grow, geographically, by pushing westward; politically, with the slow   1787
elaboration of her Constitution. Her first President was   1789
Washington, who, on the banks of the Potomac, built the
Federal capital according to plans supplied by a French   1791
architect, and on lines reminiscent of Versailles.

Republican America was not strictly democratic. For
the rule of the English King she had substituted the rule
of the great landed proprietors. In this way she smoothed
the road for the triumphal advance of plutocracy.

But her example gave the illusion of freedom. Spanish
America caught the contagion, and in a short while
achieved her own liberation. So did France, where the
word "liberty" sounded enchantment in the ears of her
people. The French King had sought to weaken England,
and in doing so had weakened himself. By supporting the
cause of the Rights of Man in the New World he had prepared his own fate. His country, by running into debt in
order to continue the American war, had now a financial
deficit which precipitated a crisis. By striking at England
France had incited the English to undertake reprisals.
Paris had helped the American Revolution; London replied by supporting the French variety.

THE FRENCH REVOLUTION

The Revolution in France was the logical outcome of
events. The moment that the monarchy showed itself to be
incapable of defending itself its day was ended. Louis XV,
who might have done much to check the rising revolutionary movement, actually provided fuel for the fire. French
opinion in the old days had been ready enough to accept
the amorous exploits of Henri IV, together with his other
characteristics. The notorious infidelities of the "Well-be-

loved" struck at his popularity. The French had grown a
critical sense. The age of Voltaire lay between the two
monarchs.

Louis XV had foreseen the inevitable coming of catastrophe. His "After me, the deluge!" was no cry of irrespon-
sible egotism, but the melancholy voicing of a lucid vision.
When the deluge did come Louis XVI was incapable of
building a dike to hold it back. That well-meaning prince,
who would have made a good artisan or a decent, peace-
loving bourgeois, could neither lead an army nor charm a
nation. He was already on the side of the philosophers.
Why should he not yield to those of whose principles he
approved?

Thus it came about that a king of liberal intentions paid
for the sins of his despotic ancestors. He recalled the Parliaments. He put Turgot in power. He signed a trade agreement with England. But all things conspired against him.
The Parliaments were opposed to reforms of any kind.
Turgot found that he had against him a coalition of the
privileged. The English treaty increased unemployment,
and a bad harvest led to a shortage of bread. The King
called the Notables together, but they rejected proposals
which by balancing the budget might have saved the
régime. He assembled the States-General. They turned
what had been a financial problem into one of politics, and
the Assembly which emerged from their meetings usurped
the duty of giving France a constitution.

The traditional monarchy was attacked from all sides—
by the nobles, who thought that they had been given an opportunity of raising their heads, only to find, not infrequently, that they were to lose them; by the financiers, who
hoped that the new movement would be favorable to speculation; by the members of the middle class, hungry to play
their part in government; by the wage-earners, who had
seen purchasing-power diminish as the century advanced;
by the philosophers, who dreamed of an enlightened despotism—with themselves as the authors of enlightenment!—

1786

1787

1789

and by the foreign agents, who worked with British gold
and under cover of the secret societies. The King committed the unforgivable sin of being insufficiently a king;
while the Queen was too much a queen. The public, conventional even in its hatreds, reproached her for being an
Austrian princess, quite forgetting that Austria was no   1793
longer the enemy of France, but her natural ally. The two
sovereigns were found guilty of the crime of negotiating
with Vienna, and lost their heads. The Sans-culottes of
France wanted to show that they were every bit as good
as the Roundheads of England. Louis XVI on the scaffold
reminded them of Charles I.

From Assembly to Assembly, from constitution to constitution, the Revolution trundled downhill at once grandiose and tragic. It was grandiose not only because it had
swept away a number of outmoded privileges, because it
had brewed a heady mixture of generous ideas, because it
had given birth to a young society, but because, too, it had
the sense of its own drama. From the taking of the Bastille
to the Feast of the Supreme Being it carefully tended its
own legend, gave to its play-acting the color of nobility,
and saw riots as epics and corrupt adventurers as great
men. It was tragic, superbly tragic, as soon as it began to
adopt a policy of wholesale slaughter, massacring the Sep-
tember prisoners, guillotining the suspects. There were
drownings at Nantes, shootings at Lyon, burnings in
Vendée. There was a scaffold in Paris. Lavoisier was exe-   1794
cuted; so was Chénier—for the crime of moderation. In
the course of a few years the Revolution succeeded in
turning a people which had long been faithful to its kings
into a people of savage republicans.

How can this extraordinary fact be explained? Was it
due to Marat's articles or Robespierre's speeches? Was it
caused by a sudden passion for the Rights of Man? Hardly.
The Liberty of Year II was a poor substitute for the liberties of the régime which had passed away. Gone was the
citizens' right to sell freely or to produce freely. Maximum

prices were fixed, but the black market laughed at maximum prices. Less than ever had men now the right to think freely, if the freedom of their thoughts did not happen to coincide with the freedom preached by the Jacobins. Catholics had lost even the right to worship freely. Equality is not of this world, and the distance between rich and poor remained unabridged. Indeed, there were some rich men behind the scenes who played a more important rôle than they had done previously, while, owing to the Assignats, the poor were poorer than ever. As to fraternity—it was born in blood.

If the Republic remained unshaken the reason was that the French now had need of it—those who had bought the property of the clergy and the émigrés with valueless paper, in order to be sure of retaining what they had got; the country at large, that the foreign conquests of the Revolution might be secured.

1792   The new France had done no less than declare war on Europe. It was her duty, she felt, to help all peoples in their struggles to shake off the yoke of tyranny. She achieved a miracle, in that she conducted a successful war. But was it really a miracle? France was still the most highly populated of all the countries of the Continent. The artillery bequeathed by the old régime had not ceased to be the Queen of Battles. The cadres formed by the military schools of the monarchy produced a whole series of brilliant generals—Lafayette, Dumouriez, Kellerman, Carnot, Kléber, Des Aix (who changed his name to Desaix), Macdonald, and many others. All these men had served in the King's armies. Bonaparte had the same background.

1793   To all this the Republic contributed (i) numbers, (ii) enthusiasm. Numbers it got by means of the *levée en masse,* which now took the place of the old system of service for pay. Gone were the small regular armies—those happy hunting-grounds of aristocrats and recruiting sergeants. From now on death on the battlefield had ceased to be the privilege of the few and was the glorious destiny of all. The Republic raised a million men—and more. For the first time in history great armies of the modern type appeared upon the scene.

The enthusiasm which animated this armed force was the product of patriotic ardor. It really did seem as though the country were filled from end to end with a new crusading spirit. The oppressed of Europe must be liberated! Unfortunately the gift of freedom was not always appreciated. The new oppression of the liberators made many regret that other oppression which had brought it upon them.

There was no unbroken sequence of victories. Fortune fluctuated. At first France had, more than once, to face invasion—a misery she had not known for a hundred and fifty years. Even later, when the Revolution had grown drunk on the intoxicating draughts of Jemmapes and Valmy, of Fleurus and Wattignies, the Great Powers found compensation elsewhere.

The foreign kings saw in the Revolution not so much a threat to their own thrones as an opportunity for making easy acquisitions. France had too much on her hands to stop them. She might decapitate Louis XVI, but Prussia 1793 and Russia decapitated Poland, whose territories they parceled out between them and Austria. Meanwhile the Rus- 1795 sians forced the Turks back behind the Dniester, and drove the Persians from Baku. England played her own hand in the Colonies and extended her gains in India. From Spain, which France was no longer in a position to help, she took part of California; from Holland, now occupied by a French army, Guiana and the Cape—a rich 1795 booty! She took all that remained of France's foreign possessions, and by blockading her harbors forced her out of the overseas markets.

For England had resolutely taken sides—not at all for the Bourbons, whom she abandoned to their fate with a light heart; not at all against the Revolution, which she secretly assisted so long as she saw in it a means of disorganizing the French navy and weakening a rival; but against France herself—the leading nation of the Continent; against France who, bursting her frontier had annexed the left bank of the Rhine.

London could not stand idly by and watch a great European state establish itself as master on the coast of the North Sea which faced her own shores. Flanders had been, to some extent, the cause of the Hundred Years' War. Because of the Low Countries England had set herself to resist the expansionist policy of Louis XIV, and now, because of Belgium, which was at once prize and battlefield, Pitt tirelessly built up a series of coalitions against the Republic.

The victorious French would not willingly relax their hold on the Belgian plain. The English stood their ground and would not abandon it. The war, constantly taking on a new lease of life, lasted for twenty years.

APPEARANCE OF A METEOR: NAPOLEON

After dictatorship came anarchy; after the Terror, corruption. The Revolution, seeking to safeguard its gains, abandoned single-chamber government and experimented with two Assemblies and five Directors. But that was not what France wanted. She was looking for a man to lead her.

And a man was ready to her hand—an undersized Corsican general who had defeated the Austrians in the plain 1796 of the Po, and had tried to shake the power of England by 1798 gaining a footing in Cairo and so threatening her road to India. An aureole of glory made him into a popular hero. 1804 He had a feeling for greatness on the Roman model. He made himself Consul. He made himself Emperor—like Augustus, like Charlemagne.

There is little doubt that Napoleon Bonaparte had dreamed, in his youth, of literary fame. The fame he won was that of the politician and the soldier. There is little doubt that he had once been a passionate Jacobin and Republican. But Fate willed it that he should restore the traditions of the monarchy. There is little doubt that he ardently desired a period of peace, so as to give himself the opportunity of perpetuating the conquests of the Revolution and his own dynasty. He was to be forced, however, into an endless war. His was a strange destiny: to have come down to history as the man who imposed his will on the whole world, yet never to have accomplished any of the things he wanted to do.

For instrument he had an immense army, constantly renewed by conscription, and reinforced by contingents drawn from the subject nations. The men lacked military training: there was no time in which to give it to them. But Napoleon was a soldier of genius. He knew how to move his troops away from their bases and make them live off the occupied territories. He knew just when to pursue a beaten enemy, when to cut off his retreat, when to annihilate him. He pounced, in rapid succession, on all the adversaries whom London put into the field against him, and crushed them. He entered all the great capitals of Europe as victor.

He redistributed his conquests. First, he created a number of vassal republics, then he annexed them, not from ambition so much as necessity, because he needed a compact mass of associated nations with which to carry on his fight against England. In this way Turin and Florence, Genoa and Rome, Geneva, Sion, Hamburg, and Mainz, became the administrative centers of French departments. He gave away kingdoms to his brothers and his marshals. He drove the Bourbons from Naples and Madrid. He resuscitated a ghost of Poland at Warsaw. Stockholm offered the succession of the Swedish crown to Bernadotte, who founded a dynasty. The Pope, who had already been forced to go to Paris for the Emperor's coronation, was dispossessed of his territories, carried off, and interned. The King of Prussia, stripped of his authority, had to seek his pardon as a suppliant. The Tsar of Russia, beaten in battle, was

compelled to enter the Napoleonic system. The Emperor
of Germany had to renounce his title for that of Emperor
of Austria, and then humbly acquiesce in the marriage of
his daughter to the parvenu general. The Sultan, remem-
bering the campaign of Egypt, was terrified lest the Ottoman Empire be divided between France and Russia.
The Corsican remodeled the map of Europe in accordance
with his wishes. He sold Louisiana to the United States.
He gave Venice to Austria and Hanover to Prussia, and,
later, took back both. This amazing man sometimes lost
himself in fantasies. He dreamed of reaching Constantinople, of creating a United States of Europe. But reality
was always renewing its hold on him, getting its hands
round his throat. He had to fight, and fight again, in order
to secure that Flanders plain which was his legacy from
the Revolution, and from which the English wanted to
drive the French forces for good and all.

For England never weakened in her determination. Napoleon claimed that he had closed the Continent against
her, but it was she who closed the world against him. At
1805 Trafalgar Nelson swept the French fleet from the seas.
London took advantage of successes afloat to continue its
policy of mopping up the European colonies overseas.
For a short while a British army occupied Buenos Aires.
Holland lost, for the time being, Java, the Malayan Archipelago, and Ceylon. Denmark was stripped of Heligoland
and the Antilles. Portugal forfeited Madeira. France was
deprived of all her sugar islands. England, meanwhile,
continued with her conquest of India, and, in agreement
with Turkey and Persia, appropriated the markets of the
Levant. Her hand was felt even in Europe. Her trade
flourished on smuggling. It was not only Napoleon's vassal
states who aided and abetted her in this, but often France
herself. The blockade, in so far as it was applied, ruined
the trade of the Continent, and especially such ports as
Hamburg and Venice. Agriculture suffered severely.
French wine, Russian and Polish cereals no longer had

an outlet. The only industries that prospered were those that need fear no overseas competition. Sugar made from beet took the place of imported cane-sugar.

Napoleon knew that his empire was shaky and at the mercy of a single defeat, and, in the long run, defeat was certain to come. The peoples were growing weary of French oppression. Russia aspired to throw off the incubus. To impose his policy Napoleon undertook an expedition to Moscow. He might have to go even as far 1812 as Tobolsk. In the vast spaces of Russia he lacked the means to destroy an army which continually melted away before him. It was he, now, who was in grave danger of being caught in a trap. He ordered his army to retreat, but the winter on the Russian plains took cruel toll of his effectives. The Grand Army had set out with seven hundred thousand men. Five hundred thousand became casualties. Unable to replace its lost cavalry, it no longer had the power to exploit victories in the field. One by one the vassal nations rose in revolt. An English army took France in the rear by moving up through Spain and Portugal. But the end was not quite yet. In the Hundred Days the Napoleonic Saga gave its last flicker. Waterloo rang down the curtain. In that Belgian plain for which France 1815 had fought so often and so hard she lost a gamble which she could not win. Napoleon, who had lived like Alexander, died like Bajazet, in captivity. 1821

No more than a quarter of a century had elapsed since the fall of the French monarchy. The marvel of Bonaparte had lasted a bare fifteen years. Everywhere, as though what had passed had been but an interlude, the kings reoccupied their thrones. The Pope recovered his territories. The Bourbons returned to Madrid, to Paris, to Naples. It seemed that tranquillity had been restored. But the Revolution and the Empire had produced so vast an upheaval in the world that the traces of their activities were never afterwards to be wholly effaced.

BALANCE-SHEET OF THE ADVENTURE

The American Revolution had not shaken the planet. It had concerned one country only of three million inhabitants. The French Revolution, because its scene had been the first of all the countries of the earth, took on the character of an example.

Nor was that all. The innovations of the American Revolution had been conducted with prudence. The movement had been political rather than social, local rather than universal. The Revolution in France, on the other hand, had flung a challenge in the face of the world. It had offered the peoples equality, and Jacques Boux and Gracchus Baboeuf had pushed the system to its logical extreme of communism. True, it had also offered liberty, which is not at all compatible with equality. For liberty exalts the individual, and abolishes all that would limit his activities—feudalism and corporations alike. In other words, it enables the rich to exploit the poor. Individualism is the springboard of capitalism.

Napoleon had done no more than give practical form to these principles. His Code established equality in the eyes of the law, individual liberty, religious liberty, and the liberty of private property. It was a bourgeois system, protecting the person even at the expense of the family. It pointed the way to egotism—and to the decline of France.

Napoleon carried forward the work of the Revolution, too, in his reorganization and unification of the country. He abolished the old pattern of provinces and the internal customs barriers. He created departments and a centralized administration. He corrected the work of the Revolution where it had been a failure, notably in matters of finance. He remodeled the entire fiscal system; the tax registers had been burned in the early days of enthusiasm and revolt. He built a new currency on the ruins of the Assignats. He founded the Bank of France.

With careful deliberation he extended all these innovations to the countries which he conquered. He swept
away the last relics of feudalism. He introduced his Civil
Code even into the Grand Duchy of Warsaw, and into Illyria, at the risk of outrage to local customs. A Code
which allowed divorce and gave liberty to the Jews was
too secular to please the clergy, whether Roman, Protestant, or Orthodox.

For the old units of weights and measures, which had
varied from country to country and from province to
province, the Revolution and the Empire had substituted
a metrical system on a decimal basis. Though the charming Republican calendar was abandoned, though the decimal division of each day came to nothing, the meter, the
gram, the liter, came slowly to be adopted in France
and throughout the world. The new standards of measurement conquered the peoples more surely than the "old
sweats" of the Imperial Guard had ever done.

It was at this time, too, that new mechanical con-
trivances saw the light in France, and went from strength
to strength. The Comte de Sivrac showed himself in the   1791
gardens of the Palais Royal astride upon a framework
equipped with two wheels. This was the "hobby-horse,"
ancestor of the bicycle. At Fleursus balloons were first
used for observing the enemy. They marked a first stage in 1794
the development of aerial warfare. An engineer named
Chappe perfected a method of visual message-transmis-
sion. It was the first stammering attempt at telegraphy.   1793

French men of science had lost nothing of their old
inventiveness. Laplace explained the universe; Lamarck
codified the first laws of evolution; Cuvier classified the
animal world; Gay-Lussac explored the properties of gas;
Monge discovered descriptive geometry. Volta, the inventor of the electric battery, was invited to Paris by
Bonaparte from Milan. An American, Fulton, who had
vainly tried to interest the Directoire in his plans for a
submarine, tried out his steamboat on the Seine.   1803

In the arts France had lost her dominant position. She still had one painter of distinction, David, who had painted a picture of the Emperor's coronation, and whose antique solidity and rigor were in reaction from the languishing graces of Fragonard and Boucher. But the iconoclasts of the Revolution had destroyed many masterpieces, and Napoleon limited his patronage to painting and sculpture, to the plundering of Flanders and Italy. The artistic treasures of those two countries were sent to France. He had a way of annexing Rubenses and Raphaels much in the same way as he annexed some common or garden province.

In literature the movement towards decadence was even more strongly marked. The Revolution could talk, but it had lost the ability to write. The Empire strangled its authors. Chénier was dead, Chateaubriand in exile. It was only later, from his grave at St. Helena or his tomb at the Invalides, that Napoleon became a legend and an inspiration to the poets. The Romantic Movement was born in other countries, true issue of that revolutionary individualism which plunged the thinker into solitary meditation and fixed him in an attitude of revolt against the conventions of society.

Outside France the moral and political effects of the Revolution went deep. Not that any other country had, of its own accord, adopted its mystical vision of revolt. It was only arms in hand that the French had succeeded in spreading and imposing their new principles. But the sense of nationalism was waking, or waking again. The Revolution had taken as its device "The Sovereignty of the People." Europe in chains had countered with "The Sovereignty of the Peoples," and so it was that the revolutionary doctrines turned against France, their mother.

But the Empire had other things to its credit. In his love for simplification Napoleon had brought together much that had formerly been divided. He established order in that chaos which the Treaties of Westphalia had carefully fostered in Germany. He gave a shape and an organization

to her component states. Now, at last, Germany had a soul. French was no longer the language of authorship. Schiller, citizen of the world though he was, celebrated the national heroes in *Wallenstein* and the liberating spirit   1798
of nationalism in *William Tell*. Fichte, pupil of the Revo-   1804
lution, brought out his *Discours à la nation allemande*.   1808
Kant was another admirer of the Revolution, and Goethe saw in Valmy the birthday of a new epoch. Both opened the eyes of Germany to her own genius, and freed her from the spiritual leading-strings of France. Beethoven gave her the sense of greatness: Scharnhorst armed her. The Germany of Barbarossa was ready to rise from the grave.

Similarly, in Italy a new patriotism took shape against French domination. The Swiss, the Dutch, were stirring impatiently under the yoke. The Spaniards had never accepted it. Revolutionary imperialism alarmed the Turks. The secular tone of the new régime alienated the French Canadians forever. They could not follow in the wake of the motherland, but they remained loyal to the language and the religion which had been her heritage to them.

The blockade had unexpected results. It separated Norway from Denmark, and threw her into the arms of Sweden. It severed Brazil from Portugal, and the bonds   1814
which once had united the two nations were never again tightened. It separated Spain of the Napoleonic era from her   1808
colonies, and Spanish America took advantage of the breach to raise the banner of her independence. Finally, from the moment that the United States, in alliance with the Emperor, resumed her war with England she learned   1811
to do without English imports. Thus was American industry born.

Among all these swirls and eddies the nineteenth century drew nearer. It would not, like its predecessors, be a French century. In the course of the saga which had worked itself out during the past twenty-five years France had drawn on herself many temporary hatreds, but she had achieved a vast prestige for the future. The influence of her thinkers was to be felt for many long years to come, as of her language, which the émigrés had carried with them through the length and breadth of Europe. But France was never again to recover her political supremacy. The wars had cost her more than a million of her sons. **1815** The peace treaties deprived her of her natural frontier on the northeast. Belgium escaped from her clutches, and the empire of the Continent was hers no longer.

The new century was to belong to her conquerors, to the English, masters of the seas.

CHAPTER TEN

The Anglo-Saxon Centuries

A KINGDOM; AN EMPIRE

JUST AS it is permissible to take Rome as the axis round which revolved the history of the centuries lying immediately on either side of the beginning of the Christian era, so is it only fair to take London as that of the nineteenth century. It was from England now that enterprise, thought, and example radiated. She was ahead of the other nations. More than any of them she was prolific and prosperous. She was rich, she was strong, she was proud. Through her navy and her business initiative, impregnable behind her defenses, she made her presence felt throughout the world.

The supremacy of England on the seas was uncontested after Trafalgar; on the Continent, after Waterloo. The bulldog characteristics of her people had triumphed. She had a free field before her. **1805**
1815

In London parliamentary monarchy had found its true pattern, a pattern which the states of Europe were to copy more or less crudely. It had found, too, its symbol in a queen who for nearly two-thirds of a century was to personify the realm and the Empire. Queen Victoria was **1837** Great Britain incarnate. She stood for both its appetites and its traditions.

The English monarchy was liberal. It gave full freedom to the strife of parties, which, though they might differ

violently between themselves, were fundamentally at one
in their sense of the national greatness. It granted the Jews
equality of rights, and permitted complete freedom of expression to the Press. It put a stop to the slave trade, and
1839   went so far as to abolish slavery altogether in its own
colonies. Its example was later to be imitated. Liberalism
in politics found its complement in a liberal economics
which was the true foundation of the country's prosperity.
Not only was private enterprise given a free field in which
to develop and compete, but customs barriers were abol-
1846   ished altogether, and England proposed to an astonished
world a universal system of free trade. Other countries, seduced by this new doctrine, followed suit, with the result
that England, without having to fire a shot, won the war
of international commerce. The prevailing fashion of liberalism provided enormous outlets for English business.

But London was not content merely to buy and sell.
Her aim was to possess. She set herself, as a first step, to
acquire bases which should assure her control of the great
trade routes. From Gibraltar, Malta, and Corfu (where
the English protectorate lasted for half a century) she
kept a close watch on the Mediterranean. Heligoland gave
her the mastery of the northern waters. She was firmly established at the nerve-center of the Indian Ocean, which
she dominated from her position at the Cape, in Ceylon
(both taken from Holland), in Singapore (built on the
very threshold of Indonesia), at Mauritius (taken from
France), and at Aden (taken from the Turks).

The British Empire grew in size until it covered a quarter of the land surface of the globe, and included a quarter
of the population of the world. Though England had lost
North America, she had great possessions in Africa, Asia,
and Oceania. In the Black Continent she imposed her
1882   protection on Egypt, a country to which the building of
1869   the Suez Canal had given quite a new importance. As soon
as it became apparent that the subsoil of the Transvaal
1899   contained rich gold deposits she set herself to subjugate

the Boers of South Africa. Later she succeeded in assert-
ing her control over all the territories stretching from the
Cape to Cairo. In Asia her hold on India was now complete. She occupied Burma, and compelled China to cede   1842
Hong Kong and to open her ports to foreign trade. In
Oceania she colonized Australia, introducing sheep-farm-
ing into the country, and getting wool and gold in return.
She took possession of New Zealand, and pillaged the
archipelagoes of the Pacific.

Her explorers and her mariners worked for her glory and
her profit. Livingstone was the first white man to cross
Africa from east to west. In an attempt to find the Northwest Passage, and so reach China by way of the Arctic
Sea, John Ross discovered the magnetic pole. MacClure
succeeded in establishing a connection between the North
Atlantic and the Pacific. Parry was the first to cross the
82nd degree of latitude, and Markham the 83rd. Towards
the South Pole Weddell established a record by reaching
a point beyond the 74th degree, only to be beaten by Ross,
who got to the 78th, and Shackleton, who crossed the 88th.
Scott, in his race to the Pole, was only thirty-five days behind the Norwegian Amundsen. By these conquests of the   1912
Frozen South man all but achieved the complete survey of
his planet.

A PEOPLE; A NATION

France ceased to be the most highly populated country
of Europe. In the course of one hundred years she moved,
with difficulty, from thirty to forty million. In the same
space of time Great Britain rose from twelve to forty-one
million. Nowhere in Europe, not in Germany, not in
Belgium, was the advance so rapid.

At the beginning of the nineteenth century the United
Kingdom contained only one city of more than 100,000
inhabitants, while France had three. Half-way through the

century she could claim eleven to France's five. At the end of it she had thirty-nine, France only fifteen. The United States still had no more than thirty-five, Germany thirty-one, Italy twelve. In the whole of the British Empire there were eighty. London throughout the century retained her position as the largest city in the world, with a population which increased from less than a million to a total of more than four millions and a half.

Demographic supremacy; economic supremacy. With **1900** her merchant fleets England ruled the oceans. The tonnage at her disposal amounted to ten million. The United States came second with no more than five. Germany had scarcely two, Norway one and a half, France one. She led the way in fishing as in freight, in exports (the total value was multiplied by thirteen in the course of the century) and in imports (multiplied by twenty-four). In all these fields London led. No port in the whole world was more active.

The City was the financial capital of the universe. Capital flowed both ways, inward and outward. It was the greatest of all markets for gold. The Bank of England, the leading **1816** issue-house, tied the pound sterling to the gold standard, and the eclipse of silver progressively compelled all the other currencies to follow the British lead. The nineteenth century was outstandingly the era of capitalism, the era that saw a tremendous increase in industrial enterprises, great companies, and large shops, the era in which amazing private fortunes were made. The five sons of a Jewish banker of Frankfurt established themselves in London, Paris, Frankfurt, Vienna, and Naples. The Rothschilds ushered in the triumphant period of international banking, and the London representative of the family held state like a sovereign. It was an age during which fiduciary money was enormously increased—the age of credit, speculation, and recurrent crises.

From statistics we can get a vivid picture of English wealth. No country absorbed more cotton or more jute;

none consumed more sugar per head of the population, nor, it need scarcely be added, of tea. Prices, which had doubled during the Napoleonic wars, reverted to their previous level, and stayed there. Well-being was becoming an adjunct of democracy.

An Industrial Revolution, which had started in England, was changing the whole rhythm of production. Mechanized labor was ousting human; workshops were being transformed into factories. Steam was the good-fairy of the period, until it was dethroned by electricity. Coal was the dispenser of energy, the creator of wealth, later helped by water-power and petroleum. There were vast reserves of coal buried in the English earth, and nowhere was so much of it produced. The country was rich also in iron ore, and the English mills were in advance of all others in their deliveries of iron, castings, and steel. Birmingham was the greatest metallurgical center of the whole world. For a long time Great Britain was the biggest producer of copper and tin. Australia enabled her to lead all countries in the wool trade. India and Egypt, as a result of the American Civil War, developed the growing of cotton, supplying Manchester, which, in its turn, supplied manufactured goods to the world at large. No country had more spindles or more looms.

In the struggle to establish her industrial hegemony England deliberately sacrificed her agriculture. She ruined her peasantry, depopulated her countryside, and was prepared to depend for food on her imports from overseas. Her Empire kept her supplied with meat and cereals, and free trade made it possible for her to live cheaply.

In spite of national prosperity and greatness, in spite of free trade and cheap food, the people of England were not contented. Poverty was as great as, if not greater than, elsewhere. Wages were low, and the purchasing power of the working class far from big. The industrial magnates had reduced their workers to what almost amounted to slavery in order to keep costs at as low a level as possible. The exploited classes came to curse the liberal—or "laissez-faire"—system and to seek other formulae of reform. The English philanthropist Robert Owen was the first man to give currency to a new word—socialism. The workers banded together into unions and began to back their claims with the weapon of the strike. A German Jew, Karl Marx, living in London as a refugee, produced a book which was to be the Bible of communism. It was in Lon-

1864   don, too, that the Workers' International was born. Industrial revolution had paved the way for social revolution.

THE REVOLUTION IN TRANSPORT

The real revolution, however, the revolution which transformed the very conditions of human existence, was to be found not in text-books but in facts. By annihilating distance it made the world smaller. The earth, which mankind had discovered with such infinite trouble, was soon to be reduced to a tiny ball which could bè rapidly circumnavigated.

Already there had been a great advance in road-building. The Scotsman McAdam improved the metaling of highways by using a technique which every country was to adopt. As a result of it the speed of land transport was doubled. But the day of the coach was over.

New roads made their appearance, but they were of iron. The railway-track, first used in the English mines, soon conquered the world. On this new form of highway steam provided the motive-power for new engines. Trevithick constructed the first locomotive, and Stephenson per-

1815   fected the invention. The first railway-line to be built was
1825   between Stockton and Darlington, the second between
1847   Manchester and Liverpool. Men attained a speed of over fifty miles an hour. Speed, power, the new means of trans-

port had everything in its favor. Belgium, France, Austria, America, the whole world, adopted the railway. Shortly after the middle of the century England, small though she was, possessed more miles of railway-track than any other country. A little later the Continent developed its own systems. America was crossed, the Andes were pierced, Siberia was brought within range of the steam-engine. Tunnels were driven through mountains; frontiers were crossed. By linking province with province the railways helped to shape the nations.

On the seas, too, steam asserted its power. For a long while yet sailing-vessels were to fight a losing battle. For the carriage of precious cargoes it was difficult to find a speedier or safer method than that offered by the slim-hulled clippers. For heavy freights there was no cheaper motive-power than wind. But steam eventually supplanted sail. The first regular line of steamboats plied between England and Ireland. Twenty years later Roberts achieved the first crossing of the Atlantic by steam alone. The Canadian Cunard, born in Nova Scotia, established the first steam service between England and America. Smith, an Englishman, suggested substituting the screw for the paddle-wheel. Ships began to be built of iron, but their dimensions remained small. For more than fifty years the *Great Eastern,* of nineteen thousand tons, remained the largest vessel afloat. The hulls of fighting ships were given armor plating, and the submarine began its career. Sailing vessels which, in 1860, made up 90 per cent of the world's fleets, had dropped by the end of the century to 20 per cent. In those forty years the all-round tonnage of the nations had trebled.

The postal services had their share of increased speed. England invented the postage-stamp, which both simplified and multiplied the activities of the mail. Ronalds invented the electric telegraph. The first submarine cable was laid between Calais and Dover. The first transatlantic cable

1818
1838

1834

1858

1840
1816

1850

1866 linked England and the United States. No people in the world received so many letters or sent so many telegrams as the English.

In Great Britain were conceived all the inventions later to prove so useful, the practical development of which was to quicken up the carriage everywhere of human thought, material goods, and men. The physicist Maxwell antici-
1848 pated the German Hertz in paving the way for the radio.
1842 Dunlop invented the pneumatic tube, which made the
1848 vogue of the bicycle possible, and the triumph of the motor-car. Henson took out a patent for the first airplane; Stringfellow was the first man to achieve mechanical flight.
1853 Carlington was the first man to design an airplane with a tractor screw. Man, who had learned to rise into the air by means of the balloon, was soon to realize his dream of flying like a bird.

THE INFLUENCE OF BRITAIN

At the height of her glory, Britain exerted influence through her men of learning and her writers. If she lacked geniuses of the encyclopedic kind, that was because science was making it more and more necessary to specialize. The days had gone by when a man could be a great painter, a great inventor, a philosopher, and a discoverer all at the same time, when he could, in short, be a Da Vinci or a Descartes. But in every branch of research the British distinguished themselves.

Essentially they were a practical people, inventing less from a love of knowledge than in the hope of making money or of improving their standard of living. But the whole of mankind benefited from their labors. Their doctors achieved wonders at a time when the battle against mortality was being successfully waged. Jenner discovered vaccine inoculation, which put an end to the ravages of smallpox. Simpson used chloroform in surgical operations.

Faraday revealed the phenomenon of induction, Joule the heating properties of electrical currents. Not all the advances in science or in the practical improvements of daily life were of British origin. But the metallurgists of Birmingham were the first to replace quill-pens with steel nibs, and London was the first city in the world to adopt gas for street lighting. It was Henry Bessemer who succeeded in transforming smelted iron directly into steel, and Darwin who revolutionized men's speculations on the origin of species.

Not all romanticism came from Britain, but it did derive very largely from Macpherson's *Ossian,* a supposed body of translations from a Celtic original, which, in fact, had never existed, and from the plays of Shakespeare. Byron and Walter Scott threw Europe into ecstasies. Their influence on the literature of all countries was profound. Both Pushkin and Mickiewicz were soaked in Byron, and the American novelist Cooper aimed at carrying on the work of Scott. In France Hugo was deeply indebted to English romanticism. His first play, *Amy Robsart,* had as theme a story already used by Walter Scott. His great 1827 "manifesto" was issued in connection with a quite unactable drama on the subject of Cromwell. Later he wrote *Mary Tudor* and *William Shakespeare*. His *Homme qui rit* has an English setting, and, when the poet went into exile it was on British territory that he took refuge.

But Great Britain in her heyday produced neither great painters nor great sculptors. She gave no plastic heritage to the world. In this respect her civilization is reminiscent of that of Phoenicia, which had produced sailors and colonists, but was more concerned about trade than the problems of esthetics. Hebrew culture too had been poor in this field. London was not a second Athens.

The high geniuses of art were to be found elsewhere: Goya and Delacroix, Chopin and Berlioz, Wagner—god of Bayreuth. England had nothing to offer but painters of the second rank and architects who slavishly copied the productions of the Gothic or Renaissance periods. Iron was 1851 used as a building material. London gave itself the glory 1889 of a Crystal Palace, Paris of an Eiffel Tower. But these achievements of the iron-master have not blotted out from men's minds the marbles of the Parthenon, some of which still slumber in the rooms of the British Museum.

But English fashions were all the rage. Paris might still be the capital of female modes, but a London now ruled the male roost, first in the person of Brummell, king of the dandies, and later in the persons of two successive Princes of Wales. English fashion dictated the laws of high life. Anglomania became contagious. All over Europe "English Gardens" sprang up, as well as imitations of the British Parliament. The mania for whist and, later, for bridge swept the Continent. Sport, before it spread across the world, was an English product. England revived horse-racing, made an industry of thoroughbreds, established a code of rules for the turf. She organized the first boxing-matches, regularized the conduct of all ball-games, including football, instituted boat races between her universities, and revived the cult of athletics.

The naturalization abroad of English words was not confined to the field of sport. They were soon to be found in politics, finance, and commerce. English is the most widely spoken language in the world. In matters of business it is universal. In the twentieth century it has acquired an equal footing with French as the medium of diplomatic exchanges, and has even outdistanced it. The Treaty of 1919 Versailles was drafted in both English and French. Since 1940 English has more and more supplanted French.

Sailors and geographers now take as their point of reference the meridian, not of Paris, but of Greenwich. Standard time is G.M.T. Yet England still clings obstinately to her old duodecimal system of weights and measures, her inches, yards, and ounces. In the hustle and hurly-burly of an industrial age she still, on occasion, uses carriages and wigs. She has achieved the miracle of blazing new trails while remaining faithful to the traditions of her past.

ON THE CONTINENT

Why, precisely, did France lose her position of leadership? The causes of her regression are to be found in a diminishing birth rate, domestic instability, and an inept foreign policy. A legal code which stressed the rights of the individual, and was her legacy from the Empire, the progressively weakening hold of Christianity on her people, an increasing love of self-regarding comfort—all these things led to the breakdown of the family. A succession of revolutions which substituted the Bourbons for Bonaparte, 1815 the Orléanists for the Bourbons, a new experiment in republican government for the Orléanists, a new Bonaparte 1871 for the Republic, a Third Republic for the second Bonaparte, were the expression of a turbulent and unsatisfied nation which had lost the secret of continuity. France in the nineteenth century was still powerful, because the days of her greatness belonged to a recent past. She had not entirely lost her old vitality, as was obvious when she established herself in Algiers, when she built the Suez Canal 1830 and reorganized her colonial empire. She had not altogether lost her great men: a string of them runs through the century—from Ampère and Fresnel, to Pasteur and Curie, from Niepce and Daguerre, the inventors of photography, to the brothers Lumière, who were pioneers of the cinema. She could still astonish the world with her poets, her thinkers, and her painters. But she was no longer ahead in every field. Though she might hate to admit it, she was definitely on the downward path.

Her worst fault was that of raising up, on the very continent which she had once dominated, the Powers which

were destined to become her rivals or her enemies. Her
favorite refrain had been the "Freedom of the Peoples of
Europe," and this altruism not infrequently cost her dear.
1830 She helped to liberate the Belgians, whom the conquerors
of Napoleon had united with the Dutch. She assisted the
Greeks in their struggle to throw off the Turkish yoke. She
waxed enthusiastic, though in vain, over the cause of the
enslaved Poles. She forged both Germany and Italy into
national solidarity, and lived to regret it. It was Hugo, in
Les Burgraves, who had summoned the Empire of Barbarossa from the grave. It was in Paris that the Italian con-
spirators were welcomed. Liberalism engendered nationalism, nationalism produced imperialism, and imperialism
turned against France.

Half-way through the century, as the result of an economic crisis (which began with a blight on the potato
1845 crop, ruined whole countrysides, caused the industrial
market to shrink, and was to result in over-production,
unemployment, and unrest), a wave of revolutionary
movements shook the Governments of Europe. The fever
1847 first showed itself in Poland, and, later, reached Italy.
1848 Paris waxed turbulent over the cause of universal suffrage,
and the autocrats of the Continent trembled. There was
fighting in Madrid, in Germany, in Austria. The oppressed
nationalities of Bohemia and Hungary began to stir. Ultimately an authoritarian reaction set in, and was successful
in Vienna and in Paris. But the seed had been sown and
was to germinate in the consciences of the peoples of Germany and Italy at the expense of that Austrian monarchy
against which France was venting her out-of-date resent-
1859 ments. Backed by the armies of Napoleon III, the kingdom of Italy took shape, with the house of Savoy as center. As a result, too, of French passivity—the fruit of blindness no less than of good intentions—the German principalities gathered about the house of Brandenburg, the
sovereign power of Prussia. Two nations were born on the

very frontiers of France—Germany fresh from the victories
of Sadowa and Sedan, the child of Wagner and Bismarck;
Italy, the child of Cavour, to which the defeat of the   1870
French gave the keys of Rome.

Germany, unified at last, was densely populated. When
it first came into existence under the scepter of William I   1871
it numbered a federated total of forty million. By the end
of the century this figure had increased to nearly sixty
million. What made her strong was her passion for discipline, her racial pride, and the fact that she possessed rich
coal-mines and mineral deposits. She was proud of her
Kultur and of her army. She had men of science, such as
Röntgen and Koch, and philosophers of the stamp of
Nietzsche and Schopenhauer. With the accession of William II her ambitions began to spread out from Europe   1888
and to include the world at large. She began to take an
interest in the Near East, planned to extend her economic
tentacles from Vienna to Bagdad, colonized parts of
Africa, intervened in China (extorting from that country
a convenient base), constructed the Kiel Canal, and
dreamed of a great fleet which should win for her the mastery of the seas. It was in Berlin that the Powers parti-   1885
tioned Africa between them, giving the Congo to the King
of the Belgians for no better reason than that they did not
want anybody else to have it. Clouds of German emigrants
descended upon the Americas. Pan-Germanism was on the
march.

Italy was not yet dreaming of reviving the great days of
Rome. She was too poor and too indolent to look so high.
But the number of her children was already great. In the
first half-century of her existence the young kingdom increased in population from twenty-five to more than thirty-
four million, and was soon to be, demographically, the
equal of France. She too scattered emigrants all over the
New World. She wanted to carve herself a colonial empire
in Africa. But the Abyssinians successfully resisted her,   1896

1881 and the French beat her in the race for Tunisia. She compensated herself in Tripolitania.

Elsewhere, too, the wine of nationalism was fermenting. Not only Greece, but Egypt, had slipped from the clutches of a decadent Turkey, and they were followed by Rumania,
1878 Bulgaria, and Serbia, in all of whom Russia took a lively interest, because they were situated on the road to Constantinople. The dismemberment of the Ottoman Empire raised problems of great gravity, because these small nationalities were at daggers drawn, and still more because the Great Powers had their eyes jealously fixed on Byzantium and the Straits, which commanded both the passage from the Mediterranean to the Black Sea and that which led from Europe into Asia.

DECLINE OF EUROPE; DECLINE OF ENGLAND

Europe's great age was drawing to a close. There had been an Age of Greece and an Age of Rome. There had been a thousand years of Christendom, an Age of Italy, the centuries of Spain and France, a century of England. Civilization's center of gravity had shifted from east to west, then from south to north. But Europe was in decline. The birth rate was falling. New competitors were arising.

Fresh forces were developing. On the very doorstep of Europe, Russia, a semi-Asiatic Power, the Russia of the Tsars, but also of Tolstoy and Dostoievsky, was growing enormously in size. She stretched now from the Caucasus to the Pacific, from the Baltic to Alaska. England barred her approaches to India, and went so far as to intervene
1855 in the Crimea, at the side of France, in the hope of keeping the Russian colossus from Constantinople. But the Muscovite autocracy forcibly Russified Poland, Finland, and the Baltic Provinces. She was ruthless, but only because she suffered from a secret weakness. Within her own fron-

tiers bureaucratic absolutism was faced by the passive resistance of her people. Abroad she found her master.

Japan, emerging from her centuries-old isolation, taught
her a lesson. In order to avoid falling a victim to colonizers
from Europe, she decided to adopt the European tech-   1868
nique. Feudal though she was in character, she took from
the civilization of the West what she needed to safeguard
her own way of life—factories, guns, ships. In the last
third of the century her population increased from thirty
to forty-seven million. She captured Korea from China.   1894
She defeated Russia in the Far East. This was Europe's   1905
first serious setback, and it suddenly opened men's eyes to
the presence of a Yellow Peril.

China, it is true, constituted no threat. She had been
compelled to humble herself, to concede ports to the
Powers of Europe. An uprush of nationalism, turning to
xenophobia, had followed. She had numbers on her side,
and was in a position to spread her emigrants thickly over
the whole Pacific region. America and Australia showed
signs of alarm. The day was not so very far off when
China, under the leadership of Sun Yat-sen—a former student of the American University of Honolulu—would get   1912
rid of her Manchu dynasty. That accomplished, she would
find the secret of renewal in a succession of dictatorships
and republics.

As in Asia, so in America nationalism was assuming an
anti-European form. "America for the Americans," President Monroe had declared. But even before this dictum   1823
was uttered the Spanish colonies had broken away from
Madrid. Responding to the call of San Martín and Bolivar,
they had won their freedom. Republics arose which, in
their search for a system of government, moved through
revolution to dictatorship. But the political situation was
no less unstable in Madrid itself, where there was continuous insurrection, restoration, and civil war. Clerics and
masonic lodges, monarchists and republicans, soldiers and

trade unionists, each, in turn, took a hand in the game of conspiracy. Spain, which once had been the dominant world power, was fast sinking into obscurity.

The Power now on the upgrade, the Power which would presently hold the foremost place, was the America of Washington. She had got over her growing-pains and successfully scotched the dangerous threat of secession. The people of the southern states, where black man-power was needed on the plantations, had long been slaveowners. The industrialists of the North wanted the protection of a tariff barrier. War broke out between them. The North, under

1865 its spokesman, Lincoln, imposed its will and saved the Union. The United States, now really united, could develop unhindered on an enormous scale. The Age of America was about to dawn.

Politically England was still powerful and still active. To some extent the weight of her hand was felt every-

1830 where. In France she had not been entirely without influence on the fall of the Bourbons. She had intimidated Louis-Philippe and seduced Napoleon III. In Belgium a British citizen had been elected king. She had kept Latin America from becoming a federation. She had checked French colonial expansion in Africa. She offered Japan an alliance, and was still mistress of the seas. The dominance of Great Britain was still a brilliant fact. The English language was steadily extending its hold. But the British Empire had received its death-blow, at the imperial no less than at the economic level.

The edifice of empire was beginning to show cracks. As once the Spanish domains, so now the British, were too widespread to be coherent. The colonial peoples were too well assured of their own importance to accept the orders of the mother country with docility. One after the other the larger colonies demanded their autonomy, and were granted the status of Dominions—first Canada, then Australia, New Zealand, South Africa. London finally gave freedom to a part of Ireland which had never ceased to protest against the guiding hand of England. The Hindu masses were agitating and demanding.

Economically England had suffered one serious check and many disappointments. Her gospel of free trade, after enjoying a temporary success, had found itself at odds with the particular interests of foreign countries, each one of which wanted to develop its own industries and to break free from dependence on British imports. London had to fight hard to maintain her position in the markets of the world. The wave of liberalism was followed by a wave of protectionist policies. The different states, instead of letting trade find its own level and leaving things alone, sought to direct their national economies, and even to control some of their industrial products. Political nationalism found its echo in economic nationalism.

But that was not the full extent of the English disaster. Coal, with which she was so well provided, lost its pre-eminence. With the invention of the internal-combustion engine liquid fuels came into their own, and of these England had none. But there was a rich natural supply of them in the United States, where they were developed by Standard Oil, and in the Dutch East Indies, where Royal Dutch had its domain. The English reply to this threat was to found Shell, which entered into an agreement with the Dutch firm, and did its best to appropriate such deposits of natural oil as still remained unexploited. A vast battle developed, but England's weapons were inferior to those of her competitors. 1870

England was losing, too, the advantage she had early gained in the industrial and scientific field. While America, Germany, Japan, and even France were busy improving their technical equipment England was content to rest on her laurels. She was the home of tradition, and she now became, to some extent, the home of routine. The automobile was born and prospered in France and Germany. Ford, 1875

1890   in America, built his earliest models. But the English law
forbade any mechanically propelled vehicle from moving
on the roads "unless preceded by a man with a red flag."
This ridiculous restriction was not removed until the latter
years of the century. Similarly, the first attempts at making aviation a practical reality were French, German, or
1890   American. Clement Ader rose in the air in a machine
1903   equipped with an engine. Lilienthal made repeated experi-
1909   ments with gliders. The Wright brothers solved the problem of human flight, and Blériot flew the Channel. England could do no more than follow the lead of others. She
did so almost with regret, for aviation constituted a threat
to her island security, just as the submarine threatened
to compromise her mastery of the seas.

Where, precisely, should we place the beginning of this
relative decline in English prosperity? Seemingly in the
last decade of the century. It was then that the United
States successfully challenged her lead in the production
of coal, iron, castings, steel, and outdistanced her in the
consumption of cotton. It was somewhat later, at the beginning of the twentieth century, that Japan's fisheries began to compete successfully with those of England, that
the United States forged ahead of England as an exporter,
that London had to take second place to New York both
as a city and as a port.

The British Empire, it is true, was still the largest producer of gold, nickel, and cocoa; but she had to fight to
maintain her position. London was no longer the unrivaled
capital of the world.

THE FLOWERING OF AMERICA

The United States had at their disposal an immense and
hitherto undeveloped territory. They had acquired Louisiana from France, Florida from Spain, Alaska from Russia. They had taken California and Texas from Mexico.

They had progressively colonized the Middle and the Far West, into which distant lands the railways were carrying new life. Now they set themselves up as the protectors of the whole American continent, compelled England to withdraw from Venezuela, and secured bases for themselves in the two oceans. They annexed the Hawaiian Islands (by request), drove the Spaniards from Cuba, Puerto Rico, and the Philippines, and laid their hands on Panama, where they pierced the isthmus with a canal. They acted as mediators between Japan and Russia.

1898

1903

Great they were by reason of their population, which rose from five million in 1800, to twenty-three million in 1850, to seventy-six million in 1900, to a hundred and twenty-three million in 1930. The flow of immigrants had been uninterrupted. In the course of a single hundred years (1820 to 1920) thirty-four million had settled in the country. On six separate occasions the annual arrivals had numbered more than a million. They came from England, Ireland, Scandinavia, and Germany. Later they were to come, too, from the Slav and Latin countries. They would have come from China in even greater numbers had not the United States, in their anxiety to maintain the predominance of the Anglo-Saxon strain, applied a quota system to undesirables. They already had trouble enough with their Negroes, whose high birth rate might well in time challenge the supremacy of the white population.

American cities developed at a pace never before seen. In ten or twenty years a village frequently became a metropolis. Chicago owed its growth to a canal; Detroit to its car factories; Los Angeles to the cinema. All three passed the million level less than a century after their founding. Similarly, gold cities, oil cities, iron cities, railway cities, competed exuberantly under the American sky.

American economy was the most powerful in the world, in part because of her rich natural deposits, in part because she developed a new system of production. England had replaced men with machines. America replaced the

290 THE HISTORY OF THE WORLD

machines with *machinism*. She introduced the assembly-line into her factories, and embarked on a vast system of standardized mass-production. She won the fight for lower costs. She paid court to her industrial magnates, her pork-packers, her oil-men, and her leaders in Press and mill. The names of her manufacturers and of her great businesses have become household words throughout the world. We speak of a Ford, a Kodak, a Frigidaire. The great thing, she early decided, was to build not for beauty or for durability, but quickly and cheaply. At that game, though Europe has striven to learn her lesson, America remains unbeatable.

She has taken front rank in many different fields. Her soil, exploited with skill, produces more corn, oats, tobacco, and cotton than that of any other country in the world. From her mines come more coal, copper, lead, zinc, oil, and phosphates than from any others. Her factories turn out more castings, more steel, more alcohol, than those of any of her competitors. Her railway mileage is the longest in the world. The Federal Treasury lends money at a lower rate of interest than any other country can equal. The United States have become the creditors of all the nations. Their monetary reserves are three times greater than all other known reserves in the universe. Three times more cars circulate on the roads of America than elsewhere.

This progress would not have been possible without much individual daring. The Americans are not content merely to produce. They invent and they explore. They were the first people to use ether for medical purposes. It was they who conceived the idea first of the Linotype, then of the Monotype, and thus revolutionized the whole craft of printing. Morse was responsible for the electric telegraph. Bell perfected the telephone, Thomas Edison the talking machine and the electric lamp. London may have been the first city to be lit by gas, but New York was the first to be lit by electricity.

The American Peary was the first man to reach the North Pole, Byrd, to fly over both Poles, though the first crossing of the Atlantic by air must be put to the credit of two Englishmen, Brown and Alcock, in 1919. In the revived Olympic Games Americans carried off the palm. Even in the realm of culture America works hard to hold her own. She has had two great poets, Edgar Allan Poe and Walt Whitman. She has given a refuge and a home to Einstein. She builds skyscrapers, which are an entirely new form of expression in terms of vertical architecture. She has introduced the world to the rhythms of jazz, which has its origin among the Negroes of the Mississippi. The films of Hollywood have invaded the screens of the world.

1927

Do all these manifestations amount to a new civilization, or are they merely the modern form of ancient barbarisms? Europe in decline regards the New World much as the Greeks regarded their Roman conquerors. Poe, obviously, was not Plato, the skyscraper is not Nôtre-Dame de Chartres, jazz is not Mozart, Charlie Chaplin is not Rembrandt. Young America, so proud of its factories and its slaughterhouses, is like a child with new toys.

THE GERMAN WARS

It has remained for the United States to carry this supremacy on to the battlefield. The might of Britain is a thing of yesterday; that of America is of our own time. But the outstanding question of the nineteenth century was—who would be the great Power of the future? Germany, Russia, Japan were showing above the horizon. The Anglo-Saxon world would be forced to a trial of strength with the most gluttonous of the newcomers.

There had been no serious threat to peace for a very long time. Fighting, of course, had taken place in the Balkans and in distant places overseas. But the great nations of the world were hesitant about embarking on large-

1899 scale hostilities. At The Hague, where disarmament had been fruitlessly discussed, a vague Court of International Arbitration had been established. This, however, did not prevent appetites from growing sharp, or imperial systems from eyeing one another askance. The nations were arming.

One of them wanted the hegemony of the world, and to achieve it was prepared, twice in a quarter of a century, to loose war on mankind. This nation was not the Russia of the Tsars, which was threatened by an internal crisis, nor was it, as yet, Japan, which was quietly growing in the

1914 shadows. It was Germany. She meant to dispute with England the empire of the seas and the world markets which

1939 she coveted. At the moment of her second bid what she wanted was a supply of those raw materials which she lacked and the living-space which her insatiable appetite demanded.

The board was set. On one side the "haves," striving to retain what they already possessed—England, France, America, Russia. On the other the "have-nots"—Germany and her satellite, Austria. The remaining Powers stood hesitating between these two groups, and committed themselves as the interest of the moment dictated. Italy was one of the "have-nots," but at first it was at the expense of Austria that she hoped to benefit, later at that of France, which explains why, in the period between the two wars, she changed sides. Turkey was torn between fear of Russian expansion, which tended to throw her into the arms of Berlin, and dread of German ambitions. Japan had an account to settle with China and with those European countries which had established themselves in the Far East. She thought it a shrewd stroke to take advantage of the first war to acquire German possessions, and of the sec-

1943 ond to impose her will on the Far Eastern territories of England, Holland, and the United States.

Gradually the conflagrations swept on until they enveloped the whole world. In such a state of universal strife there were no more neutrals. Either they were invaded, like Belgium in 1914, Greece in 1916, Norway in 1940, Iran in 1942, or they were snatched by the belligerents and enrolled in their cohorts. So it was with the Latin American countries in both conflicts, with Rumania, Hungary, and Finland, caught up in the German system in 1941, with Siam, dragooned by Japan in 1942, with Bulgaria, forced into line with Russia in 1944. The only countries which managed to maintain their neutrality throughout both wars were Spain, Switzerland, and Sweden, and they owed their good fortune more to circumstances than to firmness.

War was everywhere: in Belgium and France—the traditional battlefields of the West; in Italy, in the Balkans, in Russia; but also in Asia and Africa, and also in the very heart of the Pacific. Never before had the Old World been so shaken to her foundations; never before had so many millions of men engaged in mutual slaughter with such deadly weapons. But this fury of destruction was no more than a commonplace, even when it spared neither civilians nor the most venerable of ancient buildings. Great wars have always been marked by ferocity.

Twice the same process developed. Germany attacked and was victorious. She eliminated Russia in 1917, France in 1940. Twice she was checked—by France in the first war, by England in the second. Twice she was eventually defeated, thanks to American aid in 1918, thanks to the combined assault of Russian numbers and American manpower and industry in 1945.

On each occasion the auxiliaries of Germany were forced to let go of what they held—Turkey and Austria in 1918, Italy in 1943. Japan alone held out in 1945. Punishment of a very special kind had to applied before it was possible to tear from her grasp the ephemeral empire which she had carved for herself from the Indies and New Guinea, from Malaya and from Manchuria.

In both wars Germany showed a ferocious obstinacy. Neither economic blockade nor a coalition of the nations could break her spirit. But her courage was powerless to force a decision, and she had recourse to tactics which, fundamentally, have been those of all armies at all times (war of position in 1914; break-through in 1940), and to new weapons—gas in 1917, magnetic mines in 1939, flying-bombs in 1944. The whole German people followed their leader with fanatical devotion, whether that leader was the Emperor William II, who dreamed of ruling Europe, or Adolf Hitler, who believed that he had established German domination for a thousand years. Hitler thought that he had revived in his person the Napoleonic epic. But there was this difference between them: Hitler failed to reach either Cairo or Moscow. Germany just failed to subdue the world.

1919   From her first failure she recovered without having suffered too much damage. Though she had to cede provinces to France and to a reconstituted Poland, she strengthened her own internal unity. It was Austria who paid with dismemberment for her collaboration with Berlin. Bohemia was reborn under the name of Czechoslovakia. Prague, Budapest, Bucharest, Belgrade, and Warsaw shared between them the heritage of the fallen Hapsburgs.

1945   Germany's second defeat was disastrous in quite a different way. This time most of the cities of the Reich had been destroyed, and what remained of German industry passed into foreign hands. But in one way she was fortunate: there are still eighty million Germans alive in the heart of Europe.

She was not the only victim of these dramatic happenings. All the belligerents were left counting their losses and checking over their ruins. The two wars had cost them forty million dead and revenue equivalent to seventy wheat harvests.

Of the victorious Powers, two were at their last gasp.

France had lost many of her sons in the first conflict, much of her wealth in the second. The franc collapsed. England was exhausted. She had held out, but only at the cost of incurring enormous debts. The pound sterling was in a very shaky condition. Both nations had heard the first cracks of their disintegrating empires.

Their failure was Europe's failure. It must give up all hope now of dominating the planet. Germany had lost her colonies; Italy saw her hope of a revived Roman Empire   **1945** crumble. Holland once again, but only with the greatest difficulty, set foot in Indonesia. France had to leave Syria, where once she had hoped to establish a Frankish king-   **1947** dom, and is ready to disclaim her colonial achievements. The English have abandoned India. The West, as a whole, has given up her last remaining trading-stations in China.

Two nations only emerged from the struggle with flying colors—Russia and the United States. Both lie beyond the confines of Europe.

THE TWO CAMPS

After the first war Russia got rid of her Tsars. But she merely suffered a change of tyrants. At the cost of a bloody   **1917** revolution, and strong in the Gospel of Marx, Lenin imposed a communist régime suited to the gregarious passivity of her people. Moscow has once more become a capital. The Empire has been baptized anew: it is now the Union of Soviet Socialist Republics. But Russia remains. Strong in the increased number of her subjects, she is strong, too, because of the treasures of her soil and her subsoil. She is the largest producer of wheat, rye, barley, and potatoes. No nation has so many horses. Within her frontiers she is turning herself into an industrial country, as though in an effort to compete with America. Nor is the old Russian imperialism dead. Stalin has recovered Poland and a   **1939** part of Prussia. He has reconquered the Baltic provinces,

and is now prepared to expand towards the Balkans, Iran,
1945   and Manchuria. By crushing Germany he has made of Red
Russia the greatest single Power on the Continent.

Confronting her are the United States of America.
1945   They have emerged from the twin conflagrations with their
power enhanced. Whereas the Old World has now got to
rebuild her ruins, the United States are intact. Their military strength has been immeasurably increased by their
possession of the atomic bomb, which can disintegrate
matter. Their airplanes can fly faster than the speed of
sound. Their financial and industrial possibilities are unrivaled. They have taken from the British Empire the
sovereignty of the seas. The dollar is king. They hold almost all the gold reserves of the world, and are the great
dispensers of credit. The whole of the American continent is under their guardianship. Now that the Japanese
have been defeated, the Pacific is theirs. In them the Anglo-
Saxon Age continues.

Thus the world is divided into two camps—the Soviet
and the American. Most of the nations of the world,
whether they like it or not, must rally to one or other
of them. Stalin's Russia is building up a host of "client"
neighbors, extending from Rumania and Poland to Mongolia. She has installed reliable men in Budapest, in
Prague, in Berlin, and even in Korea. In most of the coun-
1949   tries of the world Moscow has her faithful adherents who,
in the interests of a doctrine, are prepared to act as the
spearhead of the Red Army, just as, four centuries ago,
Catholic Spain maintained her "friends" in all the Courts
of the world.

But the United States have, too, their satellites—the
nations which share their hatred of Soviet coercion, whose
reconstruction is being financed by their dollars. These are
by no means confined to the New World; far from it, for
the whole of Western Europe is going to Washington for
aid—financial aid in the immediate present, military aid
for the future. The United States stand armed and watch-

ful on the threshold of a forbidden world, in Frankfurt and in Tokyo.

The two colossi stand confronted, but one of them has feet of clay. The military might of the Soviets calls to mind that of Genghis Khan rather than of a modern state. To be policed is not necessarily to be polished. In the fields of industrial production, scientific research, and financial stability the Soviet monster is far behind the American.

It would be encouraging to think that the other nations of the world, ranked behind these two extensive powers, were on the way to achieve unity; but that seems scarcely to be the case. Duality is not unity. Furthermore, any attempt to separate the countries into two distinct but homogeneous groups is to simplify the political map unduly. Each group has its cracks. In the communist camp it is terror alone that keeps the peoples in subjection, and some of them—for example, Yugoslavia—are not wholly reliable. In the liberal sphere of influence, however, where cohesion is not the outstanding characteristic, the nations are still separated by formidable frontiers. In spite of Pan-American or Pan-European congresses, the barriers of tariffs and of monetary difficulties are greater than ever. The peoples of the world think of international exchange only in terms of increased exports, forgetting the truth that they can export only so long as others are prepared to import. They are still arranged in a pattern of jealous, self-sufficient units, which, no matter how elaborate their plans of re-equipment, are still competitive and mutually suspicious. They talk a great deal about a United States of Europe or of the World, but they seem to be quite oblivious of the fact that what they are doing is to revive the old organization of feudalism.

The world, far from becoming united, is breaking up. A scatter of small nations has succeeded to the old Austrian and Turkish Empires. India, her Western masters gone, has split in two. Lebanon has been separated from Syria, and, on the soil of Palestine, two States, one Arab, the other Jewish, are irremediably hostile to each other. The seed of autonomy is germinating everywhere, from Indo-China to the Philippines, at one side of the world, to Iceland, on the other. Tiny scraps of territory have, at one time or another within the last few years, been granted independent status—Tangier, the Vatican City, Danzig, Trieste. The world was certainly far closer to the ideal of unity in the days of the Roman Empire.

Last Chapter a Summary

THE RELIGION OF PROGRESS

No period has ever been so infatuated with itself, small cause though it has for pride.

It believes in the religion of progress, which, it thinks, can supplant all others. That progress has occurred in many fields of material achievement cannot be denied. Demographic progress has doubled the population of the globe in less than a century, raising it to more than 2000 million inhabitants. In the most advanced countries progress has produced underpopulation in the countryside, overpopulation in the cities. Technical progress has lengthened human life, has overcome certain diseases, has reduced the mortality rate. It has increased the comfort of the individual, and has put within the reach of all foods, amusements, means of transport, systems of lighting, heating, and the dissemination of news never previously dreamed of. Man has learned how to remake or counterfeit Nature. He can now produce synthetic textiles, rubber and fuel and plastic materials of all kinds. Improvements in machinery have led to a reduction in hours of work, and to a greater all-round enjoyment of leisure. The dream of the lazy is of an Eldorado where men will live at ease in a world given over to the machine.

But there is another side to all this progress. Of what use are demographic or technical advances if they are to be used only for mutual slaughter? The most wonderful inventions can be turned into death-dealing instruments. The motor-car has been transformed into the tank, Blériot's airplane into the bomber. Machinery has not brought freedom to mankind: it has merely altered the form of his slavery. The man who works on the assembly line of an American factory is no more than a slave of progress. Improvements in machine design mean only that the world now lives under a permanent threat of overproduction, recurrent crises, and poverty.

Similarly, the perfecting of credit systems has merely loosed upon the world the curse of inflation. Governments have made use of the printing-press so irresponsibly that certain currencies have collapsed entirely. Wonderful tools have got into bad hands.

Even improvements in medicine, limited though they are, have served, paradoxically enough, to lower the quality of the race. By keeping alive the weak and the diseased, at a time when wars eliminate the fit, they have counteracted the processes of natural selection.

The cult of science has induced in man such a condition of self-admiration that he thinks he can do without the gods. Country after country is becoming secularized, from France on the one hand to Turkey and China on the other. But atheism encourages the crudest forms of superstition. As the eighteenth century believed in Mesmer, and the nineteenth in table-tipping, so does the twentieth believe in fortune-telling, horoscopes, and chiromancy.

The cult of peace has led only to wars, since pacifist nations are insufficiently armed. A League of Nations, born of the First World War, encouraged men in the most dangerous of illusions. An organization of so-called United Nations now fathers a family of overgenerous dreams. Man's greatest error is to believe in his own progress.

The cult of the State has resulted in strange abuses. The individual now counts for less and less. The State takes a hand in every activity. This meddling has had many names —Communism in Russia, Fascism in Italy, National Socialism in Germany. The ecomonic life of nations is everywhere "directed." Private enterprise is dying, and with it die all human liberties.

The cult of numbers has produced a form of franchise which takes no note of sex. The result has been to enthrone mediocrity. The Press, the radio, the cinema, conducted in the interests of the masses, have lowered taste and drugged intelligence. Men's clothes are ugly. Art is often vulgar. Chicago takes pride in her canned-meat factories, Moscow in her underground railway—far greater pride than Athens ever took in the Parthenon.

Even in her trivialities, even in her errors, the Age of "'Progress" is no innovator. Monetary catastrophes are as old as—money. Famine is but an old curse revived. Hitler's and Stalin's labor camps have done no more than renew the worst forms of ancient slavery. Atheism and superstition flourished in Rome of the decadence. The pacifist illusion wrought havoc in Hellas. State control and socialism were known in Egypt under the Pharaohs, in Peru under the Incas. The dictatorships of the twentieth century take the mind back to the Greek tyrannies, which were built on popular support. The regression of the arts, the apathy of the masses, recall the Dark Ages.

In short, the centuries of the machine are comparable to those prehistoric ages which saw the herdsman emerge from the hunter. Now, as then, social life is undergoing a revolution. One was pastoral; the other is industrial. Now, as then, technical progress has improved the lot of the human animal. Comfort has made a leap forward in this Anglo-Saxon age of ours, as it made a leap forward in the days of Neolithic man. Now, as then, concern for material well-being has dealt a death-blow at the life of the spirit. The quality of art is diminishing.

Some twelve thousand years separate the two periods. Twelve thousand years, in the course of which man has undoubtedly learned to live better, but also to kill more efficiently. Twelve thousand years, in which he has discovered more about the world and very little about himself.

Index

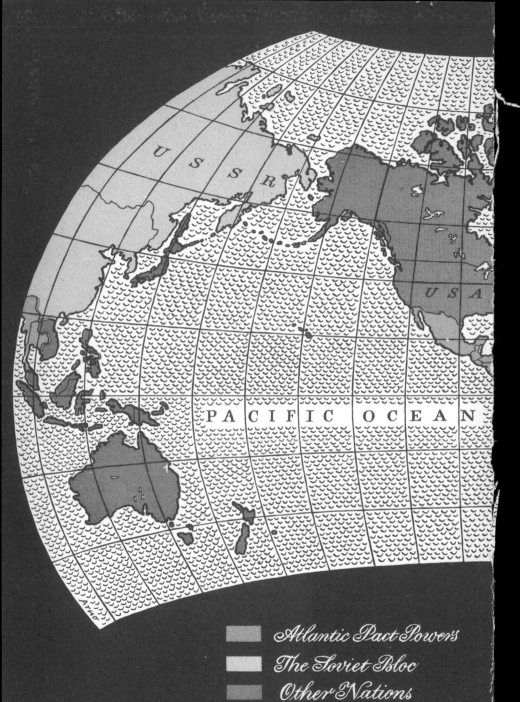

U S S R

U S A

PACIFIC OCEAN

Atlantic Pact Powers
The Soviet Bloc
Other Nations